Scale of Miles

0 5 10 20 30 40 50

BUCHAN

Buckie Banff

Elgin Urquhart

Auldearn

Old Deer

R. Deveron

Fyvie Castle

Old Meldrum

INVERNESS

Bogie Water

Inverurie

Kintore

R. Spey

R. Don

Kildrummie Castle

ABERDEEN

MAR

Aboyne

R. Dee

BENOCH

Dunottar

MEARNS

ATHOL

Stracathro

Brechin

ALBANE

Montrose

R. Tay

Forfar

ANGUS

Loch Tay

Arbroath

DUNDEE

Scone Palace

Methven

ATHEARN

PERTH

St. ANDREWS

Abernethy

FIFE

STIRLING

Kinghorn

Cambuskenneth

ippen

DUNFERMLINE

Dirleton

ckburn

Leith

Dunbar

Falkirk

Linlithgow

Firth of Forth

EDINBURGH

ROBERT BRUCE
KING OF SCOTS

BY

AGNES MURE MACKENZIE
C.B.E., LL.D., M.A., D.Litt.

OLIVER & BOYD LTD.
EDINBURGH : TWEEDDALE COURT
LONDON : 39A WELBECK STREET, W.I.

First edition published by
Alexander MacLehose & Co., London
1934

Reprinted by
Oliver & Boyd, Edinburgh
1956

PRINTED IN GREAT BRITAIN
BY BRADFORD AND DICKENS, LONDON W.C.1

AD SERVOS
NON DICTIS SED ACTIS
PATRIAE

"Antecessorum nostrum indefessos labores, pro patriae liberatione voluntarie assumptos, ad memoriam reducens."

Fordun and Bower, *Gesta Annalia*

FOREWORD

THE inception of this book is due not to its author, but to its publisher, who must not, however, be held responsible for anything it contains. I should not have ventured it of my own accord, and did so in the beginning with reluctance, because I do not share the taste of my time for a valet's-eye view of any man who has effected or even attempted much : and while I had read sufficient history to know that the war concluded by the Treaty of Northampton implied no small achievement by its leader, and counted for much in the history of Europe, I had, like most of my generation, been bred to the conventional view of Bruce, as a treacherous and rather contemptible figure who somehow, by a sudden violent conversion, was changed into the strong and beloved leader of a national struggle against heavy odds : and in spite of the psychological problem involved (whose disappearance I can almost regret) the type is not one that I would select for a subject, since I have never needed to comfort my soul by writing, for choice, of people I can despise.

One is seldom pleased, especially after an academic training, to find that one's attitude has been mistaken. In this case, however, I am glad to acknowledge that my initial point of view was false, and in spite of defects of which I am well aware, I cannot regret having ventured the attempt. The subject is not handled as it deserves. To write history well needs genius, and I have none, though at least I can claim one piece of useful equipment—in that, since I am a novelist by profession, I at any rate know when I am not writing fiction. But apart from the excitement of the chase, the detective work involved in the exercise of writing history from the raw material, I found, to my pleasure, that the academic convention as to Bruce ripped into shreds when one tested it by an examination of its own data. The popular tradition of history is very often very badly wrong, but at times it is truer than the academic. What I found was not what I had been trained to expect, but a young man sufficiently moved by desire for national freedom to sink his own claims to a throne and involve himself in family complications and a tangle of mistrusts and jealousies, through years of shiftless and ineffectual war ; who gave in at last when he, a great soldier *in posse*, knew the struggle for useless under such conditions; and who, when circumstances gave him the lead, assumed that and won, after almost twenty-two years of effort, against odds that were, in all reason, impossible. In short, I found the old folk-tradition was right, and that the old popular hero was a hero.

Such a conclusion, I know, is very shocking. To apply the word in earnest is simply not done. But an historian should speak the truth, even though it may scandalise his readers and disconcert the fine psychological theory with which he may have embarked on its pursuit. And I have done my best to speak it here.

I am indebted to those writers and editors—especially to the latter—whose names appear in the bibliography, to Miss Margot Seymour for the illustrations, to Mr Stephen Bone for the frontispiece, to Mr Ahier for the maps, and to my publisher for both faith and works.

St. John's Wood, *August*, 1934.

CHRONOLOGY

1265. *Dante born.*

1266. *? Giotto born.*

1270. *Death of St Louis. End of last Crusade. Last chanson de geste about this time.*

1273. *Rudolf of Habsburg crowned King of the Romans.*

1274. Robert Bruce born. *Death of St Thomas Aquinas.*

1276. *Death of Pope Gregory X. Death of Guino Guinicelli. Second part of the Roman de la Rose about this time. Rutebeuf.*

1280. *Conquest of Prussia by the Teutonic Knights, and its nominal conversion to Christianity.*

1286. Death of Alexander III. Turnberry Band.

1290. Treaty of Birgham. Death of Queen Margaret. Invitation to Edward.

1291. *Fall of Acre and end of Crusader states in East.*

1292. Baliol crowned.

1293. Edward repudiates promises.

1294. *Election of Boniface VIII. France and England at war.*

1295. Bruce's grandfather dies. Treaty with France. Baliol confiscates Bruce lands.

1296. Outbreak of war. Invasion of Scotland. Sack of Berwick. Dunbar. Abdication of Baliol.

1297. Insurrection. Capitulation of Irvine. Stirling Bridge. Wallace and Moray Guardians.

1298. Falkirk. Bruce holding Ayr. *Truce between France and England.* Bruce and Comyn Guardians.

1299. Lamberton added to Bruce and Comyn.

1300. English invasion.

1301. English invasion. Bruce no longer Guardian. Truce for a year.

1302. Bruce capitulates. *Courtrai.*

1303. *Death of Boniface VIII. Death of Cimabue.*

1304. Death of old Bruce. Surrender of Comyn. Band between Bruce and Lamberton. *Petrarch born.*

1305. New government for Scotland. Execution of Wallace. *Election of Clement V.*

1306. Death of Comyn. Coronation of Bruce. Methven. Kildrummie.

1307. Landing at Turnberry. War in South-west. Glentrool. Loudoun Hill. *Death of Edward I.* Rising in Moray. Bruce goes North. Inverurie.

1308. Reconquest of North-east. Truce with Far North. Reconquest of West Highlands. The Far North comes in. Edward Bruce and James Douglas in South-west.

1309. *Clement V goes to Avignon.* St. Andrews Parliament. Peace negotiations. Scotland clear to the Tay. Truce.

1310. Concilium of Dundee. English invasion. *Henry VII in Italy.*

1311. Edward II gives up invasion. Invasion of England.

1312. *Suppression of the Templars. Henry VII crowned Emperor.* Parliament of Ayr. Invasion of England. First attempt on South-east, which fails.

1313. *Death of Henry VII. Boccaccio born.* Parliament of Inverness. Capture of Perth. Scotland clear to the Forth. Reconquest of South-west and Man. Truce bought by North of England. Reconquest of South-east begun. Linlithgow.

1314. Reconquest of South-east continues. Roxburgh. Edinburgh. Bannockburn. Scotland all clear but Berwick. *Lewis the Bavarian and Frederick of Habsburg anti-Emperors. Death of Philip IV and Clement V. Accession of Louis X. Papal interregnum.*

1315. Parliament of Ayr. Act of Succession. Marriage of Princess Marjorie. Irish Expedition. Invasion of England. *Morgarten.*

1316. Attack on Berwick. Death of Marjorie. Coronation of Edward Bruce. Invasion of England. Second Irish Expedition. *John XXII elected. Death of Louis X and accession of Philip V.*

1317. Irish War. Dispute with Pope.

1318. Capture of Berwick. Invasion of England. Death of Edward Bruce. *Edward II enlists Pope.*

1319. Siege of Berwick. Invasion of England. Mytton. Truce.

1320. Pope's summons to peace. Manifesto of Arbroath. Pope excommunicates Robert. Soulis Conspiracy. Negotiations for peace.

1321. Peace negotiations drag on. *Death of Dante.*

1322. *Collapse of Lancaster.* Invasion of England. Scotland invaded in force. Another invasion of England. Biland. *Mühldorf. Death of Philip V. Accession of Charles IV. Accession of Galeazzo Visconti.*

1323. Harclay attempts peace. Official negotiations. Truce for thirteen years. Randolph deals with the Pope. *Pope quarrels with Emperor.*

1324. Prince David born. Negotiations for peace. *Edward Baliol recalled.*

1325. Parliament of Scone.

1326. Death of Walter Stewart. Treaty of Corbeil.

1327. *Abdication of Edward II.* Truce broken. Invasion of England. Weardale campaign. Another invasion of England. Overtures for peace. Queen dies.

1328. Treaty of Northampton. Marriage of Prince David. Peace with Pope. Death of Lamberton. *Deposition of John XXII. Death of Charles IV. Cassel.*

1329. Death of King Robert.

1330. Death of Douglas. *John of Bohemia in Italy.*

1332. Death of Randolph. Beginning of fresh war.

CONTENTS

CONTENTS

IV

THE WAR FOR PEACE: 1314-28

EPILOGUE

MAPS

I

THE ROAD TO DISASTER

SIX YEARS: 1286–1292

A

Quhen the Kyngis of Ingland persaivis discord, discentione, ciuil weiris, iniusteis, and diuisione vitht in Scotland, then thai forgie fenzet querrellis contrar our realme, in hope that ilk Scottis man sal be mortal enemye til his nychtbour. . . . I wald spere quhat castel can be lang kepit, quhen the enemeis seigis it cruclly vitht out, and vitht in in the said castel ther ringis mortal weyr amang the soudartis, men of weyr, quilkis suld lyf in ane mutual and feythful accord in deffens of the said castel contrar externe violens.

The Compleynt of Scotland.

CHAPTER I

TIME AND PLACE: 1286

. . . Nae war's atween the lands,
And there is peace, and peace suld be.
                              Kinmont Willie.

IT has frequently been remarked that if Cleopatra's nose had been slightly longer, the Roman Empire might not have existed, nor, consequently, might Europe as we know it. The statement is certainly an exaggeration, for Octavian, who was uninfluenced by the lady, had more to do with the founding of the Empire than any success or failure of Antony's. None the less, it is true that beauty, like other attributes of the divine, may when it manifests itself in mortals have powerful and sometimes disconcerting effects on that course of human affairs whose comprehension is the art of history: and the development of our own country, at vital nodes in that of Europe at large, shows two spectacular examples of this. If in the later eleventh century a penniless princess flying from conquered England had not chanced to be a very beautiful woman, Scotland would have lacked much of the far-sighted statesmanship that in the course of the next fifty years turned her face from Ireland and the North to Europe, at a time of intense and vital mental activity, when Scotland herself was just forging into a nation.

3

And if a couple of centuries after that, one of the ablest of the Kings of Scots had not been stirred to a hot infatuation by the beauty of his young French queen Yolette, Scotland, again at a turn in human history, would not have been left to anarchy for years, to an all but annihilating foreign invasion, to long expenditure of blood and sorrow, to a disaster in economic life that has scarred and crippled the whole of her history ; and England would have been spared a humiliation that she resents, subconsciously, to this day.

The whole of Scots, of British, and so of European history is coloured by the event of one spring night. On the nineteenth of March in the year we call 1286,[1] Scotland was ruled by a king of the ancient house that had held the throne for nearly half a millennium and created one nation out of a warring five. He was a strong man in the early forties, courageous and intelligent, whose already long reign had been a time of progress and well-being at home, of powerful and friendly alliances abroad. His own marriages and that of his lately-dead son were links with England, France, and the supreme commercial power of Flanders : he had broken for good the long-standing menace of Norway, beat back the last of more than three centuries of fierce invasion, and sealed an enduring peace with his daughter's marriage. Scotland was fortunate in her King, and loved him.

---

[1] To a Scot before the early seventeenth century, to an Englishman before the mid-eighteenth, 1286 would have begun six days later.

That was one March night, and there was a storm on the Firth, the wild cold wind of the East Coast equinox. King Alexander held council in Edinburgh, but his young Queen was at Kinghorn over the water. Dawn broke on the King lying dead below a cliff, and the sovereign of Scotland was a young foreign princess, a motherless infant at a distant court, with the North Sea between her and her kingdom. And Scotland's near neighbour was an Angevin monarch whose grandfather had lost the great French lands of his inheritance, and who held the creed of the ' natural frontier.' For twenty years there was an increasing chaos of shame and ruin, ineffectual war and growing enfeeblement. A great man rose with the promise of freedom again, to die in torment with freedom farther lost : the last thought of Wallace may well have been despair. Then another took the broken sword and reforged it, reforged the nation, won through nearly a quarter-century of war against odds more impossible than those confronting St Joan or Garibaldi, worked one of the miracles of history, and died Robert, King of free Scots, by the grace of God.

By reason, the thing should plainly not have happened. That is not a rhetorical statement, but common sense. For the Scotland of 1305 to pull herself together and not merely become an autonomous nation again but hold her own for more than three centuries and be joined at last to her great enemy not by conquest but by the peaceful accession of her own dynasty to the other's throne, becomes less rationally possible the more one investigates the actual facts. Only it happened, because by the mercy of God the man came with the hour, to rouse other men and lead them to miracle. A modern French-English historian has said finely—and he was thinking of Scotland when he said it—' Potential is of more value than mass, decision and courage of more value than numbers, and energy the deciding factor.' That is never more true than in the two-and-twenty years that begin in the late March of 1306, with a coronation like a nursery game, for the man on whose head a woman and a priest set that hasty gimcrack contrivance of a crown was one of the great dynamic figures of history. This book is an attempt to tell what he did.

The man came with the hour. Before we can see the man we must see the hour, for it was significant, and not only for Scotland. This violent wrecking of our national life, its reintegration at what cost of effort, comes at a time of transition for all Europe, at the node of two ages. All that was best and greatest in the secular side of mediaeval life flowers, in the North, in the personality of St Louis, who died four years before Robert Bruce was born. His death, and the consequent abandonment of what was to be the last of the Crusades, begin the break-up of the true Middle Ages. When eight years after Bruce's death, in 1337, Edward III of England began the long ignominious war with France that was to ruin his house and, almost, both kingdoms, the Middle Ages were definitely dying, and the modern world, for good and evil, in birth. Dante, whose life goes from 1265 to 1321, is the crown and flower of mediaeval letters : Giovanni Boccaccio, eight when Dante died, is the beginning of what we call the Renaissance. Scotland comes to her feet again, after the Lost Generation, in a new Europe.

We forget how brittle a thing is a civilisation. A thousand years before Robert Bruce was born, Western Europe was and already had been for long one great state, powerful, splendid, and at peace. From 212, all free men were full citizens of that state, bound alike by the great Roman Civil Law that is still the fundamental of our own, sharing a common political and economic life, a common language, literature, and art, a state religion : freedom from war, a very efficient land and sea police, and well-organised transport made for a wealthy commerce. Intellectually there was not the brilliance of Athens nor the reaching fire of mediaeval France, but there was a high culture, whose scholarship was freely accessible. The Christian faith was quickening in the spirit, and materially in the growing *ecclesia*, the unified communion of the Faithful. These things are not irrelevant to Bruce's Scotland, long after their time, nor to ours.

The splendid structure had forces of decay about its roots, like streams below the foundations of a building. It suffered from abandoning the soil, from concentrating its consciousness in cities, from crushing taxes, the dislocation of economic values reflected in a depreciated currency, and finally from an increasing stranglehold of bureaucracy. And outside its walls, on the frontier of Europe, the barbarians were pressing to the West. The situation is very like ours now, though the invasion of Barbarism had only negative forces of its own, lacking such positives as the film and the press : and since America was not yet discovered, it came from one side only. That was enough, however. By the third century there was growing but still intermittent border war. At the end of the fourth, the dam broke, and for something like seven centuries from that there ensues a time that we call, and not unjustly, the Dark Ages. The time between Alaric's sack of Rome and the united effort of the First Crusade, that opens the great mediaeval renaissance, is longer than that which separates us from Bruce, and the look of it, at first sight, is largely chaos. To the civilised men of the fifth century, it was the end of the world. They were not far wrong. Yet it was easier to save seed-corn than in a more fully mechanised civilisation. Men here and there, wiser and more courageous than their neighbours, or ready to follow men who were brave and wise, were working in chaos, often with small enough hope, and though many of them must have died despairing, their work was not wasted. It has for long been fashionable to mythologise history, to speak of it as the action of certain impersonal and ineluctable forces, which are called Influences, a word which sounds more scientific than Norns or Fata, and in practice means exactly the same thing. This is a merely childish point of view, a fairy-tale for those who have not reached the status of manhood, or would shirk the glorious burden of that status.

If history is science, this way of envisaging it is un-
scientific, for it ignores a large number of facts. If
history is art, it is the negation of art, for art deals with
the spirit of man in its impact on life. It is perfectly
true that most men are largely shaped by environment.
The very much greater truth, too often forgotten, is
that environment is largely conditioned by the will and
vision of individual men, one here and another there,
and very lonely.

Such men—Syagrius, Gregory of Tours, Aetius, or
vaguer figures like the Roman-British commander who
comes down in cloudy tradition as King Arthur—held
islands of civilisation in the chaos. Churchmen kept
something of scholarship alive, men like Charles Martel
beat back successive waves of barbarians : some four
centuries after Alaric—a time as from now to the reign
of James the Fifth—Charlemagne's clear brain, strong
hand, and magnificent will reforged for a time the old
unity and order in the West : the East, shrinking and
mummifying, but with yet six centuries ahead of it, still
held the unbroken but stiffened tradition of the Empire,
and kept the Eastern Gate against the Moslem.
Charlemagne's work was undone : there was chaos
again. The Moslem was held, but there were new in-
cursions from the North, and a spiritual disintegration
in high places of Church and State that make the ninth
and tenth centuries perhaps the blackest in the history
of Europe . . . so far. Yet the Spirit of God moves
always on the face of stormy waters, and there were
men willing to be His instruments. The tenth and

eleventh centuries saw the great Cluniac and Cistercian Reformation, the recovery of the Papacy that culminated in Gregory VII, the development of some sort of political order, the recovery of culture these made possible. The Church had never lost its organic structure : the civil power was developing one of its own, in the intertexture of reciprocal obligations, based on military service and the use of land, that we call feudalism. By the end of the eleventh century the great spiritual, intellectual, and political achievement of the next two hundred years was becoming possible.

Our own country in that time is something of a microcosm of Europe. There was not the break-up of the Roman civilisation, that one sees in Gaul or South Britain, for the Romans had found even the conquered South below the Forth too hot to hold for more than a little time : and above Forth was too much for even the Legions. The chaos, of course, was not less. By the middle of the Dark Ages it had roughly sorted itself into a sizable Pictish kingdom, a small but active Irish one in the West, a little Pictish enclave in Galloway, while what is now South Scotland was then the northern extremities of two states, one Celtic and the other Teutonic, whose southern parts lay in what is now Northern England—Cumbria in the west and Northumbria in the east, whose now Scottish parts were to be later Strathclyde and Lothian. Christianity had come in before the break-up of the Empire, with St Ninian, a Briton of Strathclyde and like his countryman St Patrick a pupil of St Martin in the great monastery of Marmoutier, that still, although it is a house of nuns now, is alive by the Roman road along the Loire, with St Martin's rock chapel still in its quiet garden, looking over the wall to the marching of fifteen hundred years of soldiers. The sixth century had brought a fresh wave from Ireland. Touch with Gaul had been almost lost, but Ireland was the paradise of scholars, and Northumbrian culture, fertilised partly from Gaul and partly from Iona, rose to high distinction. The little kingdoms slowly fused together—Alban and Scotia, Strathclyde, and Lothian last, taken from Cnut the Great as indemnity for his attempt to add Scotland to Denmark, Norway, and England, but with its Anglian culture secured in the treaty of cession. Malcolm III, who died in 1093, three years before the First Crusade, was king of a Scotland almost the size of ours, but minus the Isles and the two northern counties, and plus a loose hold on what is now the English county of Cumberland. And thanks to the policy of Malcolm and his Queen, she was turning her face from the growing decadence of Ireland to a Europe where had re-grown in the minds of men the very strong and clear conception of a unified culture, that transcending political divisions and some tolerably lively political oppositions, made all the West, from the north of Spain to the frontier of pagan Prussia and Pomerania, one unity that men thought of as Christendom.

It was a little Europe. A clutch of small fighting states in the north of Spain held one gate against the Moslem, who was now, and was to be for another six

hundred years, the active menace that the North had
been.   The Eastern Empire, still stretching into a
shrunken Asia Minor, held the South-east.   Poland and
Hungary were buttresses against the Slavonic pagans,
who thrust forward, in the North, over the greater part
of what became, at a later age in history, the Prussia of
Frederick.   It was a little Europe, but a mighty.   The
conception of nationality was not lacking, but loyalty
was double: locally, to a man's lord, who was master
of the soil that based his life, and universally, to the
Faith, the great international ordering of the spirit :
the old conception of tribal theologies (Luther's
cuius regio, eius religio) was a very long way yet from
its German revival.

Each of these developed a sort of corollary force.
With the international or transnational Faith went a
transnational scholarship, whose language, that of the
Church, was common to Christendom, and which was,
if limited in its incidence, free to any man, of whatever
class, who chose.   From the obligations of feudalism
grew another culture, the code of life and art we call
chivalry, whose spread was helped in that, like the
scholarship, it also had an international speech, the
French that in one or other of its forms was almost as
widely known as the scholars' Latin.[1]   *Chivalry*, nowadays, is apt to mean some vague recollection of the

[1] As late as the thirteenth century, the Italian Brunetto Latini
was writing in French, because *La parlure de France est plus commune
à toutes gens*, and even towards the end of the century one finds
French as well as Latin used in Scottish diplomatic correspondence
with *Norway*.

picturesque externals, and perversions, of its decadence: but essentially it was a very great thing. It was really, by origin, a sort of sacramentalising of that military life that was one of the essentials of fiercely threatened Western civilisation. The knight who was its type-figure had solemn consecration, like a priest : knighthood was a way of life bound by rule, an ' order ' in a sense parallel to the religious use of the word. The ideal conception, realised at times, as clear ideals are, in practice, bound him to a code that began with military and religious duty, and developed, among other things, a conception of the relations of men and women, the ' courteous love ' that for all the ugliness of its sometime perversion, the shallowness that came to its conventionalised externals, was a new thing in human evolution, and a very great one. Chivalry, largely through this new element, grew an art of its own alongside the scholarly, expressing itself first in the lovely lyric poetry of South France, that beginning about 1100, sent its inspiration rapidly north and south. Music and painting were elementary still, though they had often beauty : but there has been no nobler age of building than the round-arched Romanesque of the eleventh century, or the lovely aspiring Pointed of the twelfth and thirteenth.

The revival in the Church that comes with Cîteaux and the First Crusade, the defining of feudal political and military organisation—the two were, and had to be, inseparable—the chivalric code of life, the renaissance of scholarship, and the splendour of the arts that grew out of them, are the main positive notes of this Christendom. As for the negative, men were as greedy then as they are now, and the different ratios of time and distance made it easier for them to express this greed directly. They were no more intelligent than they are now (except in artistic matters, to be sure) and had as many, though different, superstitions. And their lives were even more precarious. But it is the positive side of an age that matters for the evolution of man that is history. What I have said is an outline, rough, as it must be for brevity, of the ideas which gave it standards. Those standards were by no means always attained, but they were at least those currently held desirable : and what a man values will always shape his life.

Within this unity of Christendom there were other, smaller, unities growing defined. Feudalism was in theory as much a single unity as the Church, with the Emperor for its head, as the Pope of that. In practice, men naturally looked to the smaller, nearer, unit. In face of a Saracen, a man thought of himself as belonging to Christendom. But in face of a man who held of the Count of Toulouse, he became conscious that he was a Breton. These local attachments were fairly narrow at first, but they fused before long into something not unlike a recurrence of the old tribal consciousness, and larger areas reached the imagination, especially those that were fairly homogeneous racially or culturally and occupied land with very visible boundaries. England, a part of Scotland, a part of France, begin to think of themselves as nations, with a sort of corporate person-

ality : and the first and third grew—very slowly in
France's case, and shattered in England by a foreign
conquest—to a kingdom identical with the nation.
Scotland reversed the order. She was a kingdom while
she was still several nations, two nations for centuries
after she was a kingdom. That has affected her history
to this day.

It was to this Europe, then, that Scotland turned her
face, towards 1100. And the infusion of new vitality
was helped not only by the deliberate action of Malcolm
and Margaret, but by the chance of the little succession
war that followed, between Malcolm's eldest sons and
their uncle. This sent the youngest sons, Alexander,
the sixth of them, and David, the seventh, who were
still small boys, to the shelter of their sister's English
court, which at that time could give them most useful
training, for it was, of course, not English but Norman-
French and the Normans had not only a political and
administrative genius that made them, wherever they
went, an organising force : they were also in full
contact with France at a time when her intellectual
leadership was as unquestioned as in the *Grand
Siècle*.[1] We think of twelfth-century Normandy as

[1] Queen Margaret's own upbringing had not been, as it is so often
called, English. Her paternal stock was English enough, of the
House of Cerdic, that had been royal for over five hundred years.
Her mother, Agatha ' the Hungarian,' seems really to have been of
the Imperial house of the stirp of Henry the Fowler, and was cer-

attached to England, but in fact it was the other way
about. And the Norman sea-rovers had so assimilated
the culture they had first begun by wrecking that
Normandy was the intellectual core of North France.
Moreover, both King and Queen loved the things of
the mind. Henry's nickname was ' the Scholar,' and
Maude of Scotland was her mother's daughter in all
things but energy. The two young men grew up in a
stimulating atmosphere, and when first one and then
the other was unexpectedly called to his father's
throne, they threw all the fiery energy of their house into
the spread of the most modern thought, David in
special supporting the reforms of the Church, and
founding many houses for monks of the new orders, to
the great enrichment of both scholarship and agriculture. The civil reforms which he inaugurated were
based not as is commonly but loosely said on ' English '
institutions, but on Norman. The England that was
known to Margaret's son, the England of her son-in-
law and his nephew, was far less English than David's
own Lothian, whose native institutions had been
granted continuance at its absorption, as those of the
rest of England had not been at the conquest by
Normandy.

tainly a near kinswoman of Queen Gisela of Hungary. She was
born in that country, and spent her first twelve years at the court
of Gisela's husband St Stephen : she grew up in that of her uncle
Edward of England, who was half Norman by blood and whole
Norman by upbringing and predilection. And her great friend
and adviser was Lanfranc of Pavia, the Lombard abbot of a Norman abbey, made Primate of England by the French prince who
had usurped her brother's kingdom.

David appreciated the practical advantages of the Norman civil organisation, and introduced them. He had, it must be remembered, ' been in practice ' already as a Norman baron, for he had married, at his brother-in-law's court, a daughter of the latter's cousin, who was heiress of a great earldom that considerably increased the resources of the Scottish crown, and brought a complicating factor into Scots politics. Many of his personal friends were young Norman nobles, and when he came north, at Alexander's accession, to rule over South Scotland (for the land was divided) many came with him, and most of the great Scoto-Norman houses date from this time. His influence was strongest in the South, for he ruled there for seventeen years before he was king, in a relation to King Alexander that parallels that of the Princes of the Lilies (especially the Valois Dukes of Burgundy) to the Kings of France. It is these seventeen years as Prince of South Scotland that strengthen a really English influence, not imported from King Henry's court, where there was none, but there already, native to Lothian, which province so throve, under his excellent government, that it became the commercial centre of Scotland.

All through David's reign and that of his eldest grandson, Scots friendship with Norman England was persistent, and with England and Normandy under one crown gave us an easy bridge to the Continent, and the vivid impulse of France. Till 1174 the friendly relation was constant : it is typical that Henry II of England received his knighthood from David and bestowed it in turn on the young William I, who as both an allied sovereign and a baron of England served along with him in his French war. Such English wars as there were during that time are not invasions of a hostile country, but support of one side in an English civil war, by David to help his niece the Empress Maude, or later by William to help his friend ' the Young King ' (i.e., the heir) Henry of England against his father. It was this last intervention that brought disaster, and the wrecking, for some years, of the good relations. The weak, impetuous William was captured at Alnwick, and the violent old Angevin gave full rein to both his anger and the greed of his house, and exacted the maximum of humiliation in the Treaty of Falaise (1174) which for fifteen years made Scotland an English fief.[1] His son Richard, however, at once on his accession, saw the advantage of the former friendship, and sold the superiority back for a sizable ransom. Richard's subjects were very much annoyed about it, but in fact they reaped a considerable gain, in a return to the old friendly relations. William bickered with John, Richard's brother and successor, but without affecting the international friendship, and English assistance helped William against a pretender.

The next two reigns, of Alexander II and Alexander III, cover the greater part of the thirteenth century, and the fourteenth looked back on them as the Golden Age.

---

[1] Nineteen years later, by the Treaty of Worms, Henry's son was forced, in exactly the same way, to make England a fief of the Empire.

Alexander II intervened in English politics, supporting
the Barons against John, but the national relations continued fair.   Alexander was not well seen at the English
court, but, partly perhaps for that reason, was personally popular in England.   He and the son of his French
second queen steered cannily through, nipped a threatened and serious Norse war in the bud at Largs, and
definitely rounded off our present Scotland, save the
North Sea Islands.   They left her hampered by great
royal estates in England, as England both had been
and was to be by the enormous Angevin fiefs in France,
which for some time she had been in process of losing.
With relations still friendly, however, these wealthy
fiefs were a great addition to the Crown Revenues : the
Kings of Scots were far less dependent financially on
taxation than their contemporaries to the south.   In
spite of occasional tension between the two govern-
ments, relations were friendly till Alexander III died,
and for some time after.   His first queen was a daughter
of Henry III and sister of Henry's successor Edward I,
and his father's first wife had been Henry's sister.

In the long peace and the growing national unity,
Scotland throve enormously.   The thirteenth century
is a time of rapid political, commercial, and intellectual
advance.   Scotland was coming to be, very definitely,
Scotland, but without losing her sense of being part of
Europe.   Scots soldiers, scholars, and merchants were
to be found anywhere from Sweden to Sicily, from
Moorish Spain to the Crusader lordships in the Levant.
The linguistic habits of the Scot helped this freedom

of movement and outlook : Scotland was polyglot
beyond any country. Our neighbours, besides the
universal Latin, had two languages, but between them
was a *horizontal* social division. One was a gentleman's
tongue, the other was not. The ' mother-tongue ' of
a Scots gentleman under the last kings of the Macalpin
house might be Gaelic, English, or Norman French,
and naturally, in the circumstances, he was likely to
speak more than one of these tongues. Alan of Galloway, of a line of Gaelic princes, had a Norman mother,
and his daughters married the Norman Earl of Winchester, in the extreme south of England, and the
Norman, or rather Picard, Baliol, who had lands in
Scotland, England, and North France. The tongue of
the commons was probably seldom French, but it
might be Gaelic (that most often, a great deal) or
English, more rarely Norse, and there was even a
Flemish element, mostly among the wealthy merchant
class, though not limited to these, for the heads of four
great Highland clans and of at least one great family of
the Lowlands are of Flemish stock. And any man who
as courtier, soldier, administrator, churchman, or merchant, had to go about and mingle with his fellows had
naturally to speak more than one language. As late as
the middle fifteenth century, a writer makes an Englishman, chaffing a Scot, address him in a mixture of English and what is meant for French and Gaelic.[1]

---

[1] Robert Bruce, Randolph, James Douglas, Comyn, and Wallace
probably all grew up bilingual in French and Gaelic : the four
former at any rate would probably have spoken in French if sud-

This point of language has been dwelt upon at length, not as a picturesque or interesting detail, but because it has a very important practical bearing. The state of things which it reveals did a good deal to condition the events of the last decade of the thirteenth century and the first of the fourteenth.

The effect of the racial mixture must not, however, be exaggerated. Precisely because it *was* so thoroughly mixed, a national feeling had been growing up. The racial difference marked by language was recognised, but so was something else. David I's proclamations might address ' the Normans, English, Scots, and Galwegians of the realm : ' the last Alexanders might have added ' the Norse and Flemings ; ' but they were all, increasingly, ' of the realm.' It ought not to be necessary to add—though unfortunately, to judge by journalism, it is—that this salad of races grew less and less distinct, especially in the very mobile ruling class. Unless possibly in Galloway, in a few pockets of Perth and Inverness, and among the Irish colony round Glasgow, modern Scotland has no such thing as a pure Celt : which is very fortunate, for Celtic blood, though its addition seems to improve any other, is like those wines invaluable as admixtures but not to be recom-

denly wakened. It is not known that any of them spoke English, and if he did it would be as an acquired tongue. Keith and the rest of the few Lothian gentlemen possibly spoke it, though their normal tongue would be French. Hardly any of the men on the English side of the war, above the rank and file, would be able to speak English much, if at all. Of the great mass of political documents of the time, the only English one I can recall is a translation of the Latin statutes of 1318.

mended for drinking neat. And similarly, there is no such thing as a pure Teuton Scot . . . though north of the Pentland Firth one may find pure Scandinavian, that is, Gothic. By the thirteenth century the racial mixture was beginning that was to leave Teuton coloured with Celt in the South-east, Celt, of two kinds, with a Teutonic infusion, in the South-west, and Celt, again of two but apparently closer divisions in the Highlands (that is, if the extensive Pictish race was Celtic) very strongly tinged with Norse in the West and North, where often indeed it is rather Norse tinged with Celtic, and rather less strongly with Teuton in the East. And the Flemish strain is perceptible in the North-east, where it is the basis of ' the Aberdeen Story.' [1] This growing consciousness of a *national* unity binding together differences of race and speech grew first and most strongly in the common people, who moved about less and had a less cosmopolitan outlook than the gentry, who frequently owned lands in two or more kingdoms, doing allegiance for them to as many sovereigns, and moving from one to the other indifferently. In Scotland, as in England, France, and Spain, there was growing a strong but as yet vague sense of the Nation, not simply as property

[1] Of the seventy-nine Highland chiefs whose arms are given by Adam, fifty-four are of stock originally Celtic ; thirteen of ' Lowland,' apparently Anglo-Teuton ; five of Norse ; four, including the second farthest north, of Flemish ; and three, including the farthest north, Norman-French. Thus practically a third of the great houses of Gaelic Scotland are not of Celtic origin. Those of the South are naturally even more assorted. And of course, all these families intermarried extensively.

of the *Dux* or *Rex* or of the *Comes regis*—one's leader, for whom one must fight, who owed one protection—but as something belonging to all free men, to which each of them severally belonged and owed something. But this conception, for another generation, had hardly risen into the ruling class, whose allegiance was not to a place, but to a man, their lord, and beyond him to their order of chivalry and its discipline, and to the culture of Christendom, of which that order had developed as bulwark.

These things must all be remembered during what follows, the events set in motion by Alexander's death.

CHAPTER II

THE INFANT QUEEN

FOUR YEARS : 1286–1290

' Scote miser, plora, tibi flendi iam venit hora.'
English Song, c. 1300.

ALEXANDER the Peaceable was dead, and they buried
him in St Margaret's great abbey of Dunfermline in
Fife, that his brother-in-law was to burn within twenty
years. Scotland had no active sovereign, but her nominal one, for the moment, was clear enough. For the
next four years, Scots politics were conditioned by the
fact that the baby Princess Margaret of Norway was
legitimately Margaret Queen of Scots. Her status as
such had already been admitted, for her grandfather,
finding himself childless on the death of his promising
son Alexander, had in 1284 called his great vassals into
council at Scone—eleven bishops, thirteen earls, and
twenty-seven barons—and settled the Crown on her in
default of further issue. (Her mother had died at her
birth the year before.) As he was a healthy man in the
early forties, with every intention of marrying again, it
is possible that no one took the matter very seriously,
least of all one baron by the name of Robert de Brus,
who as son of the cousin of Alexander's father had
already seen a similar settlement on himself, when a

24

similar situation had arisen in the preceding reign, on the failure of issue to Alexander II's first marriage. That king's second marriage had produced a son and made the succession clear. Queen Yolette might be as obliging as Queen Marie.

According to the Lanercost Chronicler, the lady did her best, announcing that she was left pregnant, and attempting a Warming-pan Plot of the sort later credited to James VII and Mary Beatrice. If she ever did, she had no luck with it. Little Margaret, not three years old, was Queen, and none of her subjects liked the situation. They had already had some painful experience of the minorities that for half a millennium were a recurrent curse.[1] This was worse than any. The sovereign was a girl, and not even in Scotland.

The Council did the orthodox thing in the circumstances, appointing a Commission of Regency, whose composition is worth a little remark. It consisted of six *Custodes* or Guardians, three for the North, and three for South of Forth. For the North there were Bishop Fraser of St Andrews, a Norman; the Celtic Earl of Fife; and the Celto-Norman Earl of Buchan, a Comyn, whose Scoto-Norman father was a great-great-nephew of Malcolm III, and whose wife was a daughter of the Earl of Winchester and a grand-

---

[1] Except Robert II and Robert III, who were both too old to be very useful rulers, no sovereign between Robert I and Charles I was more than sixteen at his accession, and only two were more than seven. Only four sovereigns between David I (acc. 1124) and Charles I (acc. 1625) did not have a more or less lengthy minority.

daughter of the Celtic Prince of Galloway. For the South there was the Bishop of Glasgow, Robert Wishart, a very able man and a patriot ; another Comyn, John the Black, Lord of Badenoch and Tynedale ;[1] and James the High Steward, whose family, originally Celtic from Brittany, had come to England with William the Norman, to Scotland with David I, and had held the Stewardship now for five generations. These three southern Guardians were to play a conspicuous part later, as were Fraser, the daughter of Fife, and the son of Buchan.

The Lord did not make the world with a committee, and from the beginning it was a dubious omen that the two parts of Scotland should still need a separate administration. National feeling, as has been said, was growing : but even in this present century it is not always strong enough to overcome sectional—even geographically sectional—feeling : the present writer, not many years ago, was called ' a Highlander ' by an angry Lowlander in a tone that suggested the epithet was intended to be opprobrious. In the thirteenth century, and frequently later, much of the South preferred England to its northern fellow-subjects, though

[1] The House of Comyn were enormously powerful, and play a leading part in the affairs of the next twenty years. They were originally Normans who had come to Scotland under William the Lion, who gave their progenitor, probably a grandson of the Conqueror's Earl of Northumberland, and already Lord of Northallerton in Yorkshire, lands about Roxburgh. This progenitor's son married as his second wife the heiress to the earldom of Buchan, and both this Buchan line and the senior one throve tremendously, as these two appointments show. The genealogy appended to this volume gives some idea of their connections.

we need not fall into the error of those historians who
have taken seriously a characteristic jape of Andrew
Lang's, and call in evidence the famous Burgh Seal of
Stirling, which is frequently referred to in this connection by gentlemen who seem to be unaware that its in-
scription has no capital letters. It bears a bridge with
a crucifix in the middle and armed men facing each
other with spears and bows. The legend is HIC ARMIS
BRUTI SCOTI STANT : HIC CRUCE TUTI. The most probable actual translation is ' Here stand the Bretts and
Scots in arms, shielded by the Cross,' [1] but the version
adopted (quite seriously as a rule) by most historians
is, more or less, ' Here are the Hielant brutes standing
in arms, here the douce Christians.' And the mistranslation is not without excuse in actual history,
while the attitude of mind that lies under it, and makes
it still possible in modern times, is not hopeful for
united resistance against invasion.

The assorted Regency found itself very rapidly in
trouble, though racial clashes had nothing to do with
the fact. The reign of a female sovereign was an innovation, and the English experiment of the preceding
century had not been encouraging. Moreover, the
principle of inheritance had not yet been very definitely
established, certainly not with an unquestioned usage
that covered such unprecedented circumstances. The
old Pictish principle of succession was by female descent,

[1] The Bretts and Scots appear in the name of the old code of
laws abrogated by Edward of England after the apparent conquest of
1304.

a sister's son being preferred to a brother's. By the old Tanist principle, the actual succession was confined to males, to the senior male capable of ruling : the early Macalpin successions are said to show the Irish form of this, in the alternation of the two branches of the house. Under Malcolm II, who died in 1034, this had been abolished in the case of the Crown, and (perhaps through the influence of the new province of Lothian) the Teutonic rule adopted of succession to the senior line of descendants. The attempted change, however, had not prevented war between Malcolm's grandson, Duncan I, and the gentleman who did not murder him, Macbeth, or, on Malcolm III's death in 1093, between the 'tanist' heir Donald Bàn and the 'primogeniture' heir Duncan II : but Donald, even after Duncan was killed, had to make terms with the new principle, keeping only the North and leaving the South that held it to his nephew, Duncan's brother Edmund. Edmund died, childless, and his next brother Edgar succeeded to the throne, and having no son, divided the kingdom again between his brothers Alexander I and David I. David joined it again and passed it to his grandson Malcolm IV, but the North tried to split off. Malcolm, however, in spite of his youth, frail health, and the vow of chastity that has got him into disrepute with Protestant historians, who are curiously nervous on that subject, was a bonny fechter, and left a united kingdom to William his brother. None the less, the principle was still rather vague, and for William's son to elect an heir from among his kindred, and for the said heir to wish to implement the arrangement when the direct male succession failed, was not surprising, nor that he should find backers, who thought that Scotland would be better with a grown man at its head than with a girl-child, or even a committee.

On the 20th of September, therefore, six months after the King's death, certain nobles of Scotland gathered together at Turnberry on the coast of Carrick, and in the traditional manner of Scots lords in revolt, made a band, refusing to accept the little Queen Margaret. They were Patrick Earl of March and his three sons ; Angus Macdonald, Lord of the Isles, and his son ; James Stewart, one of the Guardians, and his brother ; their host, the Earl of Carrick, and his brother ; and the father of the last two, Robert Bruce, the old Lord of Annandale.[1] Of the seniors, March and the Stewarts were Normanised Celts, Bruce Scoto-Norman, Macdonald a Celtic Gael. Associated with them as allies were two foreigners, the Norman Earl of Ulster, Richard de Burgh, who was James Stewart's brother-in-law, and nephew, by the way, of a Princess of Scotland ; and another Norman, Thomas de Clare, first cousin of Carrick and brother of that Earl of Gloucester who was son-in-law of King Edward. Their

[1] To speak of *Bruce* and *Stewart* is an anachronism, but general usage makes it sound pedantic to write *de Brus, le Steward, de Comyn, le Waleys, de Dufglas*, which is what these gentlemen would have called themselves, and I shall refer to them normally as Bruce, Stewart, Comyn, Wallace, Douglas, etc., retaining the particle only in case of definitely territorial names, like *David de Brechin*.

candidate for the throne was one of their number, Bruce of Annandale, the father of their host. He was then a very old man of nearly eighty, but with two sons and a thriving brood of grandsons : and the grounds for the choice were Alexander II's decision of forty-eight years previously, when that king, finding himself without an heir, had named this man, then young, the son of his cousin Isobel, and his nearest male relation, since Isobel's elder sister had only daughters.

The paternal stock of Bruce demands a word here, since his grandson's career is the subject of this book. The root of the stirp has been traced, rather vaguely though not improbably, to the Norse Jarl Sigurd of Orkney, who married a daughter of Malcolm I in the mid tenth century, and had a son named Bruis who settled in the Normandy of the early Dukes. Certainly by the eleventh century, the family were established as lords of a castle in the Cotentin from which they took a name that is spelt Brus, Brix, Braose, Breaux, Bruys, Bruyse, and Brutz, and were powerful enough for one of them to have married a daughter of Alan Duke of Brittany. His young son came to England as a page of Emma of Normandy, Queen successively of Ethelred Unred and his vanquisher Cnut of Denmark. Later, two of the family helped Emma's great-nephew to conquer England, and were richly rewarded, the younger receiving thirty-four manors in Yorkshire. Robert, the son of this latter, was a trusted friend of David I, who gave him the Marcher lordship of Annandale. He left his Scots lands to Robert his younger son, and the family throve in Scotland as it had done already in France and England. This Robert's grandson, Robert, called 'the Noble,' married the niece of William the Lion, and their son was the Robert of the Turnberry Band, the man William's son had chosen as his heir. This man, born about 1210, and known, to distinguish him from his son and grandson, as the Competitor, was a man of great lands in both Scotland and England, some of his manors lying as far south as Essex. He had fought at Evesham on King Henry's side, was Governor of Carlisle and Sheriff of Cumberland, and his personal interests seem to have lain mainly in England. He married Isobel de Clare, daughter of the Earl of Gloucester and Hereford, one of the great Marcher barons, and had two sons. The elder of these, another Robert, known later as Robert de Brus *le viel* (the elder) had served in the last Crusade, and on his return had married the young widow of a comrade-in-arms, Marjorie, Countess of Carrick in her own right : Turnberry, the scene of the gathering, was her castle, for she came of the old semi-royal Celtic stock of the South-west, her father being great-grandson of that Fergus Prince of Galloway who had given so much trouble to Malcolm IV. Countess Marjorie bore her husband a large family, of whom three were to die upon a foreign scaffold, two more to spend long years in foreign prisons, while two were to be kings and one a queen : and the eldest of their boys had been given the traditional family name of Robert, and at the time of this Turnberry Band was just turned twelve, having been born at Turnberry, or as some say at Lochmaben, on the eleventh of July, 1274.

What happened after the band is not very clear. There seems to have been at least some attempt at an armed rising in old Bruce's favour. The castles of Dumfries, Buittle, and Wigtown were forcibly taken, and the affair was formidable enough for Jedburgh, Ayr, and even Edinburgh to be strengthened. Apparently, however, it fizzled out, effecting nothing, but without anyone being brought to book by the Guardians. It must have done something to familiarise the boy Robert, then just of an age to begin his page's training, with the notion of his family's claims to the throne.

The course of affairs becomes clearer by 1288, when apparently the Bruce family had given up the idea of pressing their claim by arms. The Guardians by this time were reduced to four : the two earls in the Northern trio were dead, leaving only their coadjutor, Bishop Fraser, a fact which may have something to do with what followed. And at this point a new force comes into affairs, in the person of Edward Plantagenet, King of England, fourth of his name but known in the casual English fashion as Edward I, and great-uncle of the little Scottish Queen. Edward's personality and dynastic position were to be so important in the next eighteen years that it is best to say something of them here at his first appearance. Like nearly all the nobility of England, he was French, but unlike the most of them, not Norman. He came of the sinister

house of the Counts of Anjou of the race of Fulk the
Black, a strange tigrine stock, with a touch in it of
what we should call mania and mediaeval men described as a devil. They were mad, but with a lucid
and able madness, with an energy, in action or anger,
of incredible violence : the greatest of them, Edward's
great-grandfather, would throw himself on the floor
when he was angered, biting the rushes and howling
like a beast . . . and the process was not allowed to
work off his rage until some more practical event had
followed. With this, most of them had an uncommon
personal charm, most of them hated their own blood-
kin like poison, many of them were brilliant war-
leaders and some good civil ones, nearly all had courage
to match their ferocity, and with scarcely an exception
they were as greedy as the grave, though it won them
little, for when they went under at last in the wolf-pack
worry of the Wars of the Roses, all they had to show
for a couple of centuries of wars of aggression was
Wales, rankling memories of France and Scotland, and
the long poison of Ireland in their flank as substitute
for the huge and lawful dominions to which Henry II,
their first king, had succeeded.

Now, Edward was very much a Plantagenet. His
father was a scholar and a dilettante—he made Westminster Abbey : his mother, Eleanor of Provence, was
the daughter of that very astute politician Raymond
Berenger, who had turned his four daughters from a
liability to a brilliant asset, and held the balance of
power in the south of Europe. He was a very brave

c

and able captain, one of the foremost soldiers of his time, and a great innovator in the art of war : and it may have been the Berenger strain in him that made him, at the same time, a lawyer by hobby. He did useful service to the English law, and would have made a successful barrister, if scrupulous judges might not have liked him much : an Englishman of his own day said of him, ' The way whereby he arrives at what he will, crooked though it be, he calls straight : whatever he likes, he declares to be a thing lawful.' One of the chief modern English authorities on the period, Professor Tout, calls him the greatest of the Plantagenets and speaks of his ' rare nobility of purpose,' admitting in the same breath that ' equivocation and chicane were his worst faults.' Like his descendant the Black Prince he was devoted to the law of chivalry : he adored his very charming Spanish queen : and it is he who formulated the English penalty for high treason, that so neatly combined the maximum of mess, suffering, and humiliation, that his grateful country stuck to it till well on in the eighteenth century.[1] He broke his own oaths with public and shameless frankness, and—probably quite without conscious

[1] The details are usually glossed over by historians, but so many of the men of whom we shall have to speak made their practical acquaintance, so many others had to think about them, that it is worth while to consider exactly what they were. The victim was hanged for the sake of the humiliation, but carefully not allowed to be more than half strangled : he was then castrated, his belly ripped open, and his entrails torn out and burnt in a brazier, after which the living heart was torn out of his body, and then he was beheaded and cut in quarters—all, of course, before an appreciative crowd of spectators.

hypocrisy—had *Pactum serva* carved upon his tombstone. He had great personal charm and a splendid presence, unmarred by the slight stammer of his speech : an English writer said of him in his youth that he combined the lion and the panther, and the crouching ambiguous beasts of the English shield, between lion and leopard, were his just device.

In 1288 he had reigned for sixteen years, and was at the height of his power, royal and personal. He had learnt war in the last of the Crusades, and against that strong leader, Simon de Montfort. His consuming ambition was to make good the enormous loss of the French lands of his house. His great-grandfather had inherited Anjou, Maine, and Touraine from his father, Normandy, England, and a ghost-lordship of Ireland from his mother : he had married Poitou, Marche, Saintonge, Périgord, Gascony, Béarn, the Agenais, the Limousin, Auvergne. He had married his son to Brittany, to its unlucky half-Scots heiress Constance, got a grip on Wales, and for his last fifteen years even on Scotland. And when John his youngest son went to his own place, all that was left was England, a sketchy hold on Wales and Ireland, a part of Saintonge and a part of Gascony, that made up between them the fief known as Guyenne. Edward was grandson of John, and he wanted it back. He had reconquered Wales in the early years of his reign : the tiny principality fought well, but it had no allies, and was close to the heart of England. It whetted his appetite for larger game. He wanted the French lands, and like every King of England from Cnut to Henry VIII, he wanted Scotland, the more as Scotland, though friendly to his own country, was also on very friendly terms with France. In the present state of the Scottish royal house he saw a good chance for a more intimate alliance, on peaceful terms, that could later be used to give him what he desired.

The connection was already very close. His peaceable father, brother-in-law himself of a King of Scots, had given his daughter to that king's successor. Half the great vassals of the King of Scots—that is probably an underestimate—were vassals of his own for lands in England, while some were his fellow-vassals to the French Crown, and might be useful allies in opposing it. Indeed, there was every reason why a marriage between his young son and the Queen of Scots should be welcome to the nobles of both countries. She was, to be sure, heiress-presumptive to Norway, which therefore would expect to have a say : but Eirik II, who was only nineteen, had borrowed money from him, and was finding it inconvenient to pay back.

It is probable that there were some private *pourparlers*. Matters would not reach public discussion for a little. Norway agreed. The Scots Guardians were divided, James Stewart, who had signed the Turnberry Band, being against the match, perhaps as blocking the Bruce claims. The two Bishops and John Comyn were in favour. In 1289, three years after the little Queen's accession, the affair was put formally in train. Eirik sent ambassadors, Edward appointed to act for him the Earl of Pembroke, the Bishop of Winchester, John de Warenne Earl of Surrey, and the fighting Bishop of Durham, Anthony de Bec. The Scottish plenipotentiaries were three of the Guardians, being the Bishops and John Comyn of Badenoch, and for a surprising fourth, old Robert de Brus, who in spite of Stewart's disapproval was evidently statesman enough to see the possible advantages of the match, for both countries, and to subordinate his own claim to these. It is worth observing that even at this stage of the affair their commission bears the cautionary clause that they are to discuss the matter *salvis tamen in omnibus et singulis et per omnia, libertate et honore Scotiae*—'with due care, in all possible contingencies, for the honour and liberty of the Scottish realm.'

They all met at Salisbury in the autumn. Edward had already sent an envoy to the Pope for a provisional dispensation, as the bridegroom and the bride's mother were first cousins, and the marriage therefore required ecclesiastical permission. The Conference of Salisbury went peaceably. The Norwegians agreed to send the Queen to either Scotland or England, but without prejudice to the question of her marriage. The English agreed that if it was in England that she landed, she was to be delivered to her own country as soon as it was quiet—*bien asseure et en bone pees*, this probably as a reminder for Robert Bruce. The Scots on their part undertook to make it quiet, and without as yet committing themselves to the match, undertook not to marry the Queen without the consent of her father or without consulting her great-uncle, and further to remove any Guardians to whom Eirik (which meant Edward) might take exception, this last being intended against the absent James Stewart, who had been recalcitrant over the Queen's claim.   In the case of any Guardian being thus dismissed, a successor was to be chosen by the *probi homines* of Norway and Scotland, Edward to act as umpire in case of disagreement. Affairs were thus put in train for the betrothal, which was not, however, actually concluded, as the precise terms had not yet been decided.

The idea of this Union of the Crowns was well but cautiously received in Scotland.   For a hundred years there had been friendship with England, and the relations of the two countries were quite exceptionally intimate.   The intellectual relations of the clergy, the social and even the blood relationships of the nobles, the commercial interests of the Third Estate, were all closely interwoven.   That the union should take place would be an excellent thing, strengthening both, *provided that it was on satisfactory terms.*   That proviso shows in the Commission quoted above, and one sees the strength of the growing sense of nationality in the care taken to define these terms.   They were drawn up by the professional lawyers, who were churchmen : and the strong national feeling of the Scots church, to be so vital in the next twenty years, is in revealing contrast to the casual attitude, at the time, of most of the nobles.

All through the winter of 1289 the diplomats were busy.   The general tenor of the terms of union shows in Edward's answer to a lost Scottish *communiqué*. On the 20th of June he wrote to ' the Guardians, Prelates, Nobles, and Communitas of Scotland,' in response to certain questions on their part, which he repeats. They have asked him to ensure a suitable jointure for the young Queen : he is willing to observe this condition. They have asked him to undertake that the laws, liberties, and customs of Scotland shall not be infringed, and that the kingdom of Scotland shall remain divided, by its recognised boundaries, from England, and free in itself, without any attempt to claim its subjection : his reply is a formal assent to the separation according to the marches, ' as they have been *or may be altered in future*.' (The italics are decidedly not Edward's, for the clause slips in as casually as may be.) The question of the claim to ' Subjection ' is quietly ignored, and the letter goes on politely to other points. Apparently, the blank roused no suspicion : the document, of course, was a mere informal stage in the discussion, and the formal treaty had yet to be ratified. The Estates were apparently satisfied as to Edward's general intentions, and formal consent to the marriage was sent to the Kings of Norway and of England, signed by all the Guardians, by forty-four dignitaries of the Church, by twelve earls, including Carrick, old Bruce's son, and by forty-seven barons. Edward also wrote to Eirik, inviting him to send his daughter to England. On the 18th of July, 1290, four years and four months after Alexander's death, the Scots and English Commissioners met at Birgham on the Tweed, close to the old

victorious field of Carham, and there the terms of a
treaty were concluded, and Edward of England undertook to observe them.

The rights, laws, liberties, and customs of Scotland
should remain forever inviolate. In case of the failure
of issue to Margaret and her husband, Scotland was to
revert to the Queen's next heir, wholly, freely, and
without any question of feudal subjection. So long as
the union of the countries subsisted, the kingdom of
Scotland was to remain separate, in an equal federal
union : a clause has been added here, ' saving the rights
of the King of England . . . which may justly belong
to him.' It is probable that the Scots Commissioners
took the second phrase as safeguarding the first : it is
also probable that Edward was trying already to make
a loop-hole, for he had used those phrases already in
English domestic legislation, in his Forest Law, and
his interpretation of them had not endeared him to his
subjects. Besides these general terms, there are a
number of specific safeguards. The liberties of the
Church are carefully guarded. No vassal of the Crown
was to go out of Scotland to do his homage. No Scottish subject was to be answerable at law to a court outside the kingdom. The Great Seal was to bear the
Queen's name only, and the Chancellor, the chief Law
Officer of the Crown, must be a native-born Scot and
reside in Scotland. The other great officers of state
must also be Scotsmen, and the Crown Records were
never to leave the country.

These terms were all agreed to by King Edward, and

he set his seal to the Treaty as it stood. The matter was now in fair train. Such a union of the two countries, welcomed by both, and with the possible addition of Norway, would have been an interesting factor in European politics, though it may be that it would not have fulfilled all hopes. It is true that the similar union of Aragon and Castile through the marriage of their king and queen in the fifteenth century laid the foundation of the great power of Spain : but it is also true that the marriage of a later Queen of Scots to the Earl of Darnley was equally sound politics . . . if the gentleman's character had not been what it was. And Edward II, when he grew to manhood, resembled Darnley rather than Ferdinand. Historical marriages that do not come off, like Anne of Brittany's to Maximilian or Henry VIII's rejection by Marie de Guise (who had, as she told him, a very slender neck) provide the speculative historian with a fascinating game, but in practice serve only to remind one (which, however, is a valuable lesson) that nothing in history is ' inevitable.'

Things went on thus smilingly through the summer of 1290. Edward appointed the Bishop of Durham as his representative in Scotland. There seem to have been rumours, or rumours of rumours, of some sort of armed opposition to the match, for Edward demanded that the castles of Scotland should be handed to him as a guarantee. The Guardians' reply was a polite refusal, and a promise to give up the castles in proper course to the young Queen and her consort, the Prince of Wales, and the sufficiently preposterous suggestion was not allowed to disturb diplomatic relations.

Preparations went on. Edward sent up a handsome gift of plate, and fitted up a ship to send for the Queen. He did it thoroughly : she was ' weel graithit ' and with stores of food, including sweets, fruit, and two stone of gingerbread. We know all about that ship, how much of the stockfish went bad and was thrown overboard, how much of the sugar melted (*evanuit*) and how *nuncii asportaverunt* the cake. But Queen Margaret never sailed on her. The ship reached Norway in May, and something may have aroused Eirik's suspicions. At least she returned next month without the Queen, whom King Eirik sent over on a ship of his own, by way of his own territory of Orkney, where her subjects were to meet her. Edward could not well protest against the arrangement. He sent up an embassy, the Earl of Surrey, the Dean of York, and the active Bishop of Durham, to make the best they could of the Pentland Firth . . . and what happened then is more than anyone knows. Edward himself made hay of the Scots records, and the Norse ones for this time have suffered also. Absolutely the only contemporary document that casts any light at all on what happened in Orkney is an anxious letter to Edward in early October, from Bishop Fraser, the only survivor of the three Northern Guardians.

Fraser's letter (a private, unofficial one) announces that there is a rumour of the Queen's death, and that there is fear of consequent civil war, unless Edward

himself takes measures to prevent it : that the rumour
has been contradicted, but that everyone is anxious, and
. . . will Edward, if John Baliol should come to him,
handle him carefully, ' so that your honour and advantage may be preserved ? ' (Now, this Baliol, like old
Bruce, was near the Throne.)   Finally, he comes into
the open, and begs Edward to hurry towards the
Border, so as to be at hand to set up the rightful heir,
' if so be he will follow your counsel.'   This letter is
the sole contemporary record of the Queen's death,
and we know neither when nor how *Margareta sub-*
tracta est de praesente luce.[1]

The business was of the most cloudy, even then.   A
girl was burnt at Nordness in 1309, for claiming to be
the Queen, kidnapped in Orkney, and she held to her
story even at the stake, though Haakon's court pro-
nounced her a German from Lubeck.   There certainly
were rumours of foul play, both kidnapping and
murder.   The former, at least, does not seem very
likely, for a body appears to have been brought back
to Bergen, and accepted by King Eirik as that of his
daughter.   But the child of two children would bear a
fragile life ; and certainly, whatever happened to her,
that is the end of Margaret as Queen of Scots and
heiress of the line of the Macalpins.   And it was the
end too of Edward's excellent plan for a matrimonial
Union of the Crowns.

[1] A phrase from Pope Boniface's Bull of 1300.

CHAPTER III

THE DISPUTED SUCCESSION

TWO YEARS : 1290–1292

'Unhappy man retains in nothing so much a desire to be like
his Maker, as in that he would be supreme.'
Sir George Mackenzie, *The Laws and Customs of Scotland
in Matters Criminal.*

SCOTLAND was in a worse condition than she had been
four years before, a worse than France was to experience
thirty-eight years later. Some head to a feudal state
there had to be : but now there was no heir, or there
were too many. To a modern eye, the thing looks
completely simple, but in fact at the time it was very
far from that. The principle of succession was not
determined, nor was there established machinery that
had a clear right to determine it. In the vagueness,
there appeared a swarm of pretenders. Every eldest
son who was descended, legitimately or not, from
David I, laid claim to the Crown, with the exception of
the Duke of Brittany, whose moderation seems difficult
to account for. There were eleven of these, and a
couple more, a deil's dozen of fighting gentlemen,
mostly of powerful families, each convinced that he
ought to be the King of Scots, and ready to invoke
whatever principle of law or force would raise him to
that desirable position. The claimants belong to four

44

different generations, and it will make matters clearer to arrange them in groups. (There is a genealogy at the back of this book.) Two of them, as has been said, were not among the descendants of David I. One was Eirik of Norway, as heir to his wife and daughter, a claim that by feudal custom would have been strong if his wife had survived her father, which she had not, but which, at the weakest, had a good deal of a case. The other was one of the Guardians, Black John Comyn of Badenoch, who founded on a descent from Donald Bàn : he was considerably remote from the main royal line, but apart from his position as Guardian he was head of one of the most powerful families in Scotland, and closely connected with the Earls of Mar and Buchan. Of the rest, seven were on the wrong side of the royal blanket. One came from a possibly legitimated half-sister of Alexander III, whose legitimation, and its consequences, were disputed. Five more were descended from illegitimate progeny of William I, and another from his bastard half-sister, daughter of David I's son, Henry Prince of Scotland. Even in an age where illegitimacy was no great slur, its most serious consequences were, precisely, in regard to inheritance, so that these seven could not be considered serious starters. There remained the four legitimate male descendants of David's son, Prince Henry. One came from his daughter, Ada, Countess of Holland : this was Florent V, Count of Holland, whose father had been William, King of the Romans—that is, Emperor, or rather anti-Emperor, Elect. The other three were

descendants of Prince Henry's youngest son, David
Earl of Huntingdon, brother of Malcolm IV and
William I. David's sons had died without heir, but
his three daughters had all left children, the first and
third being now represented by grandsons, John Baliol
Lord of Galloway and John Lord Hastings, and the
second by a son, old Robert Bruce. Of these four,
Florent's claim, being through a daughter whose
brother had living descendants, was inferior to that of
the others : he tried to back it by a vague assertion
that Earl David had been guilty of high treason, but
his main support would rather appear to have been
that as son of a more or less *de iure* Emperor he was the
most important person going. In fact, however, his
claim by descent was inferior to that of the descendants
of Earl David's daughters. Daughters, normally, were
counted co-heiresses. If that applied to kingdoms, all
three—Baliol, Bruce, and Hastings—should share. If
it did not, Lord Hastings' claim did not stand, and there
remained only Baliol and Bruce . . . who, as it happened, were both immensely wealthy and very powerful. And each was sincerely convinced that his claim
was the better.

In fact, they had justification for so believing. On
modern assumptions, there is no doubt about it.
Baliol was descended from the eldest daughter, Margaret, and Bruce from Isobel, who was the second. A
modern court, if such an obvious matter should ever
reach it, would decide in sixty seconds at the most, or,
allowing for legal language, in ten minutes. In 1290,

however, the matter was less clear, even in countries
where the Tanist principle of heirship had not quite
recently been in operation.   If both men had been sons
of Earl David's daughters, it would have been clearer
then than in fact it was.   But they were not.   Bruce
was the son of Isobel of Huntingdon, but Baliol was
only Margaret's grandson, and that by her daughter,
Devorgilla of Galloway, who moreover had been alive
when King Alexander died.   (She had barely predeceased Queen Margaret.)   Thus, though Baliol was
of an elder line than Bruce, he was further removed,
and by a female descent, from the common ancestor
through whom they claimed.   Moreover—this would
be important anywhere, but was rather specially important in Scotland—Bruce had actually been proclaimed heir in the past, in the event of failure of issue
to Alexander II, a failure which now had come to pass.
To which Baliol might contend that it was fifty years
before, and there had been a couple of sovereigns since.
It is permissible, I think, to imagine that the dinner-
tables of Turnberry and Lochmaben had much to say
on the subject through this winter, and that the
Countess Marjorie's eldest son, standing napkin in
hand behind his mother's chair or kneeling with basin
and ewer before her guests (he would pass from page
to esquire about this time) heard a good deal of lively
conversation.   And when he and his fellow esquires
took their meal, after their elders and betters had been
served, they would scarcely express an affection for
John Baliol.

The case, in fact, was richly disputable, and the lawyers of all Europe licked their lips.[1]   Peaceful men who loved Scotland were less exhilarated.   Some of the candidates were tolerably powerful.   Eirik's father had been a very dangerous enemy : Florent's had made considerable trouble for the Empire : and several of the rest were in control of sizable forces and had powerful backers.   There were all the makings of an extremely nasty civil war on the lines of the later English War of the Roses, with possible foreign complications as well.   It was true that nine of the Scottish or English or Scoto-English candidates could not achieve a very serious claim : but the two who were the favourites for the stakes happened to be, in practice, the most powerful : and Scotland was rapidly taking sides for them.   As Fordun, a generation later, puts it, *Causa difficilis erat et ardua. . . . Super iura varii varia sentibant et multipliciter vacillabant. . . . Superiorem non habebant, qui eorum sententiam et potestatis rigorem executione posset demandare, vel partes compellere ad observantiam sententiae.*   There was no one to give judgment or to compel its execution, because, in the absence of a recognised King of Scots, there was no one who stood as overlord to the contestants : and the law, to which their submission might have been claimed, was not clear enough to be a valid sanction.

The obvious course, if civil war was to be avoided, was therefore to find a neutral arbitrator : and the obvious person was visibly at hand, in the person of

[1] See Appendix I.

Edward of England. He, to begin with, had the advantage of status, being a crowned king, and therefore Eirik's equal. Of the others in the nearest relation to Scotland, Eirik of Norway, though more nearly akin to the late Queen Margaret, was a claimant himself, and head of a country only lately hostile. Philip of France bore a very distant relation to Queen Margaret, and he was himself a young inexperienced man. Edward, on the other hand, was brother-in-law of the beloved King Alexander, great-uncle and all but father-in-law of Queen Margaret, and himself had royal Scottish blood in him. He was also ruler of the nearest country, which for a hundred years had been Scotland's friend : and he was a mature and able sovereign, particularly skilled, as it chanced, in law, who only three years earlier had successfully made peace between France and Aragon in the thorny matter of the Sicilian Succession, and was at the time carrying on negotiations that were to reconcile the King of Aragon, a year later, with the Papacy. Moreover (and this counted a good deal) if the competitors, as Scottish barons, *superiorem non habebant* at the time, as English ones (and most of them were that too) they *had* an overlord, and he was Edward. In addition, most of them, certainly the two likeliest, knew him personally : he was a man of strong character, much intelligence, and like so many of his house, great charm. He had for the last couple of years been intimately involved in Scots politics, and had shown ability and apparent goodwill : they had his signature to the Treaty of

D

Birgham, with its elaborate safeguards of national rights in a much closer connection than seemed possible for a mere friendly umpire. They overlooked his recent handling of Wales : but it is easy to be wise after the event, and in fact it is very difficult even now to see whom else they could choose besides the Pope. And Nicholas IV had been Pope just long enough to prove himself a greedy incompetent, while his courts, if they commanded more respect, were distant from Scotland by the breadth of Europe. Edward, then, was the obvious choice : and he was chosen. Both the two strongest parties, Bruce's and Baliol's, apparently concurred in the selection.

The extant official invitations have—for reasons, probably, that events will make clear—not been preserved. The evidence for them is in two documents, of which one, as it happens, comes from each of the parties. The first is Bishop Fraser's informal letter, already referred to on page 42. He writes not in his capacity as co-Guardian, but merely as ' William by divine permission humble minister of the Church of St Andrews.' In any case, he was one Guardian out of four, and one of the rest had signed the Turnberry Band as a backer of Bruce. It makes clear, however, that one of Baliol's most important supporters was anxious to have Edward's intervention. The other document, though it concurs with this in accepting Edward, is a manifesto on behalf of Bruce. It is written in the name of the Seven Earls, who as representing the old Mormaors seem to have had some kind of special status, comparable with that of *pairs de France*,[1] and of the Bishops, Abbots, Priors, Earls, Barons, and Freeholders of Scotland, and of the *Communitas* to them adhering. Just who these latter were is rather vague, in the absence, through Edward's plunder, of the records : but whoever they may have been, and however elected, it is clear that they represented a Third Estate, and we shall hear a good deal of them later on.[2] These, speaking ' by right of the laws and customs of Scotland from time out of mind,' address John Comyn and the Bishop of St Andrews, ' who call themselves Guardians of Scotland,' and ' that small part of the *communitas* adhering to them,' and inform them that since Comyn and his supporters are about to appoint, illegally, John Baliol, in violation of the rights of Bruce and the privileges of the national representatives, they have invited Edward of England to arbitrate. And Bishop Fraser very probably smiled.[3]

This claim, of course, is a point for Bruce, and a very strong one. His old appointment as heir by Alexander II, with the ratification of the Great Council, is now

[1] Not every Frenchman of title, even so high as Duke, was a *pair*. The usage must not be confounded with our *peer*.

[2] The original Guardians speak of themselves as *Custodes Regni Scotiae per Communitatem ejusdem Regni electi* ; one would expect the word thus used to mean the united estates, the representatives of the ' community ' in the modern sense. But all through this period from 1290 onward, the word seems to be equivalent to the modern ' Commons.'

[3] It would be interesting to trace the pedigree of the common habit of historians of quoting this document as addressed to *Edward* : when a letter uses the second person and the third, it is usual to assume that it is written to the people who are spoken of in the former.

farther ratified, both by what corresponded to the Chamber of Peers, lay and spiritual, and by what claims to be a majority of representatives of the Commons. That is, Bruce's previous claim was now endorsed by such parliamentary body, hereditary and elective, as existed. It is important that this point should be remembered, for it would certainly influence the point of view of the whole Bruce party, including, naturally, his eldest grandson, just turned sixteen, and old enough to take an interest in a matter which concerned not only his house, but also himself as heir to its dignities.

So far, so good. Both the chief parties, each with strong constitutional support (though Bruce with the stronger, as two of the Guardians as well as the Seven Earls and a majority of the Estates were on his side) [1] had agreed upon the same arbitrator, not as Lord Paramount or judge by right (unless we count Fraser's private and personal letter, which never says so in so many words) but as a friendly neutral and near neighbour . . . *non tanquam superior dominus, vel iudex de iure, sed tanquam amicabilis arbiter et vicinus praestantior.* Fordun, of course, wrote that after the ensuing war : but as has been said, there is no reason for doubting the truth of the statement. It agrees with the tone of the Seven Earls' manifesto, which is the only official document we have.

A conference, to be attended by *les haus Hommes de Escoce et une partie de la Communaute de mesme le*

[1] The Bishop of Glasgow and James Stewart both appear among his auditors during the suit.

Reaume, was arranged for the 10th of May, 1291, at Norham, the great Border castle that looks at Scotland from the English side of the Tweed. And there the Competitors were faced with a shock, for Edward had been getting his tackle ready to fish in the troubled waters of Scots affairs.

He had seen his chance now of reopening the old question of the feudal superiority of the English king over Scotland that had been an English *ignis fatuus* for generations, glimmering even after the Treaty of Canterbury, a hundred and two years before this Conference, had formally settled the matter once for all, for even sixty years after that treaty, Edward's own father had tried to trap the eleven-year-old Alexander III into an admission that might be used to get round it. The boy's precocious wit, or his previous schooling, guided him to so effective a retort that Henry's sense of honour was reawakened, and the friendship between the two countries remained unbroken. Edward, in spite of his epitaph, had less scruple. Blandly ignoring both the Treaty of Canterbury and his own signature to that of Birgham, he opened proceedings with a long speech by his Justiciar, announcing that he was present to redd the dispute not as invited umpire and an impartial friend of the differing parties, but as feudal superior over the realm of Scotland. It has been asserted that his claim, however founded, was at least sincere. Since I am writing history and not fiction, I will not claim to know what was in his mind : but the evidence is strongly the other way. If he had believed his assertion, he would already, on Margaret's accession four years previously, have claimed the ordinary feudal right, incontrovertible if he were the superior, of administering her heritage while she was a minor, and of marrying her as he, her guardian, should choose. But a legal method of union had then been open, and he had gone legally about his aim, treating with Margaret, through her representatives, as one independent sovereign with another. Moreover, even if one makes the unlikely assumption that he had been absent-minded for these four years, and forgotten such a trifling affair as a kingdom, one observes that later on, at the trial of Wallace, when the point would have immensely strengthened Edward's case, no such claim is made : he is only said to rule over Scotland by conquest, which at the moment happened to be true. The theory of his legal superiority thus only appears when needed as a *pis aller*.

The Scots were thunderstruck, though Bishop Fraser can scarcely have been surprised, seeing it was the line he had hinted already. One—we do not know who—made the obvious retort, that no answer to such a claim could be legally given by anyone except the King of Scots. The others demanded time to consider the matter. They got twenty-four hours, and then asked for more time. Edward gave them three weeks . . . and called up his army to Norham.

He still hoped to manage peaceably, however, and the Angevin in him was anglicised enough to wish to get what he wanted with a respectable air of legality.

He set his lawyers to work as well as his captains. In fact, he appealed to more than his own lawyers : he sent a (carefully edited) version of evidence as to the succession to France : the author of the *Liber Pluscardensis*, a Scot in the entourage of Louis XI's first wife, Margaret of Scotland, quotes the debate *in extenso*, from the French records, and a very illuminating debate it is, since it gives the considered opinion of some of the greatest juristic scholars in Europe. Edward's selectiveness with regard to data makes them beg the question of superiority : but he had evidently given them the pedigrees involved, and it is worth noting that there was a good deal of difference of opinion. Modern students who think Baliol's claim was obvious should read the debate : it is easy enough to come by. Some, including the great Petrus de Capella, quote Louis IX's decision, not long before, that if his son predeceased him he was to be succeeded not by the latter's sons, but by their uncle, his own younger son— an analogy to the Tanist principle, on which Bruce was partly founding. Bonet, reputed the supreme authority on Canon Law, decided that the succession ought to go to the claimant who was born first, even though he was descended from the younger line—i.e., he is for Bruce. The Master-General of the Franciscans gives for Bruce again, not on this ground but as nearer in degree, adducing as precedent the biblical case of the daughters of Zelophehad and a more recent succession case in Hainault. These statements, by such high authorities, make clear not only that Bruce may have honestly believed his case, but that he had good enough reason for doing so, even apart from both Crown and parliamentary settlement.

The English lawyers, however, in the meantime, were working on something nearer Edward's heart— the question of the superiority. They were as doucely obedient as those of his grandson, who within three years gave obliging decisions, on precisely contradictory principles, over the French and Breton Succession Cases. They hunted out every conceivable piece of record of any sort of conquest of Scots territory, or of any sort of homage for English fiefs done by a King of Scots to a King of England, culminating triumphantly in William's surrender at the quite authentic Treaty of Falaise. They did not remark that if homage for fiefs in England was tantamount to homage for Scotland itself, then England was a fief of the Crown of France. They did not quote the triumph of their own chroniclers over the Treaty of Falaise, as something entirely new and unprecedented.[1]   Nor, though they adduced the conquest of Britain by Brut, son of Priam of Troy, did they mention a more recent piece of history, the treaty which in 1189 had rescinded that of Falaise *en gros et en détail*.   Nor did they refer to those clauses of Magna Charta which in 1215 had defined relations with the Scottish kings. Nor—most cynical of these fairly flagrant omissions—did they allude to the Treaty of

---

[1] Giraldus Cambrensis, a professional historian, is ecstatic over it as a great achievement, and something entirely new, that had not been accomplished before since Claudius Caesar—' Tantus, tam magnificus honor . . . perpetuum et impretabile decus.'

Birgham, which Edward had sealed rather less than a year before, and which deals with Scotland as with a sovereign state.   Sir Herbert Maxwell, after recording at all events the majority of these facts, considers that Edward sincerely believed his own case.   For 'the English Justinian,' that seems absent-minded.

The Scots, meanwhile, were less usefully employed. The rival claimants were getting up their cases, and everything they could find against those of their rivals, but no one seems to have been greatly concerned over the question that chiefly occupied Edward.   There were probably two reasons for this : one may have been that the Scots lawyers, who knew the facts and had helped to draw up the provisions for the Treaty of Birgham, did not take Edward's claim as anything more than the sort of—to use the vernacular—' trying it on ' that, like Henry III at Alexander's wedding, the English kings had frequently attempted, in rather the spirit of an Eastern salesman who knows the buyer will refuse to pay what is clearly four times the value of the goods, but begins by asking for it, on the off-chance.   The Treaty of Canterbury was perfectly clear : so was the very recent Treaty of Birgham.

This is probable : but the other reason is certain. The person immediately concerned was the King of Scots—i.e., it was a matter for the Competitors.   And all the likeliest were Norman barons.   It is essential to our understanding of the next fifteen, or even next thirty, years to realise just what a difference this made in their attitude to the claim advanced by Edward.

Something has been said already of the cosmopolitan
outlook of the feudal nobility, in Scotland as elsewhere :
and though cosmopolitanism makes very little difference to a man's willingness to attack other countries, it
is apt to slacken his readiness to defend one. This
non-national outlook is especially true of the Normans.
The most comprehensible way of putting it is to say
that in twelfth and thirteenth-century Europe the
Normans had exactly the same position, in a military
aristocracy, as the Jew in the modern commercial
aristocracy. They had a strong sense of loyalty to
their own culture, to chivalry and Christendom : but
although they carved out kingdoms and principalities
in Italy, Sicily, Greece, the Levant, and England, and
infiltrated the ruling class of every nation in Europe,
ours not least, they belonged, essentially, to a people,
not to a nation, which is a people in a defined space of
land. That people was international, not only in
language and intellectual outlook, but in its marriages
—they had nothing short of the Hapsburg flair for an
heiress—and in its chief interests, war and landed
property. An individual man might identify himself
with a place : places take hold. But it would be with
a place that belonged to him, and with no unit as large
as what we call a country.[1] That conception, as yet,
had not caught the upper-class imagination enough to
rouse a sense of nationality, let alone of nationalism.

[1] It is significant that in the very early Middle Ages, when
feudalism is coming into being, *patria* means not the *country* but
either the fief or the *mesnie* (practically = clan) to which a man belongs.

National feeling, in their attitude to Edward's claim, was something that would hardly be involved : also, of the two men most deeply concerned, Bruce, who was the more Scottish by descent, was very old, and such slight nationalism as had arisen, in his class at least, was something very new, as new as the idea of internationalism, in 1920, would be to a general of the Crimean War. And Baliol, who like James Stewart and Edward himself, was a Norman by culture only, not by race, was probably more of a Picard than anything else. He held lands in Normandy and England as well, and had inherited Galloway from his mother, but his main, and large, estates, whence he took his name, were in Picardy.

There is a further point that arises here, and is no less needful to a just understanding. This other point is the question of fealty, a legal principle frequently concerned in the history of the time at present dealt with, and likely to give rise to misunderstanding because of the needless confusion that has arisen through looking at the thirteenth century with the eyes of either the tenth or the nineteenth. *Fealty*, in modern English, has come, largely from its poetic application, especially during the Romantic Revival, to mean the equivalent of our *loyalty*. In the beginning of the feudal relation—a time passing already by the eleventh century—it did in fact mean something of the sort, mean a permanent personal relation like that obtaining, under the clan system, between a *duine uasaile* and his chief : *uasaile*, in fact, appears to be cognate with *vassal*. But times had changed by the end of the thirteenth. To the Norman noble of that period it meant, even in theory, much more in practice, nothing of the sort. It is the difference between the conception of marriage of a present-day Catholic and a Unitarian member of the Divorce Law Reform Association—to take an intensely, even grimly, respectable member of society. Fealty was now a legal relation, not one of sentiment, far less sacramental : and the relation was mutual and conditional. It did not bind for life, for better for worse : if either party broke the conditions of the bond, which theoretically was undertaken for mutual advantage, the relation was considered to determine, and the other party was no longer bound. In practice, of course, this frequently would mean that if either party wished it to determine, it was seldom difficult to find an excuse, however reluctant the opposite partner might be. Those shocked historians who talk of the perjury of gentlemen who ' break ' their feudal oath, in Scotland or elsewhere at this period, have not troubled to study mediaeval law, which understands no less fully than our modern law that there is such a thing as a contract on conditions : I signed one in signing the lease for this flat I write in, or the publisher's agreement for this book.[1]

---

[1] It seems odd that historians should not have been put on their guard by the frequency with which highly respectable people ' denounced their fealty '—i.e., intimated that the relation was at an end. In 1297 the whole of the English Churchmen who were lay barons denounced their fealty to Edward, on the grounds that he had been trying, illegally, to get money out of them. In the same year, the Marshal and the Constable of England, two of

To the Competitors, given this point of view on both nationality and feauty, the question of an admission of superiority was more or less academic. And so, for some time to come, it was to be for the majority of their class. In twenty years time the matter was very different, as different as the parliamentary attitude to a League of Nations in 1913 and in 1920. By that time there *was* a point of honour involved. But what we are considering now is 1291.

This, none the less, is only true of the gentry, or only fully true of them, at least. The popular attitude was different. In England, which was much more unified racially, and where all the Third Estate spoke the same language instead of four or five, there was a very strong sense that

> In spite of all temptations
> To belong to other nations

there was credit in remaining an Englishman, and in forcing Welsh, Scots, and French to be English too. The English nobles, under John, had been willing to be ruled by young Louis of France, but their followers were not. Scotland, being less racially homogeneous, was slower to develop this national sense : but even

the principal officers of State, denounced theirs after a quarrel with the King : the next year they were back in their offices, and both appear in high commands at Falkirk. And though Edward no doubt found these and other denunciations inconvenient, no one seems to have thought worse of the denouncers than their neighbours of the twentieth century think of a married couple who divorce. It is true, of course, that a spouse who has been divorced may even now be extremely annoyed about it, and express some considerably fervent opinions about the one who has claimed a right to freedom : and the feudal parallel holds good there also.

already the common people, those closest to the soil, had begun, between the pressure of Norway and England, to think of themselves specifically as Scots. And the First Estate, the international Church, which was in touch with the Third, that interfused it (a mediaeval Pope might be born a serf) shared this attitude, as showed in the lawyer-clerics' Treaty of Birgham. None the less, the Second Estate—that is, the nobles—were the leaders in war, and mainly, in politics. For the time it was their attitude that counted, since without them resistance was un-officered.

The Conference met again on the 2nd of June, crossing the Tweed this time, to Upsettlington. Edward arrived with the whole armed forces of the North of England. Eight of the Competitors, headed by Robert Bruce and the Count of Holland, were present, John Baliol, who had mistaken the date, arriving next day. The Chancellor of England (the Bishop of Bath) opened proceedings by renewing the claim of superiority, and declaring that he had evidence for it, and that if the Scots had better evidence against it, well and good. The Scots with no one to lead, or convoke, a national force, decided they had no evidence at the moment that was likely to out-trump Edward's fine army, ' boden in feir of war ' across the river. Whereon the Bishop went on to announce that Edward, as Lord Paramount, would obligingly settle the problem of succession, and then put to each candidate the formal question, Did he acknowledge Edward's feudal superiority ? Deciding, presumably, that anything else in the circumstances would be a waste of time, if nothing worse—he was, in fact the overlord already, in respect of English lands, of everyone except Florent, who could hardly be expected to feel nationalistic, or to know much about it—they all gave formal assent, for *bones et suffisauntes resons*, which are not specified, but may be taken to include, before any other, the impossibility of raising anything that could stand up to that immediate army.   The Bishop, finding matters peaceful so far, proceeded to claim for his master not only superiority, but definite rights of proprietorship in Scotland, affirming that as a male fief it returned to Edward on the death of the heir.   Edward's complete omission to claim its administration on Margaret's accession, which in that case was more than remarkable, is not mentioned : but as every man there had some working familiarity with feudal tenures, the omission can hardly have passed quite unobserved.

There was a protest, in fact.   The precise details are inaccessible, through the destruction of the Scottish records.   But the English ones, through a slip on somebody's part, yield a significant glimpse.   The Scottish element at Upsettlington had at least some attempt at a representative body.   We know that besides the clergy and the nobles there were also members of the *communitas*.   The English *official* records, though they note them as present, say nothing whatever of any response from the Third Estate, though they note the formal admission of Edward's claim by the others. The English, but unofficial, *St Alban's Chronicle* lets

slip the reason. It gives the answer of the first two
Estates, and goes on ' the Commons, however, said
nothing of any use (*efficax*).' In other words, their
response was of such a nature that Edward had it
expunged from the official protocol of proceedings—
rather clumsily, as they forgot to take out the record
of the question's being put. The text of the answer,
of course, is completely lost : but from the above we
can make a good guess at its tenor.[1]

The Conference, this farce being duly played, proceeded to the serious business for which it had been
called, namely the hearing of the claims. Eleven of
the thirteen were easily dismissed. The real contest,
as all the Scots at any rate knew by this time, was
between Bruce and Baliol, and in fact the claims of the
others were suspended until the debate between these
two had been heard.

It was done thoroughly. It is very plain that Baliol's
priority was by no means possible to take for granted.
Each of the two was called on to nominate a commission
of no less than forty, who with twenty-four appointed
by Edward were to debate the matter, and report.
Meanwhile, the Bishop of Caithness was appointed
Chancellor : in spite of the provisions of the Treaty of
Birgham, which had been definite on this very point,
he was an Englishman. Edward appointed his own
secretary as the Bishop's colleague, and gave a formal
commission, as his viceroys, to the four Guardians,

[1] Sir Herbert Maxwell, in pointing out the representative nature
of the assent, omits any reference to this protest.

leaving Brian Fitzalan, an English 'Norman' (the house is really Breton) and a very distant connection of the Stewarts, to serve with them as a fifth. These regents, with twenty-six nobles and one bishop, then swore fealty to Edward, what was left of the Conference adjourned, and on the 3rd of July Edward wrote joyfully to the Judges of the King's Bench that because of that feudal superiority which by the blessing of the Highest he possesses over the kingdom of Scotland, the kingdoms of Scotland and England are now conjoined.

The Commissioners for Bruce and Baliol are worth a word or two ; as being chosen, of course, from these gentlemen's certain supporters they show the even balance of the parties : the lists, too, explain a good deal later on. The greater clergy seem, for the moment, to have inclined to Baliol : he has five bishops on his side besides Fraser, with seven abbots, the Prior of St Andrews, and the Archdeacon of Dunblane, but no other clergy. Bruce has eight of the lesser clergy, but only two bishops—Dunkeld and Wishart of Glasgow—with the Abbots of Melrose and of Jedburgh. Of the laymen, Bruce has the High Steward, five earls —March, Mar, Menteith, Athol, and Lennox—and seventeen knights, among them two Sheriffs of Inverness. Baliol has four earls—Buchan, Angus, Strathearn, and Ross[1]—and twenty knights, including the

---

[1] There were actually at this time thirteen earldoms, but the Seven, supposed to represent the old Mormaors, claimed a status of their own, above the rest, though their composition varied from

E

Sheriffs of Perth and Aberdeen. Among them one observes a Sir Herbert de Maxwell, which perhaps by heredity may account for the attitude of a later Sir Herbert Maxwell to Robert I, to which there will be reference later on. Mr Barron has pointed out—it is worth noting—that of the fifty-one lay commissioners, thirty-two belong to Scotland North of Forth.

The Commissioners thus appointed met at Berwick early in the following June (1292) and for three weeks they debated on the case. Baliol founded, as a modern man would do, on his descent from Earl David's eldest daughter, the wife of his mother's father, Alan of Galloway. Bruce's case, which Sir Herbert Maxwell, in the standard biography of his grandson, omits, was a good deal more complicated. His advocates raised the various points mentioned already, and gave precedents from the Macalpin succession, where of course there were several, as has been remarked. They also adduced several foreign instances. The record is torn, and we have not the whole, but they include one from Savoy; the Castilian Succession Case of 1275, which excluded the Infantes de la Cerda in favour of their uncle Sancho IV, who at that moment was occupying the throne; and the English exclusion in 1042 of the

time to time, as there were in fact nine of the old Celtic earldoms. Of those in this catalogue it may be remarked that Athol's daughter married old Bruce's grandson Edward : Mar's daughter married Bruce's grandson Robert and his son Bruce's grand-daughter Christina : Menteith was an uncle of James Stewart. Of Baliol's quartette, Buchan was a Comyn of the younger branch, and Angus his brother-in-law. Ross's son, much later, married old Bruce's grand-daughter Maude.

son and grandson of Edmund Ironside in favour of
Edmund's younger brother Edward, an exclusion with
several earlier parallels in the House of Cerdic, and a
later one in the sons of William the Conqueror.
Finally—and there must have been a smile or two in
court—they referred politely if not quite tactfully to
the fact that Edward was wearing his own crown by
reason of his descent from his grandfather John, who
had excluded from it (*scilicet* murdered) the son of his
own elder brother Geoffrey—whose descendants, by
the way, were still alive. What Edward thought of
this awkward precedent may be gathered from the
fact that in the official record of proceedings the mention of it has been quietly suppressed.

The question, however, was still at a deadlock, as
neither party would admit the other's arguments or
conclusion : and the Commission agreed to refer it to
Edward in person. He summoned a parliament to
meet at Berwick on the 15th of October. Only the
English commissioners were asked to vote, and they, of
course, were unanimous in assenting that the King
should decide on the question ' according to usage,'
and that if none existed, or if it differed as between
Scotland and England, he should create new, with the
advice of Parliament, and that the succession to the
Crown should be regulated as in the case of earldoms
and baronies.

On the 6th November the two chief claimants were
heard, and the rest withdrew their claims, except Lord
Hastings, who still hoped for a division of the kingdom.

On the 17th, Edward gave judgment at last: it was now a full six months since the meeting at Norham. Fordun, who was born some time in the next decade, declares that Edward on the whole inclined to Bruce, and said so in private. The long-headed Bishop of Durham, however, suggested that Baliol would be easier to handle, whereat Edward, *quasi caput concutiens*, as it were with a shake of the head, said approvingly—Fordun keeps the French phrase among his Latin—' *Par le sank Dieu, vous aves beyn chante* '— ' By the blood of God, you have sung well,' and thus warned, asked Bruce privately if he really would do homage. Bruce, like Bishop Rose with William of Orange, refused to promise. Edward then asked Baliol, who did, and turned the scale. Fordun, writing at a time when nationalism was not only in being but fervent, is possibly a doubtful authority: he certainly is pro-Bruce. But the thing has a curious air of the eye-witness.

Judgment was given. Edward declared that the kingdom of Scotland was indivisible, which automatically wiped out Lord Hastings. He then came to the main point, the question of Bruce and Baliol, and what he omits to say is interesting. He does not mention the declaration of Alexander II. The point had of course been raised in previous discussion, and Baliol's side had claimed that the witnesses were ' superannuated,' though a majority of the Three Estates, and the Seven Earls, had been satisfied a couple of years before. Edward ignores this, though their reliance on that declaration was what had led to his being called in, and declares that by the laws and usages of England and Scotland regarding the succession to indivisible heritage, the more remote in degree of the first line of descent is preferred to the nearer in degree of the second. The reference to laws and usages of course begs the whole question that had been in debate by the lawyers of half North Europe, to say nothing of admitting, if it were applied, that Edward's claim to his own throne of England was less than that of the Duke of Brittany. But decision had to be made, and thus, on whatever grounds, decision was made. To John Baliol was given ' sasine of the realm of Scotland, saving always the right of the King of England and his heirs, whenever they shall choose to put it forward.'

Fordun says that a protest was registered, that the Earl of Gloucester, who was Edward's son-in-law and Bruce's nephew (his brother had been in the business at Turnberry) took old Bruce by the hand in face of the assembly, and told Edward that God would judge him as he had judged. The story, of a Norman noble anywhere, is not inherently improbable : but there is no other authority for it . . . though naturally, such a regrettable lapse from the conventions of diplomatic behaviour would scarcely appear in the English official records.

On the 19th of November 1292, the kingdom of Scotland was formally conveyed to the new King John. On the next day the Great Seal was broken in four, and the fragments sent to the English Treasury, and

John did homage to Edward for his kingdom.   It is an
interesting light on the claim that any such homage had
been previously made to learn that no one knew what
fee should be paid, though the homage-fee, in the case
of all fiefs from the great earldoms down, was as fixed
and well-known as the stamp on a modern cheque.   A
superb new seal was cut, with the customary but quite
unusually inappropriate legend, *Johannes Dei Gratia
Rex Scotorum*, and John, with an equally suitable
choice of date, was crowned at Scone on the St Andrew's
Day of 1292, rather more than two years after Queen
Margaret's death, and seven years, less some four
months, from King Alexander's.

II

THE WAR OF THE EMPTY JACKET

FOURTEEN YEARS : 1292–1306

Na he, that ay has levyt fre,
May nacht knaw weill the propyrte,
The angyr, na the wrechyt dome
That is cowplyt to foul thyrldome
Bot gyff he had assayit it :
Than al *par coeur* he suld it wyt,
And suld think fredome mar to prys
Than al the gold in warld that is.[1]

Barbour, The Brus.

[1] Spelling slightly modernised.

CHAPTER IV

TOOM TABARD

FOUR YEARS : 1292–1296

For miht is riht, the lond is laweles ;
For niht is liht, the lond is loreles ;
For fiht is fliht, the lond is nameles.
English song of the next century.

BALIOL was crowned. The Bruces, though they cannot
have liked the situation, accepted it loyally, at any rate.
Old Robert Bruce, who was by this time well past
eighty, made over his rights to his son, and vanishes
henceforth from public life, though he lived until the
spring of 1295. Carrick, thus left as head of the family,
took up a noncommittal attitude, perhaps made easier
by the death of his spirited wife a few months before.
He may have been generous enough to wish to avoid
civil war, as his father apparently had been when he
gave up the endeavour to assert his claim, and turned
instead to an attempt to forward the Union of the
Crowns. He may have been long-headed enough to
guess that Baliol's Scots backers would soon have had
enough of him. Or he may simply have been indifferent. At all events, he did not attempt to upset the
present settlement by any armed resistance. He
merely declined to compromise his own position by
doing homage to his rival for the Scots lands. He

73

settled that matter neatly and peaceably by making them over to his young son, who was still a minor, and went on a long visit to Eirik of Norway, taking with him his eldest daughter Isobel. Within a year she was married to King Eirik, and her father stayed on at their court till his own father's death.

Where his eldest son was at this time we do not know : presumably—but not at the Scots court—he was going through the usual esquire's training, perhaps on his grandfather's great English lands, or at his own *chefs-lieux* of Turnberry and Lochmaben. We do not know whence it was that the young Earl of Carrick (as he is from this time till his coronation) sent the magnificent wedding-gift to his sister that went out in the September of '93—gowns of bluet and scarlet murrey and white cameline, furred with the royal minever and vair, rich plenishing, coverlets of cloth of gold, and silver plates and dishes for her table. At Baliol's first parliament, at Scone in the February of that year, he is mentioned as a defaulter, but he came to the Parliament of Stirling the next August, did homage for Carrick, and was confirmed in its possession as his mother's heir. Thus, though the elder Bruce had been careful to avoid compromising his own claim, the two factions were ostensibly at peace.

Meanwhile, John's reign soon showed that quality that made his subjects call him ' the Empty Jacket.' John has never been a happy name for a monarch. John of England, the two luckless Johns of France, John of Jerusalem, Joan the Mad of Spain and the two

Joans of Naples—only the Eastern Emperors had luck with the name. And John of Scotland, though materially he came off better than most, is the most futile in that queer procession. Whether Fordun's story of Bishop de Bec's advice is true or not, the substance of the alleged advice would appear to be indisputable, at least. Edward, in backing Baliol for the throne, had provided himself with a most convenient weakling, ' *simplex et idiota, quasi mutus et elinguis,*' as the English Rishanger not untruthfully calls him.

His next proceeding was to bully the worm into turning, so as to have an excuse for treading on it. That seems the likeliest reason, at all events, for the course of conduct on which he now embarked, though it may be merely that he despised the man, and the feline strain in the Plantagenets made him deliberately torment his victim, merely to see how much he would endure. It is not an edifying spectacle. John, as has been already remarked, was a Picard—more Flemish, that is to say, than anything else : and although the Flemings, as they were to show very soon, were capable of a very dour resistance, they had a higher flash-point than Scot or Norman. The tail-twisting process went on for a year and three-quarters before John's hackles rose, at any rate.[1]

To begin with, a little less than four weeks from his crowning, he provided Edward's court with a Christmas treat by being called into England, to do homage all

[1] The zoology of the metaphors is somewhat mixed, but heraldic licence may be claimed in the context.

over again for his new crown. At the same time he had
to surrender the National Records,[1] with results, to
the early history of Scotland, that have been nothing
short of devastating. The theft was made, no doubt,
with the intention of supporting the English claims :
we know that the documents were carefully examined.
Nothing helpful to Edward was found, or it would have
been heard of : and the ensuing destruction, that so
obscures the early history of parliamentary and burghal
organisation, was probably not altogether unintended.

Nor was this all. Baliol had not been three weeks on
the throne when a burgess of Berwick who had lost a
lawsuit took an appeal from the Scots courts to Edward,
who heard it with a promptness that gives some point
to Mr Barron's suggestion—which is borne out by
evidence of dates and movements—that the appeal had
been rigged as a test case. Baliol protested. Edward's
reaction to the protest is notable. He did not, as his
legal mind might have done, declare that the fulfilment
of the Treaty of Birgham was contingent on Margaret's
marriage with his son. He merely declared categorically that he did not intend to be bound by any prom-

---

[1] The provisions of the Treaty of Birgham appear to have acted
on Edward's mind like the cry of ' Don't nail his ear to the pump '
in the classic story. His breach of them shows such conscientious
carefulness of detail that a modern psychologist would draw some
very interesting conclusions. It should be added, of course, that
in breaking its terms he was not technically perjured, since they
were conditional on his son's marriage with Queen Margaret.
What probably troubled his conscience was the fact that in ratifying
the treaty he had publicly admitted Scots autonomy, which a year
later, and in all his subsequent actions, he affirmed categorically
had not existed.

ises. Baliol came to Newcastle then for his second homage, and Edward summoned his suite and repeated the declaration to them : the recorded words are *non obstantibus promissionibus concessionibus confirmationibus quibuscumque litteris seu instrumentis vallatis*, which, with regard to *pacta non servata*, could hardly be a more explicit statement. Two days later, on the 2nd January 1293, the luckless puppet was forced to sign letters patent releasing Edward from all those pledges and promises in consideration of which he himself had just done homage. Edward, depositing this remarkable document at Westminster, embroidered the occasion by executing, himself, one still more edifying, a notarial protest that the King of England was not to be bound by any promises made while the realm was in his hand, or hindered by them from judging appeals brought from the Scottish courts.

Further, the regulations for these appeals were made ingeniously humiliating. The King of Scots in person was to be made a party in any suit. In the beginning of April John had to appear at Westminster in a claim by a Gascon vintner on the estate of the late King Alexander, and the summons was served by the Sheriff of Northumberland. By autumn, Edward had reversed the decision of the Scots courts on, ironically, a succession case in Fife—a purely domestic Scottish matter, that is : the Gascon had been an English subject, at least. John had to appear, and pay heavy damages. Again, Edward summoned him, as he might have done any English squire, to sit as a Justice of the Peace in Yorkshire. Baliol did protest, but not very forcibly.

Then, in October, Philip of France summoned Edward, as his vassal, to answer for the crimes of some English sailors, who had landed and sacked the town of La Rochelle. Edward disliked this taste of his own medicine. He managed to dodge a personal appearance, but had to send Philip submission and amends, making formal surrender of his French fiefs on the 5th of March, 1294. Then, having rounded up his sons-in-law, the Duke of Brabant and the Count of Bar, he made a further league with the princes of the Low Countries and of the Franche-Comté, betrothed his heir to the Count of Flanders' daughter, by the Treaty of Lierre at the end of August, and by the end of October 1294 was strong enough to denounce his fealty to Philip, and send a fleet and an army to Guyenne. Philip managed to immobilise Edward's newest and most powerful ally, the Emperor Adolf, to detach Florent of Holland, and make a treaty also with Eirik of Norway. Both sides were working by diplomacy yet, however, rather than by war, and through the winter there was little action. By the spring, Edward decided that he could make it war, and in June —that is, of the year 1295—he wrote commands to John Baliol King of Scots to join him at London with the Scottish forces, in order to share an immediate invasion of France.

Matters, however, had been moving in Scotland. King John had formed, or, it seems more probable,

had had formed for him, a sort of Committee of Public
Affairs, consisting of twelve notables of the kingdom,
four bishops, four earls, and four barons : with their
concurrence, or more probably under their urging, he
had negotiated an alliance with France, carried through
by an embassy consisting of the Bishops of St Andrews
and Dunkeld, John de Soulis and Ingelram de Umfraville. (Dunkeld and Soulis, by the way, were both
partisans of Bruce, so that the two factions were still
working together.) The treaty is concurred in by the
Estates, and bears the seals of the six major burghs : it
arranges for a defensive and offensive alliance, for the
marriage of John's son to Philip's niece, for the sending
of a French army and the immediate invasion of
England : and John, incidentally, is very shocked at
Edward's undutiful conduct towards his lord : he, like
Edward, was Philip's vassal for lands in France.

The treaty was not made public till the 23rd of
October, but Edward seems to have got wind of it
before : Bishop Fraser of St Andrews, who had
recommended Baliol's pliancy, may have sent him
word of this new hardening. At least, on the 16th of
the month, he seized not only Baliol's English estates,
but those of all Scots nobles who remained in Scotland.
Baliol, simultaneously, expelled from his court all
Scottish nobles who had lands in England, and con-
fiscated their Scottish estates. Whether this measure
was actually aimed at the Bruces is not clear : but their
Annandale lands—this was not forgotten later—were
given to John Comyn Earl of Buchan, a kinsman of

Baliol's brother-in-law, Black John Comyn of Bade-noch, the ex-Guardian.[1] The confiscation would not be the less inconvenient in that just about this time young Robert, now holder of the lands, was married, to Isobel, daughter of the Earl of Mar (who was Buchan's cousin) and grand-daughter of that Llewellyn of Wales whom Edward had dispossessed : her brother also had married, or was to marry, young Robert's high-spirited sister, Christina Bruce.

The tension between the two courts could have only one issue, and Baliol's next action precipitated that. He had a long score of humiliation to pay, and now with Philip's treaty in his pocket he screwed up his courage to formal defiance of Edward, dictating the letter, one imagines, himself, for it is not in the grave diplomatic terms, but an odd piece of forcible-feeble scolding, in the tones of a weak man who has lost his temper enough to stand up to a bully. He relieves his pent exasperation, and denounces his fealty as Edward had just done his own.

This was the *casus belli* Edward had played for. It came at a somewhat inconvenient moment : he had not reckoned on being embroiled with France. He accepted it, as he could not choose but do, and promptly declared that his puppet was deposed, summoning John to answer for his misdoings. John, of course, refused,

---

[1] Buchan was also a connection of Baliol's, as his father had married a daughter of Elena Countess of Winchester, the *elder* sister of Baliol's mother Devorgilla, through whom this latter held his throne. Buchan was not this lady's son, but his position as her husband's heir might have made him awkward.

and Edward's response to that was ' *A ce fol, selon tel foli fet. Sul ne voit venir a nous, nous vendrem aly.*'— ' Be it unto the fool according to his folly. If he will not come to us, we will go to him.'

Both countries, through the winter, prepared for war. For reasons of commissariat, forage, and transport, mediaeval wars, at any rate in the North, were seldom fought in winter if it could be helped, and neither combatant moved until the spring. Matters in Scotland were complicated by Baliol's general unpopularity : and he had as good as declared war on the whole Bruce faction by the recent confiscation of the heir's lands. Old Bruce, the Competitor, had died in the spring, and his son had returned from his own daughter's court in Norway, and before the final breach between Edward and Baliol had been duly enfeoffed of the great English estates. When, in the autumn, the trouble came to a head, the eviction of his son set him against Baliol, and decided him to take Edward's side in the quarrel. Edward, whose interest was to keep him friendly, and prevent a *rapprochement* between the two Scottish parties, gave him his father's old post, the governorship of Carlisle, with—so it is said—some kind of promise to establish him upon his rival's throne.

In the March of the next year, 1296, just ten years after King Alexander's death, what had been brewing for six years boiled over. The Hundred Years Peace flared into ruinous flame, and from then till the year 1328 there was war, increasingly bitter, between the

F

countries, becoming very soon a true national contest, to end at last in victory for Scotland . . . and almost in her ruin through sheer exhaustion. So near, indeed, did she come to such a disaster, so bitterly has our history since been conditioned by the almost mortal wounds of those thirty-two years, that many historians, not all unpatriotic, have wondered whether perhaps in the long run it might not have been better if she had been conquered. The answer to that is the history of Ireland, as written even by English historians.

Edward moved north as soon as March hardened the roads. Nobles whom Baliol had dispossessed— the Earls of March and Angus, with Robert Bruce *père* and the young Earl of Carrick his son—did homage to him at his camp at Wark. While his fleet sailed coastwise over the March North Sea, his army took the eastern road over Tweed, and Baliol's—it was Baliol's yet, not Scotland's—was moving towards the other gate of England, by the western road over the Sark, towards Carlisle. Baliol's men crossed the Sark on the 26th of March 1296, the day after the Feast of the Annunciation, ten years and one week since King Alexander died, and ten years, less one day, before Robert Bruce was crowned. They were before Carlisle on the 28th, and on that same day Edward crossed Tweed at Coldstream, and his army and his fleet closed in on Berwick.

Berwick now is, and long has been, an inconsiderable

country town, in an odd little wedge of *Scozia irredenta*.
Then its status was different. In the Hundred Years
Peace it had grown steadily, until it was the wealthiest
city in Scotland, the centre of English and Continental
trade, with customs amounting to a quarter of those
of all England. An Englishman of the thirteenth
century calls it so populous and so rich in commerce
that it might pass for another Alexandria. To mediaeval Scotland it was very much what Glasgow is to
modern : its wrecking would be an economic disaster
. . . and it was actually *on* the frontier, the end of its
bridge resting on English soil.[1] Its governor was a
certain Sir William Douglas, called ' le Hardi,' a man
of great lands in Lanark and Galloway, whose eldest
son, then a child, was to be known.

Apparently the fleet attempted a landing, but without
success. Four of the ships went aground in the mouth
of the river, and the townsmen made a sortie by the
sea gate, burnt them, and killed or captured the whole
of the crews. Edward then attacked from the land.
The town was weakly walled, with only an earthern
agger and palisade, but it resisted. Fordun says that
he then drew off out of sight, and sent forward a force
flying Scottish colours, to whom the garrison opened.
The town, at all events, fell on the 30th. Edward,
flushed with righteous indignation over the burning
of his ships and the loss of his nephew, who had been
shot through the head at the first assault, gave it up to

[1] The bridge had been washed away in 1294, and was not rebuilt
till 1376.

a sack as famous among such histories of horror as his great-great-grandson's similar one of Limoges. The contemporary figures for the dead vary considerably : Matthew of Westminster goes up to sixty thousand, the sober Hemingburgh down to eight thousand, the Scot Fordun, in the next generation, to seven thousand. Mediaeval figures are almost invariably exaggerated, and the lowest of these will probably be nearest the actual number : it is certain, however, that it was a ghastly business, the more in that it was carried out by an army only newly in the field, not exasperated by a long siege, and against people with whom their country had long been friendly. It went on through two spring days, with all the devils of murder, rape, and loot.   Flanders was Edward's ally, but the Flemish merchants, of whom Berwick had a strong colony, were bound by charter to defend their guild-hall.   They held it until the night of the first day, and died to a man there when it was fired at last.   Edward rode watching the sport, until he saw something at last too much for even a Plantagenet in a passion : a woman, in the very act of childbirth, being put to the sword.   He called off the slaughter. The garrison of the citadel, which had held out after the town, were allowed to surrender on terms, and the women with them were apparently sent into safety. Only Sir William Douglas was held prisoner.

The Sack of Berwick, as the first *fait d'armes* of the long war, was probably intended as the Sack of Louvain was in 1914 : to terrorise into inaction.   It turned a war of parties to one of nations, whose lasting hate comes up more than two centuries later in Wolsey's Attila-purr over Hertford's sacking of the Border counties, ' There is left neither house, fortress, village, tree, cattle, corn, nor other succour of man : ' or in the savage mutual Border law that made death the penalty for marriage with a national of the other country. News of it now came to the Scots army before Carlisle, which was led by Buchan as Constable of Scotland. He turned east into Tynedale, and his infuriated troops took bloody reprisals, burning the little towns of Hexham and Corbridge.

The raid, from a military point of view, was useless : Buchan had to fall back at once, as far as Lothian, presumably to cover the coastal road. But effective resistance was impossible, because there was no one who could organise it. The mild elderly man who was the nominal king was rather more useless than no leader at all. The greater nobles would not follow each other, and those of the Bruce party would not fight for Baliol, while many of them, too, were still attached, both personally, for he had great charm, and feudally, that is by interest and legal obligation, to Edward. The lesser gentry could not organise any-thing on a scale large enough to be effective. The mass of the people had nobody to lead them. As Hill Burton puts it in one of his shrewd asides, ' A soldier is not to be depended on unless he knows his coad-jutors, and knows what they will do and whether they will do it.' He is speaking of Rome, but the principle

is true of all war and indeed of all politics : and for
Scotland, all through the next terrible decade, the
doubt meant, as it always had done, paralysis, till a
man rose who could give faith and unity again. Just
now, there was none. And Edward was a brilliant
and experienced leader, one of the great captains of
mediaeval war, and had an excellent army, well trained
and equipped.

He sent it forward now, under the Earl of Surrey,[1]
who, by the way, was Baliol's father-in-law, and should
have acted as the bridegroom's proxy at the wedding of
Queen Margaret and young Edward. Buchan faced
him at Dunbar, and was badly beaten, for reasons which
have more than once brought us disaster. The Earls
of Mar and Athol, who had joined him, were on
Bruce's side,[2] and both refused to fight. And the
army, as the Covenanters did for Cromwell in the same
place, let *perfervidum ingenium* have its head, charged
from the high ground, throwing away the advantage of position, and found Surrey's heavy cavalry
riding over them. It was the twenty-seventh day
of April, just over four weeks since Edward had
crossed the Tweed. And, since Buchan's force was
the only one in being, it was the end of the 1296
campaign.

A large number of gentlemen were taken prisoner,
and sent in batches to castles all over England, even as

---

[1] Surrey is a confusing personage, since his house both called
themselves and were called ' Earls of Warenne ' and ' of Surrey '
indiscriminately.

[2] Mar was father-in-law of both Athol and young Bruce.

far south as Corfe and Winchester. Hostages were taken for the peace of the Border. Roxburgh held out for a week or two under James Stewart, but his sympathies all through had been anti-Baliol, and in May he surrendered, swearing to help Edward against ' John de Baliol, late King of Scots.' It is said by Fordun that the elder Bruce reminded Edward at this point of the promise made when Baliol had turned restive, and was answered impatiently, ' *Ne avonis ren autre chose a fer que a vous reaymys ganere ?* '—' Have we nothing else to do than to win you kingdoms ? ' Whether this is true or not, he certainly did not attempt to defend his rival. He went back to his governorship at Carlisle, and his son went to Annandale—his again now, of course, as Baliol's gift of it to Buchan was cancelled—to receive the Annandale men to Edward's peace.

Edward, having enlarged his army by an invitation issued, rather more than a week after the Sack of Berwick, to all criminals and vagabonds, marched north to Aberdeen and Elgin. Baliol surrendered, and on the 2nd July was made to sign a document in which he admits that *par mauvoys consail e faus e par nostre simplesse* he has done amiss, and that Edward is right to withdraw his kingship from him, so that he himself resigns it ' by his free will.' Five days later, in Stracathro kirkyard, he confessed his sins, *viva voce*, and resigned his kingdom : and (Edward seems to have liked his amusements repeated) he did it again at Brechin three days later, yielding up his Great Seal to be sent into England.[1]   He had lasted a little over three years and a half.

He lived for eighteen longer, in fair comfort. Edward sent him to Hertford until the following spring, but let him hunt and gave him a decent household. The outbreak of the rising under Comyn, Moray, and Wallace, which was nominally on Baliol's behalf, caused his captor to clap him into the Tower with his son, who, as he was alive in 1370, must then have been a boy.   In 1299 he was handed over to the Pope's Legate, who moved him about in North France for a while.   At the truce of 1302 he was contemptuously allowed to go, and lived on till the year after Bannockburn, when he died at his place of Bailleul in Picardy, that later Scots soldiers were to know well enough. What he thought of his rival's proceedings in that time would be rather interesting to know, one imagines. But perhaps the local hunting was more amusing.   He was some forty-two when he was crowned at Scone, and he lived after that to be about sixty-five.   And that is the end of the king called the Empty Jacket, the son of a pious and devoted lady, descended from the fierce Princes of Galloway.

[1] The said seal, by its extant impression, was a noble piece of work. It bears on the one side a very spirited representation of King John fully armed and wearing a great pot-helm with grille and crest, on a barded horse housed with the royal arms : on the other side he is seated on an elaborately carved throne, crowned, and bearing a sceptre of very unusual and graceful form, rather suggestive of the caduceus, with the snakes replaced by floriated branches that rise on each side of a trefoil-headed shaft.

CHAPTER V

WALLACE

TWO YEARS : 1296–1298

' This affligit realm quhilk is my native cuntre.'
The Compleynt of Scotland.

THE war was over for Baliol in 1296, but not for Scotland. Edward had marched north to Elgin, by way of
Aberdeen, arriving there on the 26th of July, and
turning back three days later, by way of Kildrummie,
Brechin, Arbroath, Dundee, Scone, Perth, Dunfermline, Stirling, and Edinburgh, where he arrived on the
22nd of August. He seems to have realised that the
Sack of Berwick had been bad policy, and being apparently sure of Naboth's Vineyard, to have been in a
cooler frame of mind, for he clearly did his best to
keep his army in order on the march. We have the
record of various punishments for such offences as
looting, and they show a real effort towards discipline.
None the less, he took great care to make plain that
now the puppet king had been disposed of, Scotland
was his, and should be a country no more. She was
not even to be a vassal kingdom, but only a northward
extension of England itself. He sent three chests of
the royal records to London, so much as could be
found of the royal plate, the Black Rood of his ances-

tress St Margaret, and the ancient Crowning Stone, that Fergus, first King of Dalriada, had brought from Ireland seven centuries before, and Kenneth II, four hundred years after that, from Dunstaffnage to Scone. The old prophecy came true, and the seed of Fergus were crowned on it Kings of England, as they are yet. But it seemed at the time, and it was meant to be, the abolition of a Scottish kingdom.

Edward, having reached Berwick, held parliament there, demanding and receiving homage from two thousand Scots landowners, lay and clerical, whose names are preserved in a document called Ragman Roll. The two Bruces, ' le viel ' and ' le jovene,' were among them. It is interesting to note that nothing is said in the document of the question of Superiority. That theory was not needed at the moment, and homage is recorded to Edward as King of England, Lord of Ireland, and Duke of Guyenne—that is, by his regular and lawful titles.

Edward then recrossed the Border, in early autumn, having apparently got all he wanted. The Scottish castles were filled with English soldiers, even as far north as Cromarty and Dingwall : the Earl of Surrey was left as Viceroy, Hugh de Cressingham as Treasurer, and William de Ormesby as Justiciar. Old Bruce had decided, in spite of the loss of the crown, to side with Edward, a decision to which he adhered consistently through the eight years of life that remained to him. He went back to his governorship of Carlisle, and his twenty-two-year-old son seems to have gone to his own lands. It was about this time that the latter's young wife died, leaving him with an infant daughter, who was called for her grandmother, Countess Marjorie. Edward granted him a postponement of his debts to the Exchequer : it is probable that the forfeiture of his lands had left his affairs, for the present, in some disorder.

The events of the next seven months are rather obscure, and until—and sometimes after—Mr Barron's scholarly investigation,[1] most historians are content to pass them over. Mr Barron himself has pointed out that the closing of the Border, in next January, is not, as is commonly assumed, the first sign of a Scottish insurrection, because it is merely part of a general closing of the whole English frontier, a measure which clearly has to do with the hostilities with France. None the less, it is no less clear that Scotland was beginning to recover from the ' knock-out ' of Dunbar. We have only English evidence on the point, and not much of that : but there were certainly sporadic risings in the winter, and by the spring these were beginning to organise into a formidable resistance. As far as we can make out, the man who attempted to draw together the leaders was one of the original Guardians, who had

[1] His *Scottish War of Independence*, though forbiddingly involved as a narrative, makes a most careful and thorough examination of the facts, that renders it invaluable to the serious student of this most difficult period. I am not always able to agree with his conclusions, but I must acknowledge my indebtedness, through the next six chapters, to his minute analysis of data whose intricacy, and whose scattered provenance, have caused them to be overlooked or neglected.

played a leading part in the negotiations of Queen Margaret's marriage, and after her death had supported the Bruce claim.   This was Bishop Wishart of Glasgow, who until his capture by the English in 1306 was one of the main nerves of the resistance.   As a high dignitary of the Church he was in a better position to organise a national movement than were any of the nobles, whose authority was confined to their own lands, and whose power was further diminished by cross-currents of family and political feud.   The Church was in touch with both the nobility and the commons, who were both represented in its priesthood : it was a closely-knit organisation, throughout the whole country : and it was intensely national, while Edward's attempt to fill the Scottish Church with English clergy, though it showed his sense of where the danger lay, was not calculated to conciliate it.[1]   Hemingburgh says—and when one allows for his fervent anti-Scottish bias, he is usually a good authority—that Bishop Wishart joined another of the former Guardians, James Stewart, in turning the local risings into a national one.

The chief among the various local leaders with whom they got in touch were two great nobles and a young country gentleman.   These were, first, Sir

[1] During Edward's march through Scotland one Father Thomas of Edinburgh excommunicated him with bell, book, and candle : and Edward, who dared not then lay hands on a priest, handed him over with his server, both still contumacious, to the Archdeacon for trial.   We are not told what happened to the pannels, but the odds are that they got off with an admonition . . . and whatever is archidiaconal for a wink.

William Douglas, late Governor of Berwick, now
released from prison by the apparent settlement of
affairs, and Andrew de Moray, a very young esquire,
the heir of a great house in the North-east: he had
been taken at Dunbar with his father and uncle, who
were still in prison, and had escaped. The third was
the younger son of a Renfrewshire knight, who held
his lands of Elderslie from James Stewart: and his
name was Willem le Waleys, or William Wallace.
It is worth noting, as one mentions these, that
Moray's immediate associates were a priest, his uncle
David, later Bishop of Moray, and a burgess of Inverness, Alexander Pilche.

Most of this group are forgotten by the country they
tried to save. Only Wallace stands out in popular
tradition, largely, perhaps, because in the fifteenth
century a romantic novel (as our age would call it) and
a rather good one, was written about his deeds, which
was popular right down to the time of Burns—so
popular that at the Reformation it was re-written,
carefully Protestantised. Certain historians, recog-
nising this fact, have, in a manner too common, ignored
some others: Blind Harry helped to perpetuate tradition, which conceivably might not have endured without him: but Wallace's prominence was traditional
long before Blind Harry. The evidence of that is in
his own life-time, in the hysterical hatred shown in
England, where he was regarded much as Boney, the
Jesuits, or Prince Charles's Highlanders were to be later,
or as the friends of Herr Hitler regard a Jew. And

Edward, who was in case to know the facts, fully
shared the general impression of his people. None the
less, Wallace is a cloudy figure. Besides his great
victory and his great defeat, we know curiously little
of him in detail, but that he was uncompromisingly a
patriot from first to last, and that he had certainly
the kind of courage that will not only attack incredible
odds, but will hold out, back to the wall, in a losing
fight, of intrigue as well as war, for long grey years,
and die unbroken in what seems final disaster.

Sir Herbert Maxwell thinks, characteristically, that
he *must* be the William le Waleys who when Edward's
army was at Perth in the summer, was in trouble, along
with a clerk, one Matthew of York, for stealing beer.[1]
He himself remarks, on the very page after that, that
four William Wallaces signed Ragman Roll. *The*
William Wallace could hardly be one of them, as he
was not a landowner : but the fact does not seem convincing evidence—though it is all Sir Herbert can
produce—to show he was therefore the man who stole
the beer. And that the hotly patriotic son of a Renfrewshire laird should be stealing beer, at Perth, in the
company of a disreputable Englishman of the Army of
Occupation seems, to borrow Sir Herbert's surprising
' in all probability,' ' in all probability ' rather less
probable than that Matthew's chum was a fifth William
Wallace, who appears in Edward's army as a *valet*

---

[1] Historians, including Sir Herbert, keep referring to this worthy
as a priest : but he only called himself a clerk, which need not mean
he was anything more than an acolyte.

who owned a *runcinum*—a troop-horse, otherwise the
rouncy on which Chaucer's Shipman rode rather pre-
cariously to Canterbury.

The name, in fact, is found in both Scotland and
England. The great Bruce's stepmother, after her
husband's death, espoused an apparently English Sir
Richard le Waleys, in defiance of the gentleman to
whom Edward had given her marriage. The root
meaning of *le Waleys* seems to be ' Welsh,' a word
which would apply not only to Wales but to Strathclyde and the West, especially the South-west, of
England—to a man of the old Brython-Celtic stock,
as distinct from a Gael : the English Wallaces come
from Somerset. Sir William's family were of Elderslie
near Paisley, where his father, Sir Malcolm Wallace,
was a vassal of James Stewart's : the family may have
come in with the first Fitz Alan Stewarts under David I,
or, quite possibly there, be of autochthonous stock :
the name has been used as evidence for both, with
equal justification in both cases. Sir Malcolm was
married to a daughter of Sir Reginald de Craufurd,
Sheriff of Ayr, and had three sons, of whom William
was the second. One notices that his father and elder
brother bore Celtic Christian names, while his is
Norman.

These men, then, with Bishop Wishart as their
pivot, were beginning to appear as leaders. And there
were more men to lead than men to lead them. The
nobles were yet, for the most part, of a still international
caste and not a nation : but the country gentry to

whom Wallace belonged—*noblesse de province* as distinct from *noblesse de cour*—were more in touch with the land and the land's people. It is probable that Madame de la Rochejacquelein's picture in her memoirs of the war of La Vendée, of the royalist peasants coming up to the châteaux of their countryside and begging their seigneurs to lead them against the Blues, could have been paralleled in the Scotland of that year. Three-quarters of a century later, in ' English France,' where most of the nobles were partisans of King Edward against King Charles, they declared, according to their contemporary Froissart, that if you cut open a *vilain* of Guyenne, you would find the fleur-de-lys stamped on his heart. Wallace had not to hunt for his recruits : there flocked to him, says Fordun, ' *omnes qui erant in amaro animo et oppressi pondere servitutis sub intolerabili principatu Anglicanae dominationis* '—all who were in bitterness of spirit and oppressed by the weight of slavery under the intolerable sovereignty of the English dominion. He adds, ' *erat enim mirae fortitudinis et audaciae, decorus aspectu, et libertatis immensae* '—' for he was of wonderful daring and endurance, comely in countenance, and of an unbounded generosity.'

By the early spring, then, of 1297, Edward's garrisons were in trouble over most of the country. Ross, Argyll, and Galloway, remote from each other, were all beginning to show signs of revolt. Early in May, the matter was a full war. The chief centres were the North-east, where Andrew de Moray had raised his standard at Avoch in the Black Isle ; the South-west, where Bishop Wishart had joined James Stewart ; and at Lanark, which Wallace had captured, killing Edward's Earl of Clydesdale, the extremely unpopular Andrew Livingstone of Hesilrigge, who was also Sheriff of Ayr. Gray, of the *Scalacronica*, gives a lively account of the business, derived from his father, who was badly wounded there, stripped, and left for dead, and lay out all night between two burning houses. Wallace continued these raids on English posts, harrying Ormesby the Justiciar at Scone and the Bishop of Durham in Glasgow, while Andrew de Moray made things very lively indeed in the North-east.

Edward took action, political and military. His French war was going badly, for his brother Lancaster had been defeated and killed, La Réole was lost, and the English routed at Bonnegarde in January. He decided that he must go to France himself, and, as a precautionary measure, take with him the chief partisans of John Baliol, including the two Comyns. Baliol himself and his son were sent to the Tower. There was also the other party to be considered. Now that the old Competitor was dead, their head was an easy-going, indifferent man, newly married again, and to all appearances settled quietly enough upon his great English lands. But the most powerful partisans of the Bruces, James Stewart and Bishop Wishart, were among the active leaders of the rising : and Robert Bruce had a son to heir his claims, who was now grown just old enough to be a nuisance. The lad was sent for to Carlisle, forced to renew his fealty, and then

G

sent north to harry the lands of Sir William Douglas, who as a Baliol man was not *persona grata* with the Bruces. The arrangement was a tactful one, since Sir William was James Stewart's brother-in-law, and a breach between the Stewarts and young Bruce would be a most convenient arrangement for Edward. Young Bruce obeyed orders, and captured Lady Douglas and her children : but apparently the job set him to thinking, made him look at the situation for himself. The result of his meditations was disconcerting. Instead of quarrelling with his house's supporters, he denounced his fealty to Edward, and joined the insurgents who were rising nominally in defence of his father's rival, and actually in defence of Scotland.

For the heir of the Bruces, the situation was a complex one : and it is highly probable that it turned out even more complex than it had looked. The high-spirited young man of two-and-twenty would find himself in an awkward false position. To him, his own father must by family loyalty be counted as *de iure* King of Scots. The fact that the older man would do nothing active to maintain his rights was a complication, to begin with : there would be sneers to be met, or at least suspected, from his own partisans, that would not be pleasant. Then, the rising was nominally on behalf of Baliol : to fight for Scotland was to fight for Baliol, and that meant to fight against his father, to say nothing of the surrender of his own rights. Young human nature does not change very much, and he probably expected a certain at least tacit recognition of the generosity of the *de iure* Prince of Scotland in ignoring the fact that the nominal leader of the party which, at considerable risk and cost to himself, he had joined, was precisely the very man who had ousted him. And it is highly unlikely that he got it. To those of the leaders who were Baliol's men, James Stewart would be rather suspicious already, though his hereditary position as Steward of Scotland gave him an indubitable official status. For young Bruce—well, suppose that Frederick Prince of Wales had joined the Jacobite army at Glenfinnan ! And whatever the qualities of the mediaeval Scottish noble, the predominant one would seldom appear to be tact. Nor is it common in the early twenties.

There was disunion already among the insurgents, and young Bruce's arrival would not help to decrease it. We have no details, but certain later events, of this war itself, to say nothing of what is known of later ones, are considerably illuminating : and it is not in the least surprising that the rising threatened to collapse at the start.

Edward was arming for Flanders, and fully occupied : he sent the Earl of Surrey, the victor of Dunbar, over the Border, with a levy *en masse* of the North. Surrey's lieutenants, Henry Percy and Clifford, came on the insurgents of the South-west at Irvine. There was no battle, and the reason is clear. The leaders could not agree on a line of action. One knight deserted first in sheer disgust—he said so—at the disunion of command : and the other leaders, finding the situation

hopeless, capitulated, on the 9th of July, to ' Our lord
Messire Edward, by the grace of God King of England,
Lord of Ireland, and Duke of Guyenne.' They were
the two Stewarts, Alexander Lindsay, William Douglas,
and the young Earl of Carrick, Robert Bruce. The
latter was required to give special sureties, surrendering
his baby daughter, who of course was the heiress of
the Bruces, as hostage, Stewart, Lindsay, and the
Bishop of Glasgow going surety for her delivery.
Douglas, having failed to find hostages, surrendered
to his parole at Berwick, and was imprisoned—in irons,
to his great indignation : Henry Percy, writing later,
remarks that he is *uncore mout sauvage e mout araillez,*
' still in a very bad temper and very angry.' He was
sent to the Tower a little later on, and there died sometime before the end of the year.

The collapse of the rising, however, was only apparent. The other leaders, Moray and Wallace, had
been out of quarrelling distance in independent commands, and were still carrying on very active operations.
Moray had been beaten off from Urquhart Castle, but
was a pressing danger to the English garrisons in the
North-east : and Wallace was besieging the town of
Dundee. Meanwhile, Edward's French war was still
going very badly. Philip beat his Flemish allies at
Furnes in August, and Edward went overseas, taking
with him various captives of Dunbar who were willing
to serve against a foreigner in order to get out of prison.
He took their sons or other relations as hostages for
their behaviour on the expedition, and one of the safe-

conducts for these hostages is addressed to young
Moray, who must have grinned when he read it . . .
if he ever did : it most probably never reached him.
(His father, in the Tower, would be out of hearing of
events in the North.) A second English army was sent,
by way of Berwick, to support that operating in
the South-west. The two, apparently, joined, and
moved towards the Forth, with Surrey in command.
It was harvest time, and the country was to feel the
effects of their march.

Wallace raised the siege of Dundee, and joined by
Moray, moved to meet them at the crossing of the
Forth, taking position to cover the bridge at Stirling,
then the main link between the two parts of Scotland.
His force was greatly inferior to Surrey's, not only in
number but in armament. Until Wallace, Edward I,
and Bruce between them revolutionised the tactics of
the time, the English forces relied on heavy cavalry,
whom all the accepted principles of war—until
Courtrai and Bannockburn arrived to upset them—
considered invincible against many times their number
of infantry.[1] The Scots were not only less in total
numbers, but they were, as always, very short of this
arm. Bruce, at his strongest, could never raise a full
thousand, for to begin with, Scotland was very small.
The total population of the time, of both sexes and all

---

[1] As a fully armed man on an armed destrier—the ancestor of
the modern Shire dray-horse—weighed well over a ton, his charge,
at the gallop, made him a rather formidable projectile. And as his
mount was invariably a stallion, the beast was itself an effective
fighting engine in a melee.

ages, has been computed at four hundred thousand, as against an English two million.[1] And the class which produced the pick of these shock troops was that most slowly affected by the growth of national feeling. Wallace, at the time, had something under two hundred, and had to rely on a loosely organised scratch force of infantry, against a much larger army, on a proper war footing. What determined the day was generalship, on both sides.

Wallace reached the Forth first, and posted his men to guard the road to the North, where after crossing the broad flat haughs by the river it rose abruptly to strike into the hills. (One can see the old road yet from Stirling Castle.) The haughland was bare of cover, but their post was a strong one, not only within wood but behind the huge mass of the Abbey Craig, that rises, like a second Castle Rock, steep and isolated just before the hills. The haughs were bounded on one side by this steep rise—the river front of the Craig is perpendicular—and on most of the rest by the deep tidal Forth, curving fantastically in and out, and something like twenty feet deep where the bridge crossed it.

It seems probable that his intention was to let Surrey cross, and ambush him as he climbed out of the plain. Surrey's intelligence, however, had reported

---

[1] The present-day ratio is about one to eight. Mr Belloc, calculating on the known area of English arable land, considers the two million a serious underestimate. Wales, of course, has to be added to England, as a large proportion of Edward's best infantry were Welsh.

his position, and that general, arriving at the Bridge of
Stirling (after holding up matters by oversleeping
himself) knew where the Scots were. His staff, quite
sensibly, did not like the situation. On the morning
of the 11th of September, he sent a couple of friars
across to Wallace, to try to negotiate a surrender on
terms. Wallace, confident in the advantage of the
terrain, and in the spirit of his men, declined. Now,
Surrey was an oldish man, of the old tradition of tactics,
which simply meant riding ram-stam at the enemy :
he had ridden over the Scots himself at Dunbar, and
they had not even waited to be ridden over at Irvine.
He forgot that this time he had a leader in front of
him who was in sole command, and a disciplinarian.
He seems to have lost his temper : he did lose his head,
and ordered his men to a direct frontal attack. With
Forth between him and the enemy, and no crossing
but a long and narrow bridge, it was nearly as lunatic
as Balaclava. He had no excuse. Lundin, the very
man who had left the Scots at Irvine because no one
was capable of enforcing order, intervened and
pointed out a ford further up, presumably the Roman
paved ford at Kildean : [1] but Lundin's fastidiousness
about the intelligence of his C.O. had no more luck on
the one side than the other. Surrey declined to change,
and confirmed his orders, and his vanguard, led by
Cressingham the Treasurer, began to cross. They got

[1] The Ordnance map gives this ford as the site of the bridge : but
the piers of the bridge were found some time ago a little above the
fifteenth-century bridge, close to the modern one.

over without opposition. Wallace kept his men absolutely quiet—which, with a force of Scots, says something for his gift of discipline—and let the enemy
deploy on the plain, which was probably poor enough
ground for cavalry. Then he threw out his flanks
along the wood, and marched from the high ground.
The precise sequence of movements is not very clear,
but judging by the result and the terrain (which is not
at all like some of the standard descriptions) the account
suggests that the English were drawn across the haugh
by a feigned retreat of Wallace's left flank, while his
right was thrown past their rear to hold the bridge-head
and cut down the wooden bridge. (One English
account says Surrey cut the bridge : but though
generals have murdered their own men, this seems
rather unlikely for the most incompetent.) The section
of the English which had crossed was thus cut off
from any reinforcements, and the Scots jammed them
into the loop of the river : it is twenty feet deep
at the bridge, and the tide was rising : it runs there,
even to-day, with a strong current, and it was nearly
the tide of the equinox. Some of the knights, rallied
by Sir Marmaduke de Twenge, hacked their way
through before the bridge timbers gave, and got off :
but the Scots and the river settled the rest.

Surrey watched helplessly. It was too late now to
use Lundin's ford and get Wallace in the rear, for the
tide was in. He and the rest of his force could only
look on, and at sight of the slaughter his men panicked
and broke. He followed them, abandoning his baggage,

and like Johnnie Cope later on made off for Berwick, arriving there with his poor beast so foundered that 'it never was able to eat corn again,' and leaving the Lowlands, apparently, clear of troops except for the flying stragglers from Stirling Bridge.

The battle cost something. Young Moray, who had more than proved his value, was mortally wounded. Historians repeat that he was killed, but Fordun says *cecidit vulneratus*, and his name appears on two documents that come after the battle : these cannot refer to his father, who was in the Tower, or to his son, who was only born that year. An inquiry held in 1300 describes him as having been killed at Stirling Bridge, but this need only mean that he took his death-wound. The English lost their Treasurer, Cressingham, who as head of what we should call the Inland Revenue had made himself very far from popular. The Scots, in fact, considered it appropriate to flay his body, and distributed the hide as souvenirs. Legend says they made girths, but 'a handsome man, though too fat,' does not suggest, one imagines, the kind of leather that would hold an armed man on a heavy mediaeval saddle with any sort of safety to his neck. Gray says they made *layniers* of it—thongs or strips : in fact, the dried hide of an income-tax collector might give satisfaction merely as ornament . . . in a simpler state of society, of course.

Stirling Bridge was more or less a 'snatch' victory —the Prestonpans or Valmy of the war. It did in fact show more generalship than either, but as at Preston-

pans the completeness of the success was due in large
measure to the enemy's panic. But it had its effect,
on both the military and the political situation.   It
shattered the English army at a time of year when it
was too late to organise a fresh one before the spring :
and it meant not the surprising of a town or castle by
guerillas—a thing that could be kept, so to speak,
' out of the news '—but the rout of a formed army in a
pitched engagement. The political repercussions show
at once, in the fact that only a month after the battle
Wallace and Moray were dealing, in the name of the
communitas, with the great cities of the Hanseatic
League, the immensely powerful trade combination of
North Germany, thanking them for their maintenance
of a friendly attitude, and informing them that trade
with Scotland was open again : they were evidently
already trying to repair the economic blow of the Sack
of Berwick.

Wallace and Moray—which with Moray mortally
ill, meant in practice Wallace—became the nucleus of
the resistance. The situation in England played into
their hands. Edward's Constable and Marshal, Hereford and Norfolk, the two chief of his nobles, quarrelled
with him and denounced their fealty. He tried to
raise money for his war expenses, chiefly from the
Church : the English clergy declined to render unto
Caesar the things which they considered were not
Caesar's—that is to say, a half of their year's income—
and denounced theirs too, in a body, though Edward
stormed so at a deputation of them that the poor old

Dean of St. Paul's dropped dead at his feet. He had
to shed tears at his Parliament, in fact : but he got
round them, largely by sheer personality, and succeeded in raising means to go on with the war. Actual
campaigning, with any effective force, was impossible
now before spring : but orders were issued that the
higher posts of the Scots Church should be filled with
Englishmen—an eloquent demonstration of the part
the Church had taken in the resistance : and various
minor measures were taken also. For instance, the
hostages taken from Galloway in the beginning of the
rising were sent to Lochmaben, on the 23rd October.
Hostages, by the mediaeval law of war, were entitled
to suffer nothing worse than detention. Rather less
than three years later, one was set free. He was the
only survivor, out of eleven.

Young Bruce had ' come in ' in July with his elders,
at the collapse of the futile western rising : but apparently Edward still felt nervous about him, for in October
old Bruce was superseded in command of Carlisle,
and his post given to its Bishop. No reason is given,
but it seems highly probable that his son was ' out '
again : he certainly was by the 14th of November, for
on that date the Council meeting at Westminster sent
orders to the Bishop of Carlisle to be ready to receive
him to Edward's peace. There is not the slightest
evidence that he was so received, though Sir Herbert
Maxwell definitely affirms that he was, and on the date
on which the order was despatched from a place a
fortnight's journey from Carlisle ! (I wish the fact that

my electricity account has been duly rendered would
be taken as evidence that I had paid it !)

Stevenson assigns to the autumn of this year a letter
commanding him to bring a force from Carrick to
assist King Edward: but as, in the first place, the
original letter has not a date on it of any kind, and
in the second, there is no evidence that any such
force ever turned up, the only thing it proves, even
if we accept the conjectural date, is that Edward
wanted him to take the same line as his father : which
is likely. We do know that by the Christmas of that
year the English Warden of the Western Marches was
raiding his lands of Annandale, while before the next
summer the suspension of his Exchequer debts had
been cancelled, and the goods of his Essex estate were
being distrained on. The inference is that sometime
before November, possibly after the news of Stirling
Bridge, he had learnt that the apparent fiasco at Irvine
had not been final after all, and had taken up arms
again. And in spite of the reiterated statements of
historians, repeated parrot-like from one to another,
*there is no evidence of any kind that he laid them down
again until* 1302.

The enormous moral effect of Stirling Bridge,
reversing that of Dunbar, stimulated an invasion, in
the late autumn, of Northern England. The raid had
little military value, being apparently a mere wild
wave of reprisal. Carlisle was besieged, but it was
strongly fortified, and the besiegers lacked artillery.
A band of English, headed by the English governor of

Wark, joined the Scots, perhaps in pursuance of some
family feud. Edward's attempt on the liberties of
the Scots Church had embittered the raiders against
the English clergy, who, according to the chroniclers,
suffered severely.

Wallace followed the disorderly Scots troops, and
apparently attempted to knock some kind of discipline
into them.¹ He certainly intervened to protect the
harried monks of Hexham, and it has been observed
that Hemingburgh, having recorded the incident, no
longer describes him as *ille latro*—that brigand. It
was a bad winter for both sides of the Border, with
the Scots raids on the south and a famine northward,
for Surrey's invasion had come just at the harvest.
Sometime during the winter, Wallace, who was now
the recognised leader of the resistance, made an
attempt to define and regularise his position with
regard to civil as well as military affairs : in the absence
of any regular government and the disorder of the last
two years, it is probable that things were in a mess.
He assumed the title of ' Guardian of Scotland on
behalf of King John,' and appears now as *Willelmus
Walays miles, Custos regni Scotiae et ductor exercituum*

¹ He and Moray appear by this time as *Andreas de Moray et
Willelmus Wallensis, Duces exercitus Scotiae, nomine praeclari Principis
Domini Johannis, Dei gratia, Regis Scotiae illustris, de consensu communitatis regni eiusdem,* which shows some kind of regularising of
their position. The titles are, in English, ' A. de M. and W. W.,
by consent of the Commons (or Community) of the Kingdom
leaders of the Scottish Army in the name of the most noble prince
Lord John, by the grace of God illustrious King of Scotland,' and
the formula is an amateur's, for the King's proper title was King
of Scots.

*eiusdem nomine praeclari Principis Domini Johannis Dei
gratia Regis Scotiae illustris, de consensu communitatis
regni eiusdem*—' Sir William Wallace, by consent of
the Commons (or Community) of the Realm Guardian
of Scotland and Leader of its Armies in the name of
the most noble prince Lord John, by the grace of God
illustrious King of Scotland.' [1] Looking back at it
from after the event, we can see that this move was of
very doubtful wisdom. It certainly gave him not only
something corresponding to the modern conception of
' belligerent status,' but an official position among the
nobility which as a poor knight, the younger son of a
small laird, he lacked. But it claimed a position, well-
earned though it might be, at their head, in the place
that Baliol's powerful kinsmen the Comyns quite certainly considered would be more appropriately filled by
one of them than by the younger son of a Bruce man's
vassal. The assumption of the new dignity was also a
challenge to the ugliest vice of the Lowland Scots
character, the peculiar quality of resentful envy that
is expressed in the idiom ' Set him up!' while, identi-
fying him with the leadership of a faction, it would in
addition to ruffling Baliol feeling, make him suspect to
the anti-Baliol side. Yet we cannot definitely condemn
the decision. Scotland being what she usually is, it

---

[1] Certain amateur historians have attempted to prove their
shrewdness by suggesting something fishy about Wallace's knighthood. But even the most elementary knowledge of the Middle
Ages should leave one aware that the conferring of knighthood was
not a royal prerogative. Wallace was of knightly stock, and had
won his spurs very demonstrably by this time. It would in fact
be decidedly surprising if by now he had *not* had his accolade.

was a case of Scylla or Charybdis. He chose Scylla :
and whether Charybdis would have meant better fortune is, in the circumstances, not very clear.

Edward, meanwhile, was raising fresh troops—an
army of thirty thousand. The figures are not from the
chroniclers, whose military arithmetic is apt to be as
inflated as modern currency, but from the official
orders for the levy. The terms of the levy's purpose,
by the way, are against *les enemys de la coroen e du*
Roiaume Dengleterre e pur leur desobeissance e leur
malice refreindre qe a autre chose ne entendent qe abesser
la dite Corone e lestat du dit Roiaume Dengleterre a leur
poer—' the enemies of the Crown and Realm of
England, to restrain their disobedience and their
malice, who intend no other than to reduce the said
Crown and the state of the said Realm into their
power ' : in other words, to withstand the Scots who
were trying to annex England ! The psychology of
politics does not alter.

Wallace moved back across the Border, presumably
to organise resistance, and by the middle of February
Surrey was in Roxburgh. Edward's main mobilisation,
however, was rather slow, and his action was further
hampered by the French war. It was not until the
Truce of Provins, which was signed on the 30th June,
that he was really free to move. Having piously
prayed at the shrine of that not very appropriate
saint, St John of Beverley, patron of the deaf, he led
his main force over Tweed at Coldstream, and made
his way towards Edinburgh, very slowly, delayed by

his heavy commissariat train, the nightmare of English commanders in the North. The Englishman, fed, is an admirable fighter, but he does not do his best on a slimming diet, and the Scots soldiers, who could campaign on drammock, made a standing joke of his fussiness over his rations.

They were held up by the castle of Dirleton, and it was reduced, with some difficulty, by Bishop de Bec. Edward and his staff halted at Kirkliston, beyond Edinburgh, and there seems to have been trouble with the Welsh troops, who got drunk and mutinied. There was more trouble also over shortage of rations, for stores were to come by sea, and the fleet was delayed. It seems probable that Wallace meant to avoid an engagement as long as possible, and starve them out, for he did not attempt any action. It was well on in July before Edward was in case to move, and then he had word of Wallace and his force in the Torwood, between Falkirk and Stirling. He moved towards them on the 21st, bivouacking at Linlithgow. In the morning he was kicked by a horse and got two ribs broken, but the tough old soldier could still manage to sit the high-backed mediaeval saddle, and in the early July morning they pushed on, and found the Scots in position south of Falkirk, on a hillside called Slamannan Moor.

From the military point of view the action that followed is one of the most notable of the Middle Ages, marking, in fact, the beginning of modern war and the change from reliance primarily on contact fighting to reliance primarily on the missile. Wallace showed

sounder generalship than he has been given credit for :
it is easy to pick holes in a lost battle. But he had in
front of him not only a much larger force,[1] but
a brilliant general of long experience, controlling an
innovation in armament not less important than the
breech-loading rifle. Edward, in his Welsh wars,
had seen the possibilities of the long-bow, especially
in combination with cavalry. From Falkirk to Agincourt and Verneuil all the great English victories
depend on the tactics he worked out for them : and
from Bannockburn to Formigny and Châtillon all the
great English defeats, in pitched battles, are due to
either the muddling of these tactics or their countering
by skilful use of terrain, or, in the later Plantagenet
French wars, by the development of gunpowder. The
long-bow revolutionised missile weapons. It had a
much greater rate of fire than the crossbow, a greater
range and stopping-power than the short-bow : a
long-bow shaft could penetrate thick oak planking,
and a case is reported, when the weapon was still a
novelty in England, of a shaft going through the skirt
of a knight's mail coat, the mail hose beneath, his
thigh, and the flap of his saddle, and wounding his
horse. It was in fact this weapon that did much to
bring about the change from mail to plate that made

---

[1] Sir Charles Oman reckons 2500 heavy cavalry on the English
side, with over 12,000 foot, the latter mainly Welsh ; and some
10,000 foot with only 200 cavalry on the Scottish. Dr Mackay
Mackenzie and Sir Charles agree in estimating the numbers at
Bannockburn as about 20,000 all told on the English side, and not
more than 7000 on the Scots.

H

the knight eventually useless, except as a sort of living, and upsettable, cannon-ball.

Wallace had drawn up his men on the high ground, in a strong defensive position, with his front on the broad marsh of Darnriggs Moor. His little body of cavalry was in the rear, which has been said to show that he did not trust them. The outcome proved, in fact, that he could not, but the arrangement was sound in any case, as the only use he could have made of such a small body was to throw them on a disordered enemy, where they might in fact have been of the highest value. His foot were drawn up in a formation that used at Courtrai only four years later, with no long-bow against it, had triumphant results in destroying the axiomatic superiority of the mounted knight against infantry. This was the *schiltrom*, the hollow square or circle of spearmen,[1] drawn up in two ranks with the long spears, the characteristic weapon of the mediaeval Scot, sloped outward with butt on the ground, the front rank kneeling. His handful of archers, short-bowmen from Ettrick Forest, seem to have been on the flanks, and between the schiltroms.

Edward formed up in the orthodox three 'battles' or divisions. Norfolk and Hereford, who were back again in his peace, commanded the right, and the

[1] A little later it became the chosen formation of the famous Swiss infantry. Morgarten, the first of the great victories that made Switzerland independent, comes the year after Bannockburn ... though, as it happens, it does not show this tactic. Dr Mackay Mackenzie, in his brilliant little monograph on Flodden, gives an excellent account of the Scots and Continental history of the schiltrom.

fighting Bishop of Durham had the left, Edward himself remaining with the centre. At first it went well. The English right charged, and were tangled in the bog. The Bishop, advancing, saw them in difficulties, moved round to the side of it, followed by the King, and halted, much against the will of his knights, till Norfolk and Hereford could draw back and re-form : the Scots short-bow arrows would not have much effect against men in full mail. Then both English wings charged together. The archers were ridden down, and the little body of cavalry broke and fled. But the schiltroms, like living *chevaux-de-frise*, held firm : the English knights broke against them and fell back in confusion . . . and mediaeval cavalry, undrilled, on great brutes like drayhorses, were, in confusion, very confused indeed. It might have been an anticipation of Courtrai, but for one thing.

That was the bow. King Edward halted his centre, which had not charged, and brought up his Welsh foot to fire across the marsh. The light-armed Scots archers had been ridden down, and even if they could have re-formed again, they would have been as much outranged by the long-bow as the long-bow would have been by a modern rifle. The Welshmen might have been shooting at the butts for all the resistance Wallace's men could offer, for the very strength of the position made a charge by the slow-moving schiltrom impossible even if the state of his drill would have allowed it. And there was no cover of any kind. The bowmen were ordered to concentrate their fire on given

points of the schiltroms until there were gaps. Then
the fire was held, and the cavalry charged again the
now broken ranks. In the primitive state of drill, and
cumbered with the wounded and the dead, these could
not close up before the shock of the charge, and were
scattered into mere mobs of men on foot, with swords
and the clumsy spear that, collectively deadly, was
little use when formation had been lost. The heavy-
armed knights rode them down. It was massacre.
A third of the Scottish army was left on the field.
Wallace managed to rally a part and bring them off, but
many were drowned at the crossing of the Carron.

Wallace's army represented the main effective force
of the Scots. Once it was dispersed, no real resistance
was possible. Edward seized Stirling, now unpro-
tected, and marched on into Carrick, to meet a fleet
coming up the Firth of Clyde. Young Bruce, who
according to Hemingburgh, was holding Ayr, burnt
Ayr Castle—an anticipation of his later policy, of
leaving the English nowhere to dig themselves in—
and evacuated the town, slipping apparently round the
English flank. Edward, failing to get into touch with
him, marched south by Nithsdale, taking Bruce's
castle of Lochmaben, above Annandale, which was on
his line of march, and was in Carlisle by the middle of
September, having thus, by the end of the '98 campaigning season, completely reversed the conditions
of the previous year, and left Scotland in as ill case as
after Dunbar.[1]

[1] See Appendix II.

CHAPTER VI

COMYN

SIX YEARS : 1298-1304

> . . . The [Scots,] wrong-headed, all ajar
> With envious longings, and, the other side,
> The ordered English, orderly led on,
> By those two Edwards through all wrong and right,
> And muddling right and wrong to a thick broth
> With that long stick, their strength.
> William Morris, *Sir Peter Harpdon's End.*

FALKIRK was a most serious blow to the Scots resistance, and a deadly one to the political prestige of the man who had been its most successful leader. Wallace had still some seven years to live, but it is now that his martyrdom begins. No man has yet been able to serve his country, and least of all when it happens to be our country, without undergoing some kind of crucifixion : nor can he choose the wood of his own cross. Wallace continued to fight, both in the field and in politics, till his death : but he does not appear again in military affairs as anything more than a leader of guerillas, and his active part in politics would seem to have been confined to working abroad to gain possible foreign allies : even in that he does not seem to have had official status. Any political influence of his at home appears from henceforth to have been indirect, through his friend William Lamberton, who now makes his appearance, and was to play a very

117

important part.   In the previous year, when Wallace
was at the height of his power, he had caused this man,
then chancellor to Bishop Wishart of Glasgow (the
chancellor of a diocese is its law officer) to be
made Bishop of St Andrews, in succession to Bishop
Fraser, who had died, and over the head of a Comyn
candidate.   This, naturally, would not endear him to
the most powerful supporters of the Baliol whom he
claimed to represent, but in fact the choice turned
out a very sound one, from the point of view of Scots
politics at least.   Lamberton was a long-headed lawyer-
politician and diplomat, by no means scrupulous, but
a whole-hearted patriot, whose influence, a few years
after this, was to be of immense importance to our
history.   Even apart from the rivalries of his election, the new Bishop was likely to be ill-seen by the
Comyns, as his Bishop in Glasgow had been one of
Bruce's Commissioners in the Succession Case, and
from his office, Lamberton would necessarily have
been concerned in handling the legal aspects of that
matter.

There is a cloudy interval after Falkirk, but we know
that Wallace either resigned the Guardianship or was
deposed from it.   The insurgent nobles returned to
the old plan, of a sort of consulate, or Committee of
Regency, and the Guardians now elected, sometime
between Falkirk and the end of November, suggest
that the disaster had brought about a temporary
rapprochement of the factions, for they are John Comyn,
younger of Badenoch, Baliol's nephew and heir of

John Comyn the former Guardian, and Robert Bruce, the heir of Baliol's rival. Lord Hailes remarks on the appointment that ' Bruce Guardian of Scotland in the name of Baliol is one of those historical phenomena that are inexplicable.' It is not quite that, though it would be if he had ratted before and after Falkirk, for we are justified in assuming that the young man, like his grandfather before him in 1289, was capable of subordinating his family claims to those of Scotland, and of attempting to support the Scottish cause, at such an unpromising moment, without precipitating the civil war that did in fact break out a few years later. But the position is certainly surprising, though it suggests that they were beginning to recognise possibly Bruce's value as a soldier and certainly the grave danger of disunion. The evidence for the date of the appointment is a writ in the joint names of Comyn and Bruce as Guardians, dated 2nd December of this year. A letter from Philip of France, dated conjecturally by Bain in 1302, but fitting better, as Mr Barron has demonstrated, the April (it bears that month) of 1299, shows that in the following spring they were still acting together in that capacity, while on the 13th November 1299 the Guardians who write to Edward accepting Philip's offered mediation for an armistice are still Bruce and Comyn, though Lamberton—we shall see why—has been added.

Through the next year the main action was diplomatic, not military. Lamberton had been consecrated in Rome the previous June, a month before Falkirk, and in spite of the half-dozen ships that Edward had sent out to intercept him, had returned to Scotland, bearing a letter from Philip to the Guardians. The letter is unfortunately, reticent, as it merely names the Bishop as Philip's envoy, who will give them his decision by word of mouth, but it makes plain at least that in spite of the Truce of Provins just before Falkirk both Lamberton and possibly the Guardians were still endeavouring to win Philip's help.[1] The situation was the more hopeful in that the Pope, who had negotiated the truce between Philip and Edward (though he had not managed to achieve more than a suspension of hostilities, without a settlement of the *casus belli*), had shown himself very well disposed towards Scotland. And the Pope was no longer the feeble Nicholas IV, but the vigorous and courageous Boniface VIII. Lamberton, who as has been said was a trained lawyer and a fervent patriot, had clearly made the most of his time in Rome. Philip, however, was a rather uncertain quantity, for when Wallace, about the time of his friend's return, decided that he himself would go to France, Philip clapped him in prison and offered to hand him over to King Edward. For some reason, however, he must have changed his mind, for

---

[1] It is one of the ironies of history that this truce, which left Edward unimpeded for the campaign of Falkirk, should have led to the murder of his son and heir. It was ratified by the marriage of Edward to Philip's sister, and the betrothal of his heir to Philip's daughter, in spite of the Prince's previous betrothal to Philippine of Flanders. This latter marriage led not only to the bridegroom's subsequent deposition and murder, but to war for a hundred odd years between England and France.

Wallace, instead of being handed over to England, went to Rome, and with Philip's official commendation : the letter survives.

A leader who has once failed publicly is likely to have a task to do anything right. This journey of Wallace's had an evil issue in provoking a quarrel between the two fiery young Guardians. In the middle of August —the 12th, to be precise—the various leaders of the resistance met in Selkirk Forest, apparently to discuss their future policy. Those who were present include, on the report of an English spy, the two young Guardians, Wallace's friend, Bishop Lamberton, and his brother, Sir Malcolm Wallace, with the Earls of Buchan (Comyn) and Menteith (James Stewart's cousin) who were two of the Seven, James Stewart himself, Sir David de Brechin, and Sir David Graham. Now, Graham and Buchan were both Baliol men, and Brechin was Buchan's nephew. Malcolm Wallace presumably was for Baliol, at least in name. Lamberton, though appointed by Wallace, probably inclined to the Bruce side, and had been made bishop over the head of a Comyn. Menteith and Stewart had been Bruce partisans from the beginning. And of the Guardians one was the nephew of one of the anti-kings, and the other was the son and heir of his rival, and Bruce and Buchan had the matter of the Annandale lands between them, while from all we can make out the military situation through the summer had not provided the sort of immediate urgency that, after Falkirk, had for a while at least united the parties. Instead, there had been a year's uncertainty and a futile lack of any decisive action, which would not sweeten anybody's temper.

In fact, there were all the materials for an explosion, and a detonator was not long to be lacking. It is not quite clear just how the trouble began, but somebody fell foul of the absent Wallace : Sir David Graham, incensed that the ex-Guardian who had spectacularly failed at Falkirk should take on himself to act independently, censured Wallace for going to France without leave, and demanded the forfeiture of his goods and gear. Malcolm Wallace, not unnaturally, lost his temper, and gave him the lie, and both men drew their daggers. The Bishop apparently tried to intervene, and was seized by Buchan. The young Guardians were somehow drawn into the fracas, and Comyn flew at the throat of his colleague Bruce.

Somehow, they recovered their senses and their tempers before blood was shed : one imagines, from all that is known of him, that the Bishop might have a vigorous turn of speech. But bad blood had been made, that flowed, years later, in the Greyfriars Kirk of Dumfries. The upshot of the meeting was to confirm the two young men in their guardianship, but to associate the Bishop with them. And he is given the custody of the castles, a condition which is pretty eloquent of both their attitude towards each other and that which it caused in their associates. Lamberton's appointment, incidentally, rather suggests that Graham's attack on Wallace had shamed the meeting into a more generous attitude.

Further military action was decided upon, though nothing on a large scale. Bruce and Brechin (whom he was one day to put to death) moved west and attacked the former's castle of Lochmaben, which had been taken by Edward after Falkirk. Buchan went north with Comyn ; Stewart and Menteith turned westward to raise Clydesdale ; while the Bishop remained with a force in Selkirk Forest, to watch the Marches. Late in autumn we find the three Guardians had come together, and were besieging Stirling in company. In November Edward assembled an army at Berwick : it was an uncanonical time for campaigning, and he did not advance : Trivet says the barons refused to follow him over the *loca palustria et immeabilia* to which winter would reduce the probable terrain. On the 13th of the month the Guardians sent him the letter already referred to. Philip of France has offered to act as mediator in arranging a *sufferentia* or suspension of hostilities, in which discussion would be possible, and they are willing to agree to this. Edward, however, refused to consider it, and desultory fighting continued. Stirling, later in the winter, was reduced by John de Soulis, the Guardians having apparently gone elsewhere.

This letter is Bruce's last appearance as Guardian. For the next two years the confused and cloudy annals of the time give us no information at all about him, except that sometime during that period, or just outside it, he either resigned the guardianship or was superseded in it, his place being taken by Sir John de

Soulis, who may have been chosen, as Mr Barron suggests, with some idea of conciliating the factions, as though a Bruce partisan (he had been one of the Succession Commissioners on that side) he was son of a Comyn of Buchan, first cousin to the present earl, and therefore kin to Comyn the Guardian. He was a brave soldier, and a patriot.

The absence of evidence as to Bruce's movements during the years 1300 and 1301 does not prevent Sir Herbert Maxwell from declaring categorically that ' all this time the Earl of Carrick continued to act a double part,' and that, though a Guardian, he was betraying his associates. His sole evidence for this unpleasing charge turns out, when examined, to be a single letter of 1302, in which Bruce writes to Edward to intercede for a man charged with killing another : and in citing it he quite omits to remark that (a) by this time Bruce was no longer a Guardian and (b) that the letter was written during a long truce. He does cite also a (conjecturally dated) letter from Philip to Bruce as Guardian, but as the letter demonstrably does not belong to this time, and as all that it would prove if it did belong there is that Bruce was concurring in Wallace's policy, it is rather feeble evidence of betrayal.[1]

---

[1] I regret to have to hold up my narrative with digressions of this sort : but Sir Herbert's myths have gained a good deal of credence, and in fact have become part of academic tradition. The most recent popular history of Scotland repeats them gaily, without citing even Sir Herbert's evidence. Mr Barron examined his charges twenty years ago, in the light of the authorities on whom he himself claims to base them, besides that of some others : but the examination was not made until over twenty years after Sir Herbert's *Bruce*

Affairs went on through the winter of 1299 without any conclusive action on either side. In the spring of 1300 Edward decided on a fresh invasion in force. Preparation was slow. It was not till Midsummer Day that he held court at Carlisle, and then moved north and west, heading for Galloway, where a strong Scots force was under the command of Comyn, Buchan, and Umfraville. His path was blocked in Nithsdale, by Caerlaverock. It was lightly held, but a very strong place in itself, and apparently he thought it unwise to leave it in his rear. He sat down before it, and sent for his siege artillery to come up by sea, and this delayed him for a good deal of time.

Meanwhile, affairs had been progressing abroad. According to Fordun, John de Soulis, who may (though this is not clear) have already succeeded Bruce in the Guardianship, had sent an embassy to the Pope, the envoys being the Archdeacon of Lothian, Baldred Bisset, and William of Eaglesham : and they decided Boniface to take action. What followed is absurdly misunderstood by a surprising number of historians, who are quite as shocked at Boniface's attempt to help their country as Edward's Parliament was. The Pope was the spiritual head of Christendom, and his duties in that position included the defence of international

had been published, it is difficult reading for anyone not a serious (and fairly resolute) student, and it had the misfortune to come out in the autumn of 1914, when contemporary history hardly gave it a chance.

I learn with pleasure, as this book is on the eve of going to press, that Mr Barron's work is to be re-issued.

equity and the *comitas gentium* : there are many instances of such intervention, including more than one,
before this, on the side of Scotland when relations with
England were showing signs of strain. Precisely as
the League of Nations might nowadays address an
aggressor Power, Boniface sent to Edward the bull
Scimus fili, a very strongly-worded note, declaring that
Scotland is the vassal of the Church, as were all kingdoms, the implication being that he himself has an
official status in its concerns and a right to tackle
Edward on the subject, and charging that monarch
with the violation of Scottish national rights, setting
forth in great detail the case against his alleged superiority, and finally challenging him to contest these
facts if he can, and warning him vigorously, in good
round terms, to think it over : *infra claustra pectoris
sollicite considerare te convenit.*

The note was forwarded to the Archbishop of Canterbury, with a covering letter which faced him with
the pleasing alternative of defying the Pope's categorical instructions or presenting it in person to King
Edward. And he may have remembered the luckless
Dean of St Paul's. At all events, the unfortunate cleric,
having spent three weeks in reaching Carlisle, took
six more to find out his sovereign's whereabouts,
though King Edward, during that time, was twenty-
five miles off, conducting, by no means privately, the
Caerlaverock siege. He did find the King, in August,
and apparently survived, though there was, to put it
mildly, a certain warmth. Edward, however, dared

not ignore the challenge, and the English monasteries were set to work to provide materials for a defence. They worked all through that winter, no doubt with zeal, Rishanger the chronicler being one of the men employed, and by the middle of next May they had completed a most imposing document, which includes such relevant instances as the career of Brutus, son of Priam of Troy. Sir Herbert Maxwell considers that Edward's indignation, no doubt as sincere as later was that of Japan when the League protested over Manchukuo, shows him ' playing a noble part,' and that his Parliament ' never acted with greater courage and dignity ' than they did in supporting their sovereign in this instance. It is one point of view, at all events.

Meanwhile, Caerlaverock had fallen : its garrison had only sixty men left. They were put through a humiliating ceremony before Edward's new queen and her ladies : the Lanercost Chronicler says that many were hanged, but the author of *The Siege of Caerlaverock* says their lives were spared. Both are circumstantial, but the author of *The Siege* sounds like an eyewitness, so we may give Edward the benefit of the doubt.

Comyn and Buchan attempted then to negotiate for a truce, demanding the restoration of King John. (It may have been over this that Bruce resigned. That, however, is merely a conjecture of my own : the evidence as to dates is too vague to be certain.) Edward refused, but the siege had wasted his time, and it is possible that the weather was against him, since we know from the returns that his cavalry horses suffered

very severely.   When, a few weeks later, Philip intervened with fresh suggestions for a truce, he agreed to
one, and it was signed on the 30th October, to last till
the 21st May of the next year, 1301.

Edward's case for the Papal Courts was despatched
a few days before the truce expired.   In early July he
was in Scotland again, and this time remained there
until February, though the campaign was again a good
deal of a stalemate, the English holding the country
south of Forth, the Scots that north of it, and neither
party effecting very much.   Soulis and Umfraville
just failed to recover Lochmaben, Edward did take
Bothwell Castle, and the Prince of Wales led a force
into Carrick, but had to retire.   Bruce may have been
responsible for this : it was his country : but both he
and Wallace are out of sight during both this campaign
and that of the previous year.   Bruce was certainly on
the Scottish side, however, as the Earl of March was
nominally in command of his lands.   There are vague
indications that Wallace went to Norway, and Queen
Isobel's brother may possibly have gone with him :
but *possibly* is all that one can say.   A very thick ' fog
of war ' covers Scotland at this time : all we can say is
that the scattered details we do know imply that resistance of a sort continued, but that it was neither
organised nor more than very negatively effective.

In the winter, Philip of France intervened again,
and succeeded in negotiating another truce, to hold
from the 26th of January 1302 till the 30th of the
following November.   This, in practice, meant virtual

peace for over a year, for even if hostilities were
renewed on the date of its expiration, no effective
English force could reach Scotland before the end of
March at soonest, and even that only if the spring were
droughty. It was an opportunity to recover, if there
had been anyone to organise recovery : but Scotland
had already had a similar opportunity, and had wasted
it. Wallace might have done it : Bruce, from his later
record, might have done it : but clearly neither of them
was given the chance, being excluded from any sort of
higher command. Perhaps this had some effect on
Bruce's action. He reappears now, but it is clear that
by this time his association with the Comyns was becoming intolerable. They had, as we have seen,
become heads of affairs : and the natural impatience
of a man who had the makings of a very great soldier
with the feckless campaigning in the more than three
years since the fall of Wallace, and his knowledge that
resistance, with a disunited command, was hopeless,
would not make Bruce a pleasanter associate for men
already inclined to mistrust a Bruce and ready to resent
his criticism. The fact that a man of his incontestable
courage, ability, and personal charm should for over
two years be relegated to obscurity is eloquent of the
attitude of his associates, and not less is their subsequent conduct when he did at last assume headship
of affairs. Most of the men prominent on the Scottish side of this war fought for England in the subsequent—Bruce's—one, rather than serve under Bruce.
And Scotland's allies, Philip and the Pope, before on

bad terms, were now in open quarrel with one another. Just over a fortnight after the truce was signed, Philip publicly burnt the Pope's bull *Ausculta fili*, which itself was not much less than a declaration of war.

Bruce evidently was coming to the conclusion that there was no hope for Scotland while the Comyn-Baliol party were at the helm, and decided to wash his hands of the futile business. He had spent five years —a long time for a man in his twenties—in a visibly useless struggle, sacrificing his lands, his status, and his personal dignity; and the sacrifice had effected exactly nothing. When the truce was signed, he made up his mind to take the opportunity it gave him to get out of the mess, and make the best of the position open to him in England as the heir of a house that if it must give up hopes of royalty was at any rate a great and wealthy one. A few weeks after the truce he had written to Edward to intercede for a man of his charged with killing another. Edward's answer is not preserved, but it was evidently conciliatory : it was very much in his interests, at the moment, to be on the best possible terms with the man who would one day succeed to the position of Baliol's rival for the Scots crown : and we know what charm he could exercise when he chose. Apparently it decided Bruce finally : on the 28th of April he was received into Edward's peace, and a little later was made Sheriff of Lanark and Governor of Ayr. Sometime in that year, being then twenty-seven or twenty-eight, he married again, Elizabeth de Burgh, daughter of his grandfather's supporter of '86, the

Earl of Ulster, and niece by marriage of James Stewart, whose wife, Egidia de Burgh, was her aunt. The one recorded utterance of this lady, and the difference between her treatment and that of her stepdaughter and sisters-in-law, when all four were later prisoners in England, suggest that her influence upon her bridegroom would not be in the direction of nationalism.

The truce came to an end, with nothing done, apparently, in the way of organisation. Edward sent a force north as early as February 1303, under John de Segrave, his new Viceroy, and at last there was a flicker of success, for Segrave was caught and defeated at Roslin by a force under Comyn and Sir Simon Fraser, who had come over to the Scots during the truce—in such a hurry that he left the English camp on another man's horse. The flicker was the last. By the end of May Edward succeeded in making a definite peace with France : the Treaty of Paris was signed on the 20th, and the continuance of peace was ensured by Philip's troubles with Rome and his heavy defeat, in the previous July, by Edward's Flemish allies at Courtrai. Philip pursued his quarrel with the Pope, and in fact in the autumn of 1303 was to take him prisoner at Anagni, where a little afterwards, being very old, Boniface died. Edward had thus cleared his flank, and was ready for a Scottish campaign in full strength. Philip had made a real endeavour to get his allies included in the Peace, but he was not in case to stand on terms, and these had definitely and ominously excluded Scotland. The Scottish ambassadors at the

French court wrote gallantly home, bidding their countrymen be of courage yet, but Scotland, disunited and isolated, was incapable of serious resistance.

Edward made enormous preparations, sending up great siege engines, while for the passage of the Forth two fortified wooden bridges were built at Lyme Regis, and sent up by sea, presumably in sections. Entering Scotland again, he swept over it without meeting any sort of effective resistance, except from Sir Thomas Maule at Brechin Castle. Stirling also held out : he was contented, for the time being, to contain it, and marched past it to Kinloss in Moray—some of the English chronicles say to Caithness. He then returned to Dunfermline, having left garrisons all over Scotland, and kept his court through the winter in the Abbey, which, by the way, he burnt when he quitted it, to ease his feelings over the Scots Church.

During this time, the Scots leaders attempted nothing. A fleeting glimpse of Wallace in the spring suggests he was still carrying out some guerilla operations, and Oliphant was holding on in Stirling, but that is all. On the 9th of February—that is, of the year 1304— the rest all surrendered on terms, at Stracathro, the very spot where Baliol had abdicated. Edward apparently decided to try the effect of the leniency that had worked with Bruce, for he gave them really generous terms of surrender, consenting that most of them should be exempt from any penalty of imprisonment or disinheritance. Comyn and Soulis, the Guardians, with Bishop Wishart, James Stewart, Simon Fraser, and a Sir Thomas du Bois were sentenced to various short periods of exile. Wallace had not surrendered : and Edward made it clear that if he did it would have to be a surrender at discretion : in other words, that it would be suicide. He was the only one of all the leaders who had achieved a material success, and Edward had not forgiven him Stirling Bridge.

Stirling Castle held out for a little longer. Edward called a parliament at St Andrews, attended by both Bruce and Bishop Wishart, and then set about Stirling with his whole resources. The English chroniclers are enthusiastic over his magnificent artillery, whose counterweights were made of lead stripped from the church roofs of Dunblane and Perth. It was not only numerous but of the most modern and effective type : we have a list of the pieces, with their names, the Vicar and the Parson, the Gloucester, the Belfrey, the Tout-le-Monde, and so forth, thirteen in all with one great new one of the latest pattern, the War-wolf, so dear to its commander that although it arrived too late to be used until after the negotiations for surrender, it had still to be let off, the garrison being given warning to take cover. Oliphant made a superbly stubborn defence, holding out for three months, while Queen Margaret and the ladies of her court watched the proceedings from the windows of Stirling. He was starved out at last, and surrendered with his men, a hundred and forty, on the 24th July. His defence is now very properly commemorated by a tablet within the castle, bearing his arms.

Oliphant and his officers were sent to English prisons, and Edward made special gifts to those who had taken part in the siege, for the fall of Stirling, after the surrender of the leaders, made it seem that eight years of war had been successful, and that Scotland was completely broken at last.

CHAPTER VII

THE BROKEN COUNTRY

A YEAR AND THREE-QUARTERS : 1304–1306

' God have mercy on this afflicted land ! '
The last words of Montrose.

BY the middle of 1304, then, resistance seemed over.
For fourteen years, things had gone from bad to worse :
for eight the country had struggled, with blood and
tears, to get back . . . King Empty Jacket. Wallace,
the only leader who was left, may have decided that
Scotland had no chance of recovery unless she could
find a more effective king. Lamberton, his friend,
thought so at all events. And at last one was available
to their hand, for old Robert Bruce, the other Empty
Jacket, had done his country his second greatest service,
and died, good peaceable man, sometime in March,
leaving his son unquestioned head of the house, and
responsible to nobody but himself. He was no longer
the lad who had taken up arms in the first muddled
rising and seen it collapse, but a seasoned soldier, just
turned thirty. It is true that he had not been conspicuous in the Comyn wars, but Lamberton, in all
probability, knew that he had never had a chance to
be so. It seems the likeliest reason, at all events, why
he was not, for a few years from that time, when the

chance did come, he was to prove himself one of the
greatest soldiers of history. The shrewd lawyer-priest
had been in the centre of things, and probably understood very well just why the young man had washed
his hands of the struggle.

Bruce's accession to the headship of his family, and
the fact that the rival party were out of the way, probably
fixed the Bishop's policy. Nothing could be attempted
for the present except to await some measure of
recovery, of organisation, of economic activity : the
tramplings of seven invasions in eight years, beginning
with the sack of the chief trading city, must have left
Scotland an economic wreck. Quite probably, too, he
reflected that Edward was growing old—he was nearly
seventy—and that the son who must very soon succeed
him would be a less formidable antagonist. He intended, then, to make time for recovery, but to assure
that when Scotland could act again—and he knew the
general spirit of the nation—she would have an effective head available, a man with the right to lead and
the power to do it. Before Stirling had fallen, and in
a place very near it, Cambuskenneth Abbey, just across
the river, close to the scene of Wallace's victory, he
had discussed the matter with young Bruce. I have
suggested that Lamberton took the initiative, since it
seems on the whole more probable : but it may have
been Bruce. Both were quite likely to have arrived
independently at the same conclusions.

Certainly, Bruce and Wallace's friend came together,
and presumably, since both were intelligent men, this

was their reading of the situation. It agrees with the facts and their actions, at all events, for at Cambuskenneth on the 11th June they signed a sort of personal alliance, or band. It does not specify any definite line of action : and this is presumably because they decided that the time was not ripe, and not for caution, for the discovery of the band itself would have been enough to reveal their ultimate purpose. It merely undertakes general mutual support, and that neither is to act in serious matters—matters unspecified but easily guessed at—without consulting the other. If either broke the pact he was to pay £10,000 towards the general fund for the Crusades. It was, in fact, an alliance of the Powers, of the *de iure* Crown with the Church : and the great church dignitaries were lay barons also, and controlled about a third of the fighting forces.[1]

The alliance being made, with this hope for the future, both men set themselves, until the chance for

[1] This is not the usual interpretation of Bruce's conduct in 1302-1306. But as that interpretation is based not merely on an ignoring of the complicated circumstances that led to his surrender at Irvine in 1297 and to the second surrender of 1302, when the Comyn party had practically cast him out, but on the academic tradition of two or three more surrenders, *for which there is no evidence whatever,* this does seem worth considering at least. To accept the classic portrait one has not only to ignore a good deal of solid evidence and invent several actions for which there is none at all, but to postulate a melodramatic conversion of a man capable of a number of flagrantly profitless and pointless treacheries into one capable of winning, largely through sheer personality and the faith in him he could inspire in his followers, twenty-two years' war against fantastic odds. The chief base of the academic tradition, when one examines the evidence that itself puts forward, is not fact, but fashion : see the instances of ' evidence ' already adduced on pp. 107 and 124. And I shall have to refer, in a few more pages, to another and even more remarkable case.

action should arise, to do the best they could with the *status quo*, and try to get Scotland on to her feet again. Lamberton went about the duties of his office, and Bruce did the regular homage for his new inheritance, on the 17th of June, and was enfeoffed in it, his debts to the Exchequer being respited until a full statement of those owing by his ancestors could be drawn up.

For over a year reconstruction, of sorts, went on. Edward set himself to evolve an administration, which began by making some concession to national feeling, and very large concessions to the surrendered leaders. The union was not to be entirely incorporating : there was some form, at first, of a federal element. There was to be a separate parliament. A Viceroy with a small advisory—not deliberative—council was to represent the Crown : but the council included Lamberton and three other Scots bishops, four abbots, five earls, including Bruce and Buchan, Ross, who had been in an English prison for long, Athol, and March, and with them six barons, who included Comyn.

In the spring Bruce, in his capacity as a baron of England, attended Parliament at Westminster, whither the Law Courts had returned, the Scottish War having caused them to be held, for seven years, at York. De Umfraville had forfeited lands in Carrick, which had been given to him by Edward's Lieutenant of the Marches, John de St John. Bruce, as Earl of that province, put in a claim for them, and they were granted, and Edward consulted him, with John de Moubray and the strongly patriotic Bishop Wishart

(who evidently shared Lamberton's policy) on the
representation of Scotland at a parliament to be held
in the summer. These three were in a manner Acting
Guardians, with a general commission to keep the
peace till the new Administration could get going, and
a special one to arrange for the election of the Scots
members. They went north in April, and on the 28th
of May representatives were elected at Perth for a
parliament to meet in mid-July. It had been arranged
that there were to be ten of these, in five pairs, one of
each pair from either side of Forth : two bishops and
two abbots, two earls and two barons, and two of the
Third Estate.

To the ten elected Scots representatives, twenty
English were added to form a governing body. Further, for Edward's hand was growing heavier as his
position seemed to consolidate, the old legal code was
cancelled, to be replaced by a new one, *ad hoc*. Sir
Herbert Maxwell considers that by this constitution
' Scotland . . . in spite of the enormous sums it had
cost to subdue her, in spite of the provocation her
conqueror had endured ' (*Cet animal, en effet, était
bien méchant. Quand on l'attaquait, il osait se dé-
fendre !*) ' was to receive equal rights with loyal
England.' Twenty foreigners on a representative
body of thirty, and a nice new code of laws marked
Made Abroad, is not everyone's definition of equality
with the English constitution of the time.

The newly elected members, who included Lamberton, but not Bruce, were summoned to Westminster

for mid-July. Parliament, however, did not actually meet until mid-September, and before it met some other things had happened.

Edward had long been especially eager to lay hands on Wallace. The exile of Comyn had in fact been remitted on condition that he should seek him : and Bruce himself is officially thanked for having done so ... though it is probable that Lamberton's ally had confined his search rather carefully to the large area where Wallace was certainly not. At all events, neither Bruce nor Comyn took him. He was taken, however, captured at Glasgow in the house of one Ralph Rae, who had been one of the garrison of Stirling, released on condition of securing him. Popular tradition has assigned his betrayal to the treachery of Sir John de Menteith. Sir Herbert Maxwell considers that Sir John is acquitted by the fact that he was Governor of Dumbarton and ' that there is no evidence to connect him with the treachery.' A few lines further down, on the same page, he produces such evidence himself, stating—and this time on good authority in the English accounts—that *le vallet qui espia Will. le Waleys* got 40 marks reward, the others who took part in the capture 100 between them, and Menteith £151. Menteith may not have been *guilty* of the treachery, and I am not going to accuse him of having been so : but there is certainly ' evidence to connect him with ' it.

What followed is a significant commentary on Edward's generosity towards Comyn and the rest.

They had, at one time or another, all taken oaths of
allegiance towards him. Wallace had sworn no oaths,
and had consequently, whether justifiably or not,
broken no fealty. They, however, were great nobles,
he a poor knight. No policy therefore demanded that
he should be spared, save one that had never been in
Edward's purview.

He was not spared. They took him down through
England, four hundred miles and more in the high
summer, a slow journey on dusty mediaeval roads.
He reached London on the 22nd of August, and was
taken through crowded streets to the heart of the city.
The chroniclers, the journalists of the time, reflect the
popular imagination. Reading them, one recalls the
Daily Mail of the Great War . . . *mutatis mutandis,* for
Lord Northcliffe's eloquence about the Kaiser would
not have bracketed ' Herod, Nero, and the accursed
Ham,' as Matthew of Westminster does to describe
Wallace. The official records of the trial, or rather
of the process of law, are wanting, but we have a
detailed description of the event, anonymous, but
apparently by an eyewitness, who, it would seem,
was either a shorthand writer or had some access to
the documents later on, for the indictment is given in
full legal form.

The business went quickly now the long journey
was over. They warded Wallace for the night in the
house of one William de Leyre, in the parish of All
Saints Fenchurch, and next morning he was marched
through the streets to Westminster Hall, the Mayor

and Sheriffs and the Aldermen riding in state in the triumphal procession. It is a long road, longer, one imagines, through the narrow thronged ways of the mediaeval city : one wonders if it were the stifling heat or the heavy thunder-rain of late London summer. In the Hall they set him, crowned, more fittingly than they intended, with laurel, on the south side of it to face his accusers. It was not a trial, even a mock trial. He was not admitted to plead, nor to defence. They merely read his indictment, and his sentence. The former does not lie, save in one point only. It tells, in unfriendly terms, but with accuracy, what he had done, and he must have listened as proudly as Montrose. One observes that now, when it might have provided Edward with an excuse, no claim is made to the Superiority. There was no practical need for that lie any more, and the indictment tells the cold truth there, that Edward had conquered Scotland and administered it as a conquered country. The only lie is one that begs the question of the whole charge against the man who had resisted that conquest : it is the statement that he was *fidelitatis et liganciae immemor*, unmindful of his troth and his allegiance. Wallace answered that. Neither defence nor advocate was allowed him, but he spoke in one brief sentence, at any rate. He admitted the other charges made against him, but he was no traitor to the King of England. *Respondit se nunquam traditorem regis Angliae fuisse, sed alia crimina sibi imposita concessit.* I wish we had his words. It is seldom true that great men do not speak greatly at high moments. But the unfriendly Latin gives their sense.

His sentence was read. It is phrased unctuously, with insistence on the butcherly details of Edward's code, and a good deal of moralising over them. It was carried out the same day. They took him first through the streets for a public show, chained prostrate on a hurdle drawn by horses, first to the Tower, presumably by the Strand : it is a distance of two miles and a half. Thence he was taken to Aldgate, and thence to Smithfield Market outside the walls, where stood and still stands the Hospital of St Bartholomew. The Norman gateway of the priory church, that is still there, would have seen what was to follow. When he was dead at last and hacked in pieces and the scent of his burning entrails in Edward's nostrils, they set his head on the spikes of London Bridge, to look down upon the shipping in the Pool, and his limbs went to Newcastle, Berwick, Stirling, and Perth. Newcastle hung his sword-hand above the river ' where the common sewers go down into the Tyne.' Someone wrote joyous doggerel verse in Latin. England was happy.

Edward, perhaps, was less so. Naboth's Vineyard proved to have nettles among its grass. *Debellaverat superbos* : but they had not all their heads on London Bridge, and some of the heads were awkwardly highly placed. His own very long one was rapidly breeding suspicion of what was in that of the young Earl of

Carrick. Bruce, for the three years since his capitulation, had behaved with a decorous quiet : he had co-operated, even to the point of providing assistance for the conveyance of the siege-engines to Stirling,[1] in the pacification of Scotland, *more Romano*. He had helped to draw up those plans for the new administration with which he and Wishart and Moubray had been commissioned at the March parliament. But . . . his grandfather had claimed to be King of Scots. And in the summer, Edward had grown suspicious.

There is a point that demands some comment here. I could wish it did not, for it gives me no pleasure to fall foul of another writer's work. But in the interests of historic truth, no less than of a great man's reputation, I must deal with certain charges against Bruce. The charges need not have been made : but being made, I cannot escape from examining their content, for they colour nearly all of both the scholarly and the semi-popular work on this time of the last generation. To the point, then : it has been stated, more than once, that Bruce was at Wallace's trial, and concurred in it. Now, it is one thing for Bruce to realise, after years of bitter experiment, that resistance, for the time, and under the conditions obtaining, was useless ; to submit accordingly, and to do the best possible, in the circumstances, to obtain any kind of stable government under

---

[1] The terms of Edward's letter on the subject, dated the 14th April 1304, are polite, but their tone suggests a lack of enthusiasm on Bruce's part.

which Scotland could recover from the results of some dozen years of practical anarchy and recurrent invasion. He would no doubt have been a more suitable figure for a hero of romantic fiction if he had set his face against compromise, even temporary compromise : but he was a practical politician in circumstances that are seen to be more difficult the more one examines them : and the more one examines them the less one inclines to judge. It would have been another thing, however, if he had concurred in Wallace's death, and in that death.

The authority for the charge that he so concurred is again Sir Herbert Maxwell, who talks in shocked tones of ' Bruce's repeated presence in Edward's parliament and Council at the time when Wallace was hurried to his death,' and says that in August 1305 Bruce was ' probably a witness of the trial and execution of Wallace.' Now, Sir Herbert, as support for this statement, cites a contemporary authority, a rather inaccessible one for most readers, as it is long out of print and I doubt whether more than five public libraries in Scotland, four of them university ones, would contain a copy. And if the reader has the power, and will take the trouble, to look up Sir Herbert's reference for himself, he will find in it no evidence whatever that Bruce ' consented to the death of Wallace,' ' that he swore a new and elaborate oath of allegiance,' just after that death, ' on the Lord's Body, the Holy Relics, and the Four Evangels,' or, finally, that he was present at all. The ugly story, of which

K

Sir Herbert speaks so circumstantially and with such shocked reluctance, has no contemporary evidence. The evidence which he himself offers in support is Joseph Bain's *Calendar of Documents relating to Scotland*, vol. ii, p. 457. The reference is to an abstract of the Ordinance for the Settlement of Scotland. The Ordinance is printed in full in Palgrave's *Parliamentary Writs*, and neither in the abstract nor in the full text is there any suggestion of the point Sir Herbert adduces it to prove, of which it is his solitary proof, and which is the ugliest charge against Robert Bruce, a charge whose ugliness he underlines by every possible means of emphasis.[1]

The Ordinance, however, does reveal something about Bruce—not that he was in London at Wallace's death, far less that he approved of that, but that Edward, since March, had grown suspicious of him. It refers to his appointment the previous March, with Wishart and Moubray, to see to the election of repre-

---

[1] Sir James Ramsay, in his *Dawn of the Constitution*, a standard book on the period, mentions Bruce among those who took the oath at Westminster in *October*, 1305. His authorities are Rymer's *Foedera*, and Matthew of Westminster, iii, 125. Matthew, in any case, is doubtful evidence : but as it happens, he mentions none of the new Commissioners, or Guardians, by name. The *Foedera*, which consists of official documents, would be conclusive, if it mentioned Bruce : but it does *not* say, as it happens, that he was present. What it does say is that the Scots were to give obedience to ' the foresaid Bishop, John, Robert, and John.' Sir James has apparently taken these four to be the *three* Commissioners of March, *Bishop* Wishart, *Robert* Bruce, and *John* de Moubray : but the four mentioned here are not these, but the new Guardians, *Bishop* Lamberton, *John* de Sandale, *Robert* de Kethe, and *John* de Kingston, whose names are given in full in an earlier paragraph of the same document.

sentatives, and then later states that he is to place the castle of Kildrummie 'in the keeping of one for whom he shall answer.' (Kildrummie was one of the key positions of Moray, the province that was foremost in the rising of 1297 and was to play a leading part in that of 1306-1307: and the child Earl of Mar, to whom the castle belonged, was Bruce's nephew and ward.) That is the only reference to him. There is not the slightest suggestion that he was present.

Mr Barron has made the suggestion that Bruce and Wishart had not put themselves forward in May for election as deputies to this parliament, because they preferred to remain in the North, and free from official responsibility, in order to be able to organise against the time when fresh resistance could be undertaken. This is very probable, though it must remain a conjecture. It is certain, however, that from about the time of Wallace's death, Edward's attitude to Bruce undergoes a change. Before that time, Bruce had shared in the policy of conciliation the King had adopted towards the Scottish leaders, and had been given that prominence in affairs which his birth warranted. On the 26th of October, however, pending the arrival of the new Viceroy, John of Brittany,[1] who could not come until the beginning of Lent, the custody of Scotland is given to Lamberton, John de Sandale, Robert

[1] Earl of Richmond, younger son of John II of Brittany and Beatrice of England, sister of Edward I. His elder brother, later Duke Arthur II of Brittany, had married Yolette, Queen Dowager of Scots.

Keith, and John de Kingston. Bruce, who had been a
Guardian in March, is omitted. This fact, of course,
is capable of various interpretations, but it does suggest
that he was out of favour : and the suggestion is confirmed by the certain fact that twelve days before the
Commission was appointed, Umfraville's Carrick lands,
given to Bruce in March, were taken from him and
given back to Umfraville.

One small point in official records, a little later, has
been used to suggest that Bruce, all through this winter,
was still enjoying an apparently discreditable degree of
Edward's favour. On the 8th of the next February,
there is an order that a sum of scutage, due from
Bruce on the succession to his English estates, should
be remitted. Much has been made of the fact. But it
was not a favour, any more than the return of im-
properly overpaid income-tax is a favour. The official
statement is not a remission of a charge due, but an
admission that a charge on Bruce's father's estate had
been wrongly made, scutage (exemption-money for
military service) having been charged for services of
1271 and 1282, which turn out to have been actually
rendered. If I tell the Inland Revenue Commissioners
that they have assessed my income-tax without de-
ducting the earned-income allowance, and they, admitting the error, reduce the claim, I shall be receiving
precisely such a favour. In fact, it actually happens
that I have done so. But if anyone accused me, on
the strength of it, of being on terms of improper
intimacy with the Chancellor of the Exchequer, Mr

Chamberlain and I would both be, to put it mildly, rather surprised.

It seems fairly clear that after Wallace's death Bruce was not, in fact, well seen at Edward's court. It is possible that he may have expressed himself unwisely. It is also possible that something taken on Wallace may have awakened suspicion. We do know that the papers seized on him when he was captured included, besides safe-conducts from the Kings of France and Norway, some correspondence with ' the magnates of Scotland,' which was probably compromising for somebody. Lamberton, in his agreement with Bruce, most probably had Wallace at his back, for the latter, though his influence with the nobles had been lost, was still a power among the men he had led. The papers, however, can hardly have referred to this agreement, as there is no sign of Lamberton being in trouble : but they may have hinted at some understanding with Bruce, or even suggested a possible fresh rising in the name of Bruce instead of, as before, of Baliol.

Through the winter of 1305, things were outwardly quiet, in spite of these various signs of growing tension. Then in February, there was a sudden explosion, not less disconcerting, it is probable, to Bruce and Wishart and Lamberton than to Edward. Precisely what happened is very far from clear : or to be more accurate, we know what did occur to explode the mine, but the why and the how of it can only be guessed at from a variety of conflicting (and elaborately circumstantial) stories, which cannot possibly all of them be true, and all of which may be fairly considered as biassed, either in Bruce's favour or against him.[1]

We do not know where Bruce was when the trouble began. Mr Barron thinks that he did not return to England after the spring parliament of 1305. There is certainly no evidence that he attended the autumn one : but Fordun declares he was at Edward's court in the mid-winter, which is not improbable, for Edward may have preferred him under his eye ; and Barbour also affirms that he was in London when the trouble began. Now, it appears that there had already, since Comyn's surrender, been some *rapprochement* between him and Bruce : quite conceivably he may have shared Lamberton's policy of allowing time for recovery before another rising, though this is conjecture. The details are exasperatingly vague. Whether Comyn had decided on making a fresh attempt, not this time with Baliol as figurehead, but with himself, Baliol's nephew and with a better record,[2] or with Bruce : or whether Bruce had decided that he would after all need to work with Comyn's help, even if it were purchased with the Crown, is completely uncertain. We cannot even be

[1] We are constantly warned that Scottish chroniclers are likely to be biassed in Bruce's favour. This is quite true, and the warning needs attention. But I have never seen a parallel warning, that English chroniclers may be biassed against him. Yet would anyone expect to find a perfectly full and unbiassed account of the Battle of the Aisne in the *Times*, the *Matin*, or the *Berliner Tageblatt* of September 1914—let alone the *Daily Mail* or the *Petit Journal* ? And the chroniclers were the Fourth Estate of their day.

[2] Red John Comyn, the leader of the recent wars, was now, like Bruce, the head of his great house, since his father, Black John, the original Guardian, had died in 1303.

absolutely sure that one of them did take up one of
these lines. The interview, if there was one, was not
likely to have been carried on in shouts, and although
there is plenty of evidence, it contradicts itself at
almost every point. Barbour's real narrative, after a
very perfunctory summary of the general situation,
begins at this point : and he gives the initiative to
Comyn, whose offer is that either Bruce is to have the
Crown and he Bruce's lands, or that Bruce shall have
his and he assume the Crown. Bruce, by this account,
accepted the former alternative, and they made a band
to that effect. Gray, who is very detailed, reverses
this, making Bruce put the same suggestion to Comyn,
but giving place and occasion differently—not ' riding
from Stirling,' as Barbour has it, but at the Greyfriars
of Dumfries, on the day of the quarrel that led to
Comyn's death. Fordun's story agrees with Gray
about the terms, and gives the initiative, as he does,
to Bruce, but agrees with Barbour in setting the interview on the road from Stirling, though he dates it, for
another complication, in 1304, the year of Comyn's
surrender and also of Bruce's band with Lamberton.

Barbour, Gray, and Fordun, who thus contradict
each other, are among the best of the authorities. Of
the three of them, Barbour is the most likely, from his
official position, to have had inside knowledge, if any
one of them had : but the affair of the band and its
consequence is not one on which precise information
would be very likely to be available to the writer of
memoirs, any more than the precise terms of an im-

portant and dangerous conversation between, say, Herr
Schuschnigg and Signor Mussolini, over a matter of
secret diplomacy, would be to-day. Both men, in such
an affair, were risking a very unpleasant and messy death
if Edward should gather a whisper of what was toward.
All three stories agree on the general terms, however,
Gray adding two further points as being made by
Bruce, that Edward was growing old, and that Baliol
was useless even as figurehead, since *son droict e la
fraunchise du realme ad lesse perdre*. We may take it,
on the whole, that there really was some such discussion,
though the place and the date are impossible to determine, any more than the distribution of the arguments
used. The time for action, and its nature, were probably not agreed, any more than in the band with Lamberton. But at the beginning of February, action was
forced.

Again the circumstances are obscure, and the best
authorities contradict each other. Hemingburgh says
that Bruce set on his brothers to murder Comyn, but
that the latter received them in such friendly fashion
that they politely refrained, and contented themselves
with bringing him where Bruce could murder him.
Gray repeats this, with circumstantial—too circumstantial—detail : that either Bruce or his brothers
should repeat the elaborate conversation that Gray puts
into their mouths is, to put it mildly, rather improbable.
And there is a further and conclusive point against
any suggestion of planned murder, which will be mentioned later. Barbour says Comyn sent the band to

Edward, which he might have done on thinking the matter over. Fordun agrees. John Major, writing much later, blames *Lady* Comyn, which again is possible, as she was a sister of Edward's general Aymar de Valence : but one would like some earlier evidence. Edward himself, in writing to the Pope, says that Bruce made proposals to Comyn which Comyn rejected : which would suggest that Comyn did betray the matter, but is not, all the same, an adequate proof that he did. Diplomatic correspondence, with a third party, has been known before now to be inaccurate.

In any event, whether through Comyn, Lady Comyn, or otherwise, it appears that Edward got wind of the affair. Barbour says that he forthwith challenged Bruce, who had the presence of mind to win time by an expedient : but the expedient suggests confusion with a later incident concerning Lamberton. Fordun's story is that the old King was so pleased at the news that the same night, ' when the wine glowed in the cup,' he supped too well, and at his *coucher* revealed his satisfaction that the Earl of Carrick would soon be out of the road. The Earl of Gloucester heard : he was Edward's son-in-law, but Bruce's kinsman and friend. He sent him twelve silver pence and a pair of spurs, and Bruce, having tipped the messenger with the money, took the hint, and put the spurs to immediate use, riding north on the instant with only his secretary and another man. As he reached the Marches he met a man of Comyn's, whom one of them knew.

Something roused his suspicions, and, the man being searched, they found letters to Edward, urging Bruce's death.

Now, all this story is perfectly possible, and on a different plane as regards probability from a statement as to the time and place of a secret agreement, or even as to its terms. But we cannot take it as absolutely certain. The next thing that happened, however, is clear enough. Apparently by appointment, Bruce and Red John Comyn met on the 10th of February, in the Kirk of the Franciscans of Dumfries. The details of the affair are vague again. Apparently they met before the high altar : all the accounts agree in mentioning that, and it means that the interview was not in secret. A Presbyterian reader may need to be reminded that a Catholic church is open at all time to all comers, and very rarely altogether empty : one can certainly never count on its being empty. And ' before the high altar '—presumably at the gate of the Friars' choir—would be the most conspicuous part, though in a large building it would be quite possible to carry on a private conversation there in the low tones that men would naturally use in such a place. Whether Bruce confronted Comyn with his man's letter, accused him, on suspicion, of betrayal, was threatened with it, or whether the long hostility came to a head, one asserting his rights and being given the lie by the other, or one taunted the other—Bruce Comyn with the futility of the war, Comyn Bruce with surrendering before the rest—two hot-tempered men forgot where they were

standing. They quarrelled : steel glinted, and Red
John fell, and Bruce rushed from the church. Barbour
gives no more, save that Comyn's uncle, Robert (he
calls him Edmund) was killed there with others. The
other account is that Bruce struck Comyn down, then,
possibly realising the sacrilege, rushed from the
church and cried to his friends who were waiting, presumably with the horses, that he thought he had killed
him, whereat one, Kirkpatrick, ran into the church
and promptly finished off the wounded man. One
may agree for once with Sir Herbert Maxwell in re-
marking that Kirkpatrick's traditional pun, the delight
of generations of Scots schoolboys, is very unlikely in
its traditional form, as Kirkpatrick was hardly likely
to speak Scots : Sir Herbert appears to have forgotten,
however, that a parallel one is possible in French,
between a *je me doute* and a *pas de doute*. The episode,
pun and all, is in fact not unlikely, and so is the suggestion that there was a fight of sorts in which others
were killed. A great noble would not have ridden by
himself.

How, or why, Comyn was dead, at all events, and in
a church. To a knight of the time, to stab a man in a
sudden passionate quarrel was not commendable,
assuredly : but it was at worst an unfortunate accident
that might happen to any quick-tempered gentleman
in a moment's carelessness over the controls. Their
attitude was in fact much that of the modern motorist
over running down a pedestrian. It ought not to
happen, of course : still, it does happen, and nobody

minds very much except the victim. But sacrilege was
a very different story. The mere scene of the killing,
to anyone who knows the age, and the dependence of
Bruce, in any rising, on the help of the Church, is convincing evidence that whatever caused it, the thing was
not premeditated murder. To kill Comyn at all meant
an immediate blood-feud with one of the greatest
houses in all Scotland, not to mention all its numerous
connections—and incidentally, with one that was
pretty consistently nationalist. To kill him in church
meant forfeiting the support of his strongest ally. And
the deed that added to his enemies and stripped him at
the same time of his strongest friends thrust him into
premature action against Edward.

He rode back to Lochmaben, and thought it over.
There were three lines of action from which he had to
choose. He could surrender, which meant certain
death, and the leaving of Scotland, in consequence,
without leader. He could go into hiding or go abroad,
to his sister's court, the Queen Dowager now of Norway : and this alternative must have looked promising.
Or he could challenge Edward, and fight it out.

The whole future of Scotland lay in the decision of
that February day : not only the future of Scotland,
but that of Europe. What he chose was to raise the
Royal Standard at Scone.

III

THE ROAD TO MIRACLE

EIGHT YEARS: 1306–1314

Anglicana natione . . . Scotos multifariis multisque modis iniuriis, flagellis et caedibus sub diro iugo servitutis crudeliter affligente, misericors Deus . . . suscitavit eis salvatorem et propugnatorem . . . Robertum de Bruyse nomine, qui eos in lacu miseriae prostratos et omne spe salutis et auxilio destitutos videns . . . tanquam alter Macchabaeus manum mittens ad fortia pro fratribus liberandis, innumeros et importabiles diei aestus et frigoris et famis . . . subiit labores, non inimicorum tantum sed etiam falsorum fratrum insidias, et taedia, inedias, et pericula laetanter amplectendo.

Fordun and Bower, *Gesta Annalia.*

CHAPTER VIII

KING HOB

ONE AND A HALF YEARS : 1306–1307

' Nu Kyng Hob in the mures gongeth.'
English popular song, c. 1306.

ON the 27th of March, 1306, being then in the thirty-second year of his age, Robert Bruce Earl of Carrick was crowned King of Scots. It was twenty years and eight days since the death of Alexander III, ten years and a day since Baliol's men crossed the Sark : and during that time, Scotland had fairly been wiped from the map of Europe, had vanished out of national existence with the apparent completeness of pre-war Poland. Bruce was assuming the headship of a country whose strong places were all garrisoned by the enemy, whose commerce and agriculture were in ruins, whose man-power and whose spirit—so one would think—were drained by ten years of futile, shiftless, and unsuccessful war. He had against him, not on his frontier but flooding his whole kingdom to beyond Inverness, an enemy from five to eight times more numerous than what should have been his own full strength : and by way of assistance in confronting these odds, he had a civil war on his hands as well, against the very men whose past sympathies had been nationalist, while of the rest of his nobility many powerful men sided with the foreigner.   And in addition to the numerical odds, incalculably increased by these complications, he was challenging, with a country economically wrecked, one thriving and wealthy, and barely touched, on the fringe of her poorest provinces, by the war.   His only allies abroad were fighting each other : his own rash act, in a moment's loss of temper, had set him at odds with his chief friend at home, the Church.   In fact, in the whole history of Europe, it would be hard to find a more lunatic venture.

The English court were uproariously amused, and somebody promptly christened him ' King Hob,' which is as one might say nowadays ' King Bobby.' Scotland, by all the standards of common sense, was a conquered country, if ever there had been one.   It had taken ten years—an absurdly long time for the job : but as an English song of the time remarks,

> Post hos et huiusmodi bellicos labores,
> Angli velut angeli semper sunt victores,
> Scoticis et Wallicis sunt praestantiores.[1]

Even Bruce's wife cried out when she got the news, ' Alas, we are but King and Queen of the May.'

Common sense, however, though no doubt admirable, is not always a safe guide to future history.   By

---

[1] More or less literally, in its own key,

> If there's a war
> We give them what for.
> God's Englishmen
> Have done it again.
> > We're better than Scotland or Wales, O,
> > We're better than Scotland or Wales.

all rational standards, Bruce should have failed in six weeks, gone under, and for good, with ignominy. Instead of that, he fought steadily on for eight years, and completely and magnificently succeeded. It took, indeed, another fourteen years of war to consolidate what was won at Bannockburn. But that also was achieved : and though danger came on his work again and again, there were always men (it was once a priest and a woman) who had brains and resolution to hold it off, and in course of time, when the two countries came together at last, they came in peace, and it was Scotland who gave her king to the two. The last chapter of Bruce's adventure is 1603. Since then the dangers have been of another kind.

The miracle, of course, like all miracles, becomes explicable when one knows its causes. The new King's case, on the most hopeful reading of the facts, was almost fantastically desperate, but there were certain elements in his favour, though one of them—and it is fairly important to our minds—was something that would not have struck a man of the time, very largely because he would simply take it for granted. In the long run, and while man endures on this planet, the end of a war will ultimately depend on personnel. But the increasing mechanisation of life has made matériel of huge importance. It has always counted, long before Napoleon at Eylau raised artillery to be the predominant arm : in this very war, Falkirk was won and lost on armament. But before explosives— and they did not enter this war until a year or two

L

before Bruce's death—matériel counted for less in actual fighting. Bruce's task may have been prolonged by the lack of siege engines : but Edward at Stirling, a first-rate soldier with the full army of England and a splendid siege-train of the latest model, was held up for weeks by a couple of hundred men. Commissariat, in a wrecked country, was a problem, but the Scots had the shorter lines of communication, and could fight harder on worse rations than any efficient fight-ingmen in Europe. The lack of either funds or munition-works was not felt as it would be in a modern war, though the lack of a fleet was an obvious handicap.

The King would not see all this, nor would any man of his time, as we do, looking back. But he would see two other things that counted greatly. One was the country. Scotland—her very earth—could fight for Scotland. Edward could make his fleet serve him on the East as it had done against Wales, but it dared not venture in among the Isles, and the West from Kintyre north was safe from it. Further, to reach Scotland in force, an English army had to cross the most barren part of its own country : the English base for mobilisa-tion was York, which is almost a hundred miles, as the crow flies, from the nearest point of the Border. The once rich provinces of Southern Scotland were wrecked with seven invasions in ten years, and parts even of them were wild country for campaigning by an army that more than most required heavy rations : while beyond the Forth great stretches of wilder hills gave the Scots, if they could once get those provinces clear, a retreat into which it was difficult to follow.

The other thing that he would see was the men. The English were in earnest about the war, rather as Great Britain was in 1901 about the Boers. They had expected a picnic, and had not got it : and now they felt their prestige involved in winning. But the Scots were fighting for their country's freedom, and a man will do more than he can for the sake of that. As Cardinal Mercier said in 1914, when his Belgium was in the case of Bruce's Scotland, ' *Une nation qui se defend ne périt pas.*'

There is one more point, too, that he would not see, that is visible to us as we look back. That was sheer luck . . . if that happens to be the word for anything when a man works in faith : to work in faith does not mean believing that things will be all right somehow or other, but that *if* one does, to the utmost, all one can, in a right cause, one's strength will be reinforced. The luck, if one is to call it that, came from the chance of English politics, that allowed Bruce to dispose of his civil war before the foreign one mustered its full strength. That point, however, may be taken later, though it cannot be passed in a general discussion of the event of the ensuing eight years. The fundamental factor of them all was the principle that I have quoted already, of Mr Belloc's. ' Potential is more than mass, decision and courage of more value than numbers, and energy the deciding factor.'

That was the situation, then, and those the odds, when

Bruce rode north from Lochmaben to Bishop Wishart, down Clydesdale in the February weather, when spring stirs in the rain and the sound of the burns in those smooth yellow hills. The Bishop had waited that hour for some sixteen years. Now it came bleakly enough, but he was ready. He brought out from his treasury where it was concealed the old forbidden flag of the Kings of Scots, and the Lion within his tressure of scarlet lilies took the wind again. He gave Bruce absolution for Comyn's death. It is easy and cheap to sneer at both for that, but the repentance was like to be real enough. There is nothing in any of Bruce's history that suggests him a man to practise political murder. Fierce temper, and steel too ready to his hand, had caused what it was well within the man to repent when his blood cooled : and the Church has never refused (nor did her Master) reconciliation with the penitent. Wishart gave Bruce absolution, at all events, and if he was wrong he paid for it with long years of prison and the loss of eyesight. Then he rode with the Bruces to Scone for the coronation, ransacking the vestment-chests of his cathedral for such poor pomp as there could be at such a time, and a goldsmith hurriedly made a circlet of gold.

It was on Palm Sunday that the crown was used. The stately and terrible mass of that festival, the Sunday before the Day of the Crucifixion, must have come with strange colour to the minds of men who were some to die very soon for that day's work, and all of them in peril of their lives—the procession with its exultant palms and lights, but the veiled crosses and the violet colour of mourning on priests and altar, the long and awful Gospel of the Passion, preceded by the Psalm of the Dereliction. And the hymn for the evening offices that day is the terrible joy of the *Vexilla Regis*, that commemorates the Battle on the Cross. I do not think any of the men with Bruce, as worldly as they might be, could have heard them lightly.

We know some of those men, and their names deserve recollection, with those others ' who have no memorial.' There was the Abbot in whose great church they were gathered, and three chief bishops, Lamberton, Wishart, and the Bishop of Moray, the uncle of that young comrade-in-arms of Wallace who died in his youth before he had seen the son who was to serve Scotland also in his time. There were Bruce's own kin : his four brothers, three knights and Wishart's scholarly young Dean ; Thomas Randolph, who was to be Earl of Moray and a great captain, and who was some kin to Bruce, just what is not known ;[1] and an English knight, Christopher Seton, who had married the young widowed Countess of Mar, Bruce's brave

---

[1] He is commonly described as Bruce's nephew : but the word was used almost as loosely as ' cousin.' There is no trace of the marriage of any of the six Bruce girls to a Randolph, and in any case none of them could be born before 1272, which even with the early marriages of the age would not leave time for a son who was old enough to witness a document in 1292. Sir James Balfour Paul thinks his mother may have been a daughter of Robert Bruce *le viel* by an unrecorded first marriage, which, in the state of the records, is possible, the more as to judge by the known age of his father he was not young at his marriage to Countess Marjorie. Randolph's father was Sheriff of Roxburgh, Great Chamberlain, and Lord of Nithsdale.

sister Christina. Of the rest, there were two great
earls from above Forth, Lennox and Athol, who were
two of the Seven ; Hay of Errol and his brother ;
Barclay of Cairns ; Alexander Fraser, Somerville of
Cairnwath, David de Inchmartin, Robert Boyd, Robert
Fleming, and a lad who was to be the greatest soldier of
all, save Bruce himself. (He had been a student in
Paris when his father died in the Tower, and after that
he was Lamberton's carving-squire.) This was young
James Douglas, who was to be ' Good Lord James.'
Most—all the great men except Bishop Wishart and
the disinherited Douglas—were from north of Forth.
Nine, by the end of the next year, gave their lives, and
three of the churchmen saw years of an English prison.

The rite went through as it could. Bruce's own son
David II was the first King of Scots to be anointed,
and the two essential points of the old form were the
placing of the King on the Sacred Stone, and his
crowning by the head of the House of Fife. The
Stone was in London : so was the Earl of Fife, who
was a young lad. It was counted ominous at Baliol's
crowning that he was too much of a child to officiate
there.

But the young Earl's sister had word of what was
toward. She was distantly akin to both Bruce and
Edward, for her mother was a daughter of Gilbert of
Gloucester by his first marriage with the latter's
cousin. She was also the wife of John Comyn, Earl of
Buchan : but she calmly commandeered her husband's
horses, and rode to Scone to act as her brother's proxy.

The coronation was over when she came, but partly
for tradition, partly, perhaps, out of courtesy to an
heroic lady, they repeated it on the Tuesday, which
was that of Holy Week, and the crown was duly lifted
to its place by one of the old great house. She was
risking both her life and her good name, for of course
she got herself jeered at for Bruce's mistress. She
may have been. But the Whigs brought the same kind
of charge against Flora Macdonald, and called Hen-
rietta Maria, a fool but certainly a devoted wife, ' a
Popish whore : ' and the English brought similar
charges against St Joan. The accusation is a handy
one for a woman who dares support an inconvenient
cause : and Matthew of Westminster, who makes it
with the unction of a Kirk Session, calls Bruce *coronatus
fatuus* in the same sentence, which his worst enemy
now would admit is a lie. There has never been any
dearth of Scotswomen who would risk all they had for
a cause that they believed in : and yet a recent historian
of Scotland repeats the charge in a sniggering aside.
I would need more proof of its truth than that it was
brought, which it undeniably was. But I have not
come on any, in some research.

The coronation was ultimate defiance to Edward.
Bruce set about gathering men to support the defiance,
and all over Scotland the priests took up his cause,
Wishart and Moray leading the Crusade, and preaching
—so Edward later complained to the Pope—that it
was as worthy to fight the King of England as to fight
the heathen Saracen in the East. Edward's statement

sounds a little more convincing than the rider he gives
it—a pious wail of regret that these sinful Scots have
prevented him from going on the Crusade that is
nearer his heart than anything else on earth !

Bruce's recruiters had no bribes to hold out. They
could have used the words of Garibaldi. ' I offer
neither pay, nor quarters, nor provisions. I offer
hunger, thirst, forced marches, battles, and death.
Let him who loves his country in his heart, and not
from the lips only, come with me.' And as with
Garibaldi, there were men found who accepted these
stern gifts.

We have the names of a hundred and thirty-five
landed gentlemen who joined Bruce in that spring of
1306. Sixteen come from Perthshire, among them
the Earls of Athol, Menteith, and Strathearn. There
are twelve from Angus and the Mearns, another twelve
from Aberdeen and Banff, and eight from Moray.
Seven are from the Lennox, four from about Stirling,
four from Argyll, among them Angus Macdonald and
Neil Campbell, younger of Lochow, the husband of
Mary Bruce. Dumbarton and Clackmannan send one
apiece. South of Forth, there are fewer, and these
mostly from the West, where the Bruce and Stewart
influence was strongest. There are two from Berwick,
seven from Roxburgh, six from Peebles and Selkirk,
and twenty-seven from Ayr, Renfrew, Dumfries, and
Galloway. There are no names of men from Lothian,
and that province was the last to be recovered. It was
not until the last month of 1312 that Bruce could

attempt to tackle the South-east : and then the attempt was a failure for the time. Lang's statement that ' the war was won by Lowland Scots, in origin mainly of English descent,' is rashly repeated by many historians : but it does not bear any detailed examination of what is known—and that is a good deal—about the identity of Bruce's followers, in 1306 and later. The Lowland element all through the war is predominantly not from ' English ' Scotland, but from the Brython- and Gaelic-Celtic South-west.

Edward, who was at Winchester, heard the news. He wrote in fierce indignation to the Pope, not Boniface VIII now but Clement V, the first of the exile-popes of Avignon. His fury was hottest against the Scottish Church. It does not seem to have occurred to him that even if his conduct towards Scotland had not broken the mutual obligation implied in allegiance, the man who made Edward's declaration of the 2nd of January 1293, and repeated it later on publicly and in cold blood was in no more case to complain of a breach of fealty than a bigamist whose second wife has left him. The Pope, who until lately had been Archbishop of Edward's city of Bordeaux, and relied on England for support against Philip IV, obediently wrote back authorising the Archbishop of Canterbury and the Bishop of Carlisle to excommunicate the shocking King Hob, which, on the 5th of June, was duly done, though the Scots clergy took no great heed of it.[1]

---

[1] A casual attitude to excommunication, especially foreign (even though papal), is remarkable all through the Middle Ages. Robert II

Meanwhile, Edward also applied the secular arm. Aymar de Valence, Earl of Pembroke, who had a blood-feud with Bruce, as his sister was the widow of Red John Comyn, was sent up to be Governor of Scotland, in the place of John of Brittany. Edward gave orders that all those taken in arms, and all who sheltered them, were to be hanged or headed, while those concerned at all in the death of Comyn, and those who gave them countenance or support, were to suffer his full invention in the way of disembowelling and castration. No jousts were to be held till the war was finished, but he held a magnificent pageant of his own. The Prince of Wales, aged twenty-two, was to be knighted : the King held a gorgeous function in the Temple, at which two swans were brought in bound with chains of gold, and all the knights present took solemn oath on these never to rest till Scotland should be conquered, while Edward himself offered a pious vow that when the wrong to Holy Church of Comyn's murder was duly avenged, he would never bear arms again against Christian man, but set out for Palestine and the Crusade. ' Our old English God ' was no doubt greatly obliged, and by way of encouraging the terrestrial forces, the lands of Bruce and of his followers were distributed among the gentlemen present, Henry

of France, known precisely, and with some reason, as the Pious, is merely one spectacular example : and his clergy backed him, although the excommunication in his case had clear moral grounds as well as political. The principle was that an excommunication was null if its motive was manifestly incorrect : and this could apply even to a papal sentence, as Papal Infallibility was not yet *de fide*.

de Percy being given Bruce's earldom of Carrick, and Wallace's captor Menteith the earldom of Lennox. Then Edward began his journey to the North, but he was too ill to travel with any speed : indeed, it was spring before he reached Carlisle, nearly a year after Bruce's coronation. His fever of anger shows in the urgent letters with which he bombarded his generals in the North.

Pembroke, of course, had moved a good deal faster, even with a considerable army. Lothian gave him no trouble. He struck straight across Forth, and on the 8th of June took Cupar Castle, capturing its Governor, who was no less a person than Bishop Wishart. At midsummer he reached Perth, cantoned his force within the walls of what was counted the strongest city in Scotland, and waited. What happened is told by the English chroniclers, and as Hemingburgh, Gray, Trivet, and Rishanger, who include three of the best authorities, agree, we cannot consider the story a Scots invention. Bruce was at Methven, half a dozen miles off. His force was smaller, but apparently he decided to put matters to the test of a definite action. He could not, for lack of artillery, tackle the city. What he did was typical of one side of the age. On the 26th of June he came before the town and challenged Pembroke to surrender it, or to come out and fight. Pembroke politely replied that it was Sunday, but that he would be delighted to oblige next morning. Bruce accepted the arrangement, characteristic of the age even much later. (Cf. Froissart *passim* and

Edward Bruce's famous agreement over Stirling.) The
Scots force drew off again, and camped for the night,
relying on Pembroke's military parole. He saw them
out of the road, led out his men, and marched them to
Methven in the long summer dusk. The thing was
clearly a complete surprise. Hemingburgh says they
timed the attack for when the Scots troops would
be cooking supper or *recumbentes secure*, and that they
fell on them before they could mount, which suggests
what is, even after the arrangement with Pembroke, a
rather surprising neglect in the matter of pickets.
Gray represents the Scots scrambling to arms and
horses, and charging all anyhow.

The surprise attack was a complete success. The
Scots were shattered before they could manage to form.
The King was unhorsed and taken, but rescued, or let
go : Gray says one John Haliburton had taken him,
not knowing who he was, since he was wearing *vn
chemys blaunk*—a white linen surcoat to keep the sun
from his mail, not the emblazoned one he would wear
in action—and that, when he found who he was, he
let him go.   Six of the men who had stood at the coronation were taken likewise, and with less good fortune.
Of the rest, Edward Bruce, Neil Campbell, Douglas,
Hay, and Athol, got off and fled with the King, and
those who could.

Three months to a day from that hazardous coronation, the cause of Bruce was to all appearance ruined,
his army was scattered, and he in flight for his life, and
men he could very ill afford to lose were killed or in

prison. Lamberton joined these last in the next month, and the Abbot of Scone was also apprehended. Edward was delighted with the capture of the churchmen, though his pleasure in it was a little dashed by the fact that the Bishop of Moray had slipped between Pembroke's fingers, and got away to Orkney. Edward wrote wrathful despatches to poor Pembroke, who was certainly doing his best, and in spring to King Haakon : but he did not succeed in capturing Bishop David, and had to do what he could with what he had. He dared not hang two Princes of the Church, but he had them sent to Winchester and Porchester, and kept in irons. Wishart never saw Scotland again. They released him in 1314 : but he was blind then.[1]

The laymen could not claim benefit of clergy. Early in August sixteen gentlemen were hanged at Newcastle without trial, the charge being ' killing the King's lieges at the battle ' (of Methven) ' and being taken in the field.' They included Sir David de Inchmartin, Alexander Scrymgeour, whom Wallace had made Standard-bearer for Scotland, and a brother of Christopher Seton. Seton and another were ' drawn,' the rest hanged merely.

Bruce, meanwhile, with what followers he could rally, made west for Athol, probably to raise men, for its Earl was with him, and the Highlanders, as Gray remarked later on, were *gentez legers a mouvoir countre*

---

[1] Edward II seems to have mitigated their captivity, for a few years later they were allowed a chaplain and two servants apiece, which suggests they were now treated as prisoners of state.

Engles. He then fetched a compass eastward, and betook himself and his force to Aberdeen, where he met an addition that was probably as surprising as unwelcome. Edward had hit on an original way of harassing him : he had not only stripped his followers of their lands, but had also outlawed their womenfolk.[1] ' Outlawry ' is apt to suggest, to the modern mind, a cheerful and sporting picnic in the greenwood. What it actually meant was that the protection of the law was removed : in more concrete terms, that anyone who chose might rob, murder, or violate any of them at pleasure, and the law would neither prevent nor penalise him. The ladies had done the only thing they could, and sought their men's protection, such as it was. Nor could the men, in the circumstances, refuse this very hampering addition, which in fact brought several of them to their deaths.

The English army marched on Aberdeen. The town seems to have shown itself not unfriendly, but the King was in no case to stand up to Pembroke, and he and his companions took to the heather, making south-westwards. By what we know of their route, it seems probable they were making for Kintyre, for shelter with Angus Macdonald. August in the Grampians is not commonly a dry month, and they were half-starved : Barbour remarks that young Douglas

---

[1] The authority is Fordun : the truth of his statement is borne out by the known conduct of the ladies. They would never have been permitted, under any less compulsion, to share the hardships, and increase the dangers, of a scratch force moving in peril of their lives.

was distinguished above the rest for his success in catering for the ladies. That uncommonly resourceful gentleman would no doubt have the makings of a first-rate poacher. They seem to have headed by Deeside and Glen Tilt, and then along the march of Breadalbane by Loch Tay and into Glen Dochart. On the 11th of August they met with disaster. John of Lorne, old Macdougall's son, was seeking them. (His mother was the aunt of Red John Comyn.) He came on them at Dalry, near the head of Glen Dochart. Bruce and his party got away, with a sharp rear-guard action. It was here that the three brothers set on the King : one sprang on the crupper and one caught the bridle, while the third got the King's foot and tried to throw him, but by his address and courage he slew them all.

The affair apparently decided the King that it was going to be impossible to get the ladies through Argyll and Knapdale : the further south they went, the worse grew the danger. His sister, the Countess Dowager of Mar, was with them : he determined to send the ladies to her son's castle of Kildrummie, an exceedingly strong place on Upper Donside, which apparently was not in English hands. With them as escort he despatched his brother Neil, with Athol, Lindsay, and Boyd, and apparently all the horses of the party : he may have meant them to make it their winter quarters, or intended them to reach Orkney, or perhaps Bergen. Having thus parted with his wife and child, whom he did not see again for the next eight years, he with the

two hundred men whom he had retained made their
way towards Kintyre, apparently giving up the route
by Real Argyll, and going south by Menteith.   Loch
Lomond lay in their way, among dangerous country.
Douglas found on the shore of it a small sunken boat,
and they managed somehow to raise and bail and patch
her, and crossed in her two at once, for that and the
oarsman were all that she would carry.   Those who
were good swimmers swam alongside with their kits
tied to their backs, and the King, waiting through the
slow business on the shore, passed the time by reading
aloud from a French romance.

Their rations were done, and they scattered to kill
stags.   Lennox, who had got back to his own countryside after Methven, heard of poachers at work and
went after them.   He had had no news of the King
for nearly two months.   He and the raiders recognised
each other :   they embraced, and wept, as Barbour
carefully explains, for joy.   In time they got to the
coast, Lennox joining them.   Neil Campbell, who had
gone ahead to forage, had shown the talent of his
eminent clan, and had ships and food :   they were
glad enough of both, for pursuit was up.   Lennox, in
the last ship, was nearly taken, but resourcefully hove
his baggage overboard, and got off while the pursuers
stopped to salvage.   It was a long row, and hard work.
The knights took their turn at the unaccustomed oars,
and as Barbour says, hands more used to the spear lost
a good deal of skin in the process.

They got safely to Dunaverty, however, where

Angus Macdonald gave them kindly welcome. It was a strong place, but even then not safe, for the galleys of John of Lorne had followed them, and by mid-September it had been invested . . . too late, for they slipped out before the lines could close, and the King disappears from sight for the next four months.

We may guess at wanderings not unlike those of Prince Charles, but the record is in tantalising glimpses. Barbour sends him to Rathlin, off the Irish coast, and gives a lively description of the crossing. Mr Barron thinks it a mere literary convention, after Homer : but though the good Archdeacon clearly enjoyed his set-piece, and may have attempted some Homeric colour, there is a suggestion of the eyewitness about the actual substance of the description, with a fair wind but a high sea running in the strong tidal current of the North Channel . . . so high a sea that the small ships in the trough lost sight of one another and of the land. (In fact, a fair wind—which for a mediaeval ship meant a following one—from the Mull of Kintyre to Rathlin, or *vice versa*, would probably mean a sizable cross sea, with the tide running and anything of a swell.) Barbour, however, is pretty certainly wrong in leaving the King in Rathlin through the winter. He is apt to be very accurate in the detail of his episodes, but to muddle their chronology, at times rather badly, as one would expect in a writer getting much of his story from men who would remember what had happened, but be rather uncertain whether it was before or after something else in which, perhaps,

M

they themselves had not taken part. The King, in all probability, *was* at Rathlin. He may have gone there from Dunaverty, and he was pretty certainly there in the next January. But he could hardly have spent the winter there, certainly not if his followers were with him. That the island belonged to a house on the English side is not, perhaps, a very cogent argument : its lord did not live there, and either a Scots or an Irish countryside has a remarkable talent for keeping a secret . . . and the native Irish had no cause to love their masters. What is more to the point is that Rathlin is rather more than six miles by a mile.

Neither Gray nor Fordun mentions Rathlin. Both speak simply of the Isles, and the latter adds that Bruce was succoured there by a noble lady, Christina of the Isles, a name that suggests a kinswoman of Angus. There is a Mackenzie tradition, set down in a MS. of 1669, but clearly much older in itself, that Bruce was received this winter at Eilean Donnain off the coast of Kintail, the *chef-lieu* of Iain Mòr, the young chief of what was still a quite small clan. Iain fought at Inverurie the next winter, and was at Bannockburn seven years after that, so it is not inherently improbable.[1] The English chroniclers, except Gray, say, sometimes in some detail, that Bruce was in Norway,

---

[1] He was one of those who put national feeling before partisan, for his mother was a daughter of old Macdougall of Lorne, and therefore sister of John of Lorne and first cousin of Red John Comyn. He himself, according to the clan historian, later married Edward Bruce's niece by marriage, Margaret of Athol, grand-daughter of Red John : but he does not seem to have shared in the Athol-Bruce quarrel.

and there was a Scots tradition to that effect also, that appears more than two hundred years after Bruce's time, in a book encouraging resistance to Henry VIII.

These tales are various on the face of them, but quite probably all of them are true. Norway (or, as Mr Barron suggests, the Orkneys, which were Norwegian territory) was a natural refuge for the brother of its Queen Dowager. (Queen Isobel was a widow by this time, as Eirik II died in 1299.) We know that King Haakon's Jarl of Orkney sheltered the Bishop of Moray, and the events of next spring, which suggest co-operation between Bruce and the Bishop, might have been concerted there, while Bruce might possibly expect to meet the ladies, who were certainly sent off in that direction when they left Kildrummie.

Coming south after a short stay, the King might have halted a while at Eilean Donnain, gone south down the Sound of Sleat to Ardnamurchan or Islay—both Macdonald country—and been received there by the Lady Christina. He seems to have been well south by January, for at the end of the month orders came to Bisset of the Glens of Antrim, the laird of Rathlin, to join the fleet that was hunting for King Robert. The King slipped through that, however, and early in February of 1307 he was in Arran, in sight of the shore of his own earldom of Carrick. There he found Douglas, who had been provisioning his little force by raiding supplies intended for John Hastings in Brodick Castle. They were glad to meet, and having met, they took counsel. The spring was at hand, when Edward's

armies would be able to move in force. The King, it
would seem, decided to forestall them by some action
that would give him a base for operations. It is possible that he may have concerted, with Bishop de
Moray, an attack on the South-west—his own country
—timed to correspond with a rising in the North. The
trouble was one inherent in mediaeval war. ' The fog
of war ' is a real thing even now, with wireless and
aeroplanes to assist a commander. With no mechanical
means of communication, and even roads, where there
were any, in such case that a man riding light and in a
desperate hurry took a fortnight to get from London
to Carlisle, it was blinding. And the King had been
wandering, away from the mainland, for months : he
did not even know of affairs at Kildrummie. He sent
a servant across the Firth to scout, a man named Cuthbert, who was to learn how things stood, and if they
gave a chance for a fresh rising, to light a beacon fire
on Turnberry Head.

Cuthbert went, and they watched the shore, and by
and by saw the fire that was the signal. They set sail
in hope and crossed the Firth and landed, and Cuthbert
met them in horror, for the fire was not his but chance
muirburn, fired early in the dry days that often come
then before the spring rains, and he thought it had
betrayed them to their deaths, for he had news, any
amount of it, and all the news was as bad as it could be.

Indeed, it would have broken a smaller man's nerve.
To know what some of it was, we must go back, to the
parting after the action at Dalry. Neil Bruce and

Athol then had gone with the ladies, to the strong castle of Kildrummie, in the lands of the King's young nephew, the Earl of Mar. In early September, when they could not have been there for more than a few days, they had word that the Prince of Wales was marching against them. Neil and Athol decided then to hold the place, but apparently tried to send the ladies to safety, perhaps to get them out of Scots territory. There may in fact have been some tryst with the King to meet them in Orkney and take them to Queen Isobel for shelter. But they never got as far as the Pentland Firth. They reached Easter Ross, a journey of something like a hundred miles. But the Earl of Ross, who was a Baliol man, had come down on Edward's side : he heard of the party, and gave chase. They made for Tain, on the shore of the Dornoch Firth, and the famous sanctuary of Saint Duthac, and there he took them, forcing the sanctuary—Queen Elizabeth, the child Princess Marjorie, Christina and Mary Bruce, and Lady Buchan, and possibly—she was taken about this time—a Lady Wiseman, wife of the Sheriff of Elgin, and such small guard and attendance as they had.

Meanwhile, in Kildrummie, things had gone no better. The castle, like many of that time and later, was stone walls and flanking towers, round wooden buildings : [1] and there was a traitor in the garrison. Neil, probably, had counted on holding Prince Edward

[1] As late as 1345 the buildings of so great a castle as Durham were of wood within a stone wall of enceinte.

for a long siege, for the castle was not only strong but well provisioned. But the traitor flung a hot plough-share high on the grain, and the girnel took, and before they could get it under the whole mass of the wooden buildings was in a blaze. They owed their lives to the fact that at Kildrummie there was the unusual feature that the *chemin de ronde*, the fighting-walk at the top of the castle walls, had not only a parapet but a parados, and they could crouch in some shelter between the two, till the furnace burnt itself out within the enclosure.

There was no hope now, however, of holding the place, for their stores were ash. The garrison had to surrender at discretion. Athol escaped somehow, but was recaptured, and Neil Bruce, Alexander Lindsay, and Robert Boyd were taken also. Simon Fraser, some time before the castle fell, was already dead in London, and his head by Wallace's skull over London Bridge. Athol also was sent to London, and hanged there on the 29th October. Being some kin to King Edward, he had a gallows thirty feet higher than common : that he was grandson of the last native Prince of Wales would not endear him to that country's con-queror. One chronicler says that affairs were so arranged *ut majores cruciatus sentiret*, but others say he was spared torture, being semi-royal. Matthew of Westminster notes pleasantly that the news of his death helped Edward to bear his own illness.

There were other invalid comforts for that monarch. Neil Bruce and the others suffered also, at Berwick. Neil was the youngest of the five Bruce brothers, a

courageous lad and of an uncommon beauty : even
Matthew of Westminster speaks of his death with com-
passion. Edward concerned himself eagerly with the
prisoners. We have the official orders respecting
them. The men whose lives were spared were sent
to various castles over England, and their treatment
does not seem to have been gentle. Where ' in irons '
has been omitted in one warrant, it is carefully added.
Young Mar, a boy of ten or thereabouts, received certain concessions. He is to be allowed to walk in the
garden and to be free of irons, though added to this is
the clause, in a different ink, *tant come il soit de si
tendre age*—' so long as he is a child.'

The disposal of the ladies is thought out in detail.
It varied a good deal. Queen Elizabeth, whose father
was not a man with whom Edward dared quarrel, is
treated as a state prisoner, not a criminal. She was
sent to Brustewick, and given a little household, with
five servants—English, of course, and no doubt intended to be warders as well : it is specified that the
women must be *nyent gayes*. She was to live in the
best house of the manor, and have freedom to come
and go in the park, and apparently to hunt, for she
had three greyhounds : and she is to have what fish
and venison she needs.[1]

In the case of the rest, no policy intervened. Lady
Buchan's cage at Berwick is traditional, though modern

[1] In June of 1308 she was moved from Brustewick, whither is not
stated. In February 1312 she was moved to Windsor, and in March
of 1314 there is a warrant for her removal from Barking Abbey to
Rochester.

historians carefully explain that she was really comfortable enough. Unfortunately this academic tradition depends entirely on a mistranslation of a technical
term, and the popular one is a good deal nearer contemporary record. Her cage would seem to have been
under cover, but otherwise it is nearer the bird-cage of
folk-tradition than the ' decent apartment ' of the
modern scholar. It is to be made of strong beams, *en vng
turelle* of the Castle of Berwick, which suggests that it
was probably under a roof, but also suggests cramped
space and some lively draughts in that uncommonly
east-windy spot. The famous ' comfort ' depends on
the injunction that she is to have *eesement de chambre
cortoyse*. This does look like ' comfort of a decent
chamber : ' but if historians had taken the very small
trouble of looking up Littré instead, for a hundred
years, of cribbing Lord Hailes, they would have discovered that *chambre cortoyse*, in mediaeval French, has
a technical sense, of the sanitary accommodation with
which the average mediaeval castle was profusely if
somewhat primitively equipped, even in its dungeons.
It is the only instruction as to equipment : but she was
better off than St Joan at least, for besides this concession to the decencies her gaolers were to include
either one or two women. That she should be exposed
to public view is not definitely stated in the original
order : but that was apparently the purpose of the
cage, for the tradition that she was so exposed is neither
a later nor a Scottish invention, since Matthew of
Westminster, Rishanger, Hemingburgh, and Gray, all

English and the first three contemporary, all state in categorical terms that she was. Matthew remarks with joy that 'she was hung up out of doors that she might be given, alive and after death, for a sight to passers-by and an everlasting scorn '—*sub divo forin-secus suspendatur, ut sit data, in vita et post mortem, speculum viatoribus et opprobrium sempiternum.* Matthew alone would be dubious evidence : he was, as I have said, Northcliffian, and the ' out of doors ' does not tally with the order, while the others have nothing equivalent to ' hung up.' But Rishanger, a sober official, has ' she was placed in a certain wooden hut above the ramparts of the castle of Berwick, so that those who went by could see her '—*in domuncula quadam lignea super murum castri Berwici posita est, ut possent eam conspicere transeuntes.* Hemingburgh, uni-versally recognised as one of the best authorities, has ' she was confined in a wooden structure [1] so that she could be seen and recognised by the passers-by '—*in tristega lignea fixa ut sic a transeuntibus videri posset et cognosci.* Gray, an English knight of distinction, who knew personally many of those concerned in this war, and whose estate was in Northumberland, says that she was confined in an open cage, ' the walls latticed so that all could stare at her as at a curiosity '—*lez parrays eschequerez qe touz la pourroient agarder pur meruail.* So it seems tolerably clear, at least, that her prison was

[1] It is not easy to know precisely what is meant by *tristega.* Ducange and Maigne d'Arnis both give it half a dozen glosses, varying from ' a belfrey ' to ' a latrine.' None of them, however, suggests ' a decent chamber.'

meant as a permanent pillory. The poor girl—she was probably not out of her twenties—spent four years there : then Edward II commuted her sentence to confinement in an English convent : three years after that she was transferred to the custody of her husband's nephew and heir, one Henry de Beaumont, and apparently died. No more is heard of her, and there seems to be no record of her release.

For some reason it would be interesting to know, Mary Bruce, the wife of Neil Campbell, was also given a *kage*, at Roxburgh. That the two ladies dealt with so severely should be placed, unlike most of the prisoners, in Scots castles, seems intended deliberately as terrorisation. There seems to have been less vindictiveness towards Mary, for after three years her exchange is more than once spoken of. But she was at Newcastle, still a prisoner, on the 2nd of November 1312, though some time after that she was released.

Lady Wiseman was also sent to Roxburgh, though there is no detailed order in her case. The most important of the prisoners, Bruce's heir, the child Marjorie, who would be somewhere between ten and twelve, had a cage too, but well south, in the Tower, with orders that she should have no communication with anyone. Later on she was handed over to Henry Percy, who held her father's earldom. He already had charge of her aunt Christina Lady Seton, the mother of young Mar, now widowed once more, and one hopes that the two were allowed to be together. Their imprisonment, though probably less painful than

Lady Buchan's, does not sound luxurious. The allowance made for a knight prisoner was fourpence a day
for food, and twenty shillings yearly for his clothing.
Princess Marjorie and her aunt had threepence a day,
and thirteen and fourpence yearly for their wardrobe.
It was probably enough to nourish them better than
the fare of Lady Buchan, who was *in arcta dieta*—on
short rations : but it does not suggest much scope for
the vanities. They were released with the Queen,
after Bannockburn.

Bruce, landing hopefully on the coast of Carrick,
heard of these captures of his wife, child, and sisters,
and of the gallant lady who had crowned him, of the
execution of his friends and young brother, the capture
of his ally Lamberton. The immediate situation was
no more cheering. Carrick swarmed with English.
His own Turnberry was held by Percy, with a strong
garrison. The whole country was trodden down, and
had lost heart. No one, even in this province of her
fathers, was willing to rise for Countess Marjorie's son.

He would not go back to Arran, however, but took
to the heather and awaited his chance : and before many
days there was bad news again. The Turnberry landing seems to have been intended to synchronise with
one in Galloway, by the younger of the King's surviving brothers, Alexander, the Dean of Glasgow, and
Sir Thomas. They landed on the 9th of February,
with a Highland force, in Lochryan, and were met by

Macdowalls, who were connections of Comyn's. A
sharp action scattered their men, and the two young
Bruces and Wallace's uncle, Sir Reginald Crauford,
were taken to Carlisle, and followed Neil.

Before a year was out from that wild coronation most
of the men who had surrounded the King were dead
or in prison : their women were in prison. Those
supporters who were still free had given up the apparently futile struggle, and some of them, including his
nephew Randolph, had made terms with Edward.
The English had firmer grip of the land than ever, and
all its King held was under the soles of his feet . . .
and their contact with that was made precarious by the
imminent chance, or high probability, of the English
hangman's rope about his neck, as prelude to the further
ceremony already undergone by three of his brothers.
But for all that he did not choose to go back to the
Isles : and there were men who chose to stay beside
him.

CHAPTER IX

DEBOUT LES MORTS !

A YEAR AND THREE-QUARTERS : 1307–1308

> 'And men in desert places, men
> Abandoned, broken, sick with fears,
> Rose singing, swung their swords again,
> And laughed, and died among the spears.'
> John Masefield, *Fragments.*

In the last war, the French army had a tale how a post of some key-importance was under fire so heavy that no reinforcements could get near it, and all its defenders were down save one sergeant only. Then the Germans rushed it : the one man left knew that it must be held. He shouted, turning to meet them, ' Up, the dead ! ' and the shapeless creatures beyond human living dragged up from the mud and the blood and the relics of men, turned on the enemy, and held the trench. When the reinforcements arrived, they had fallen again, as if dying twice, but the post was held and saved. Quite possibly the story is not a fact. But it has been true, and many times, for all that, in that war and others. It was never more true than in Scotland in the spring of 1307.

The last crazy venture had been made and failed, had seen its Culloden at Methven. It was all over. Bruce had followed Baliol, Wallace, Comyn, Soulis : even the heads of the Church were in English prisons,

and soldiers hunting the priests who had preached the
war : they burnt Paisley Abbey sometime in that year.
It looked like ruin : and that was just what it was.
Only Bruce was one of those men who have it in them
to arouse the faith that moves, not mountains, but
men : and when men are moved by that faith, the
mountains melt.

The failure of the landing in Lochryan may very
well have seemed like final disaster. But the King, in
spite of it, would not go back. He was in his own
countryside, that he knew well, and he possibly knew
that from the people of it he could count on neutrality
at any rate. They would not follow him, but they
would not betray. What he did was to disappear into
the landscape—it is a fairly commodious one for the
purpose—while Douglas went off with only a couple
of men to see if there was anything could be done on
his own family lands in Douglasdale. There he celebrated Palm Sunday, the anniversary, by the Church's
calendar, of the coronation, by the first success, after a
year of war.

He risked making himself known to men of the
estate, and the risk succeeded. That *fortis malleator
Anglorum* had a personality that men willingly followed.
Barbour describes him as a tall, powerful man, black
haired and sallow-skinned, not handsome, but with
singular charm and gentleness of manner, and lisping
a little—Barbour remarks defensively, ' so did Hector.'
We may add, from his known deeds, and effect on
others, that serenity, the sense of moving in a clearer

air, that marks the great man of action. In any gallery of varied portraits, it is the thing that these all have in common. Barbour speaks of his effect on the men he led, that

> " the maist coward
> Stouter he made than a libbard,"

and his gift of sheer leadership was no less important than the cool and audacious resource in his choice where to lead.

He found some men then who were willing to take a long chance. Douglas Castle was garrisoned, and impossible to take by direct assault with the resources at present at his disposal. But it had a commander who took things easily, considering, no doubt, that the local natives were sufficiently overawed by the might of England. On Palm Sunday he paraded the garrison and marched them piously to the local church, leaving only a sentry on the castle gate and a cook to take charge of that sacred English institution, the Sunday dinner. Douglas heard of this, and sent rapid word, rallying his men about the parish kirk. One nearly spoiled the affair by raising the Douglas cry a little too soon, and giving the alarm before the English came out from their devotions. There was a wild fight then, in the church itself, and the thirty Englishmen were killed or taken. The Scots went to the castle, quietly roped in the sentry and the cook, and finding the Sunday dinner all ready laid, sat down and saw that a good meal was not wasted.

To hold the castle was quite impossible. They

helped themselves to what clothes and arms were of
use, and proceeded to wreck the place, broaching all
food and drink in a heap in the cellar, flung the bodies
on to that in a ' foul melle,' long known in tradition as
the Douglas Larder, spoilt the well by throwing in salt
and the dead horses, burnt what would fire, and left
the resultant mess to edify the local English troops,
having made one of the strongest holds in the country
entirely useless to their enemies, and laid the foundations for the nightmarish terror with which Douglas's
name affected these later on.   The fantastic circumstances of the destruction are neither pure savagery
nor a very young man's taste for the melodramatic,
but the first instance of the quality that Douglas
possessed *in excelsis*, the power of working on the
enemy's imagination with very upsetting results to his
morale—a gift of the first importance in such conditions, as Guesclin proved in similar ones later.   When
Clifford came, he found a ruined castle, a blandly innocent expanse of country . . . and a certain uneasiness
among his men as to where trouble would descend
from next.

The moral effect of the business worked on both
sides.   The tale went about the country.   More men
joined Bruce.   His little force, together or in detach-
ments, lurked in the drying moors in the spring
weather, risking their lives at every hour of the day.
The situation, in fact, was sufficiently warm.   Pembroke with 4000 men was to the south, and the Galloway men were up under Macdowall, with their recent

victory to encourage them. Percy was on the coast, at
Turnberry. Sir John Botetort was inland with a strong
force. Clifford was guarding the crossings of the Cree,
between the Sheriffdom and the Stewartry. John of
Lorne's Highlanders were moving south through Kyle,
and Moubray with a strong force of English archers
was beating the country, trying to drive Bruce into
one or other of these. In effect, the King and his
force were entirely surrounded.

They had some very exciting weeks of it. There
are many tales of the King's own adventures and hair-
breadth escapes, that since they are unlikely to happen
in contemporary Princes Street, would mean a charge
of sensationalism if I told them : and there are quite
enough improbable things in this war that cannot be
left out of any story intended to give a just impression
of it. Most of these tales, very probably, are true,
though some may have been transferred from other
men. They show the King's inexhaustible resource,
his buoyant cheerfulness in adversity, that make
someone—probably Burton, I imagine, since he is one
of the few Scots historians who have heard of other
countries than Scotland or England—compare him to
Henri IV. There is a likeness. Both, under their
recklessness, had a level patience, a *mens aequa in
arduis*, and a cool and lucid appreciation of odds, and
both were leaders as well as strategists. The incident
of De Bohun, the white plume at Ivry . . . both reckless gestures are quite characteristic of the level-headed
politicians who made them, though the *Vert Galant*

N

would have kept his temper better if he had met with Comyn at Dumfries.

About a couple of months after the landing, some-where between late March and early April, the King's enemies came to grips with him at last. He was in Glentrool, under the Merrick and the great Range of Kells, when Pembroke got word of him, and sent a force of 1500 up Creeside. Bruce charged them from the hill, with the tactic of Claverhouse at Killiecrankie, and they broke and scattered, leaving many dead, while he slipped off north, between Botetort and Percy.

Pembroke raised a stronger force, and beat the country. On the 10th of May they came on Bruce again, in the valley of the Avon, inland from Ayr. Bruce turned and defeated them in a pitched engage-ment. He took up his position where the highroad to Ayr runs along the flank of a small height, Loudoun Hill. The road runs on a strip of hard ground, flanked by mosses, and Bruce narrowed this strip by digging three sets of trenches, so that horsemen could not get round to his flank and rear, and Pembroke was forced to attack on a narrow front, that cramped his cavalry. Pembroke was beaten off, in such disorder that he had to take refuge in Ayr, and within a few days the King had met Botetort, and sent him after the unlucky Pem-broke. Indeed, he was strong enough to invest them in Ayr, which probably annoyed them very much. A fresh concentration against him, however, compelled him to raise the siege in a very short time. But as a

gesture no doubt it had some effect, if it was only on
poor Pembroke's temper.

On the 7th of June, at Burgh-on-Sands over Solway,
within sight of Scotland, old King Edward died. The
country that should have fallen into his hand like a
ripe apple was still unconquered, after eleven years'
war. Its upstart King had held out for fourteen months
now, and the last news Edward heard from the Carrick
front was that Bruce, in six weeks, had thrice defeated
his generals, including the Commander-in-Chief for
Scotland, and was still at large. He died like a Plantagenet, giving orders to bear his bones at the head of
the army. The orders were not obeyed, for the new
young king took his father's body south, and buried it
politely at Westminster, where *Pactum serva* was
carved upon its tomb. It probably did not occur to
anyone to accent that most admirable injunction by
adding beneath it the date ' 2–1–93 ' and the figures
of eleven years' killed and missing.

It was August before the young king was in Scotland
again, to find things much as they had been when he
had left it. Pembroke and his men were probably
somewhat lighter from much active exercise in the hot
weather : the unfortunate general undoubtedly worked
hard. But Bruce and his little force were still at large.
Edward brought a sizable army, but did nothing. He
came of two extremely hard-fighting stocks, but in
spite of a splendid body and great physical strength he
had a sort of fretful impulsiveness instead of his
father's steady dynamic force. His accession, in fact,

a good deal lessened the odds. He had huge advantages of man-power, munitions, and money : but Bruce could use what he had to the full, and put some more in it of his own, while young Edward could not even choose good lieutenants. Like most Plantagenets, he had hated his father, and almost the first thing he did on his accession was to discharge the latter's high officials, and replace them from his own set. Pembroke, with more excuse perhaps than most, was one of those thus superseded, his command being given to John of Brittany, whom *he* had superseded the year before.

Edward stayed at Cumnock in Nithsdale till the 25th of August, then simply turned, army and all, and went back to England, to the great encouragement of the national forces. It is possible that, as no action was offered, he thought that a demonstration in force was enough to overawe any project of resistance. Bruce sped the parting guest by taking the offensive, and raiding the country of Sir Dugald Macdowall, who had sent his brothers to their deaths in spring. The raid had more purpose than mere vengeance, however : it showed his enemies that his strength, for all their six months of hard work, was growing, and it would give some needed provision to his men. It must be remembered that throughout these early wars they had to follow him without any pay. His estates were all in the hands of his enemies. Some of his followers might be better off, but he could not be sure of a penny of his own, even if his Scots tenants tried to pay double rents, as the Highlanders did for the Jacobite chiefs in exile. Rations had either to be cajoled or forced from the country itself, to keep body and soul together—from a country that on top of eleven years' war and foreign occupation had been crossed and recrossed by troops for the last six months.

So far, events had been set in the South-west. By the autumn, however, things had begun to happen elsewhere. They decided the King to change his base of operations. He had held out in the South-west for six months, and won four small victories : his force was increasing. But proceedings were none the less at a stalemate. He was not strong enough to clear the country : it was still swarming with English troops : and a cordon of any strength up Nithsdale and down the valley of the Doon would cut him off, if he let himself get inside it, from the mass of Scotland. Moreover, it must be remembered—he could scarcely forget it—that he had *two* simultaneous wars on his hands. He had to face not only Edward, but most of the old Comyn-Baliol faction, his comrades-in-arms of the War of the Empty Jacket. He would certainly have to deal with them sooner or later, and Edward's withdrawal, so early in the season, gave him a breathing-space in which to do so. What probably clinched his decision was news from the North. The middle North—Moray[1]—had taken up arms, apparently thanks

---

[1] Moray included not only the modern counties of Nairn and Moray, but all northern Inverness-shire as far across as the head of Loch Duich.

to the efforts of its Bishop, who had raged through
it like a human Fiery Cross. The King determined
to leave Douglas in command, to keep the English
garrisons amused, while he went north to deal with
the civil war. That decision is the turning point of
his fortunes. For the next two years the strategic
centre of the war, and its first effective successes, are
north of Forth.

The change marks the beginning of larger-scale
operations, but events in the middle autumn are
rather obscure. Inverness Castle fell about this time,
perhaps taken by Andrew de Moray's old comrade
Pilche, and the King himself was in Moray in October.
This brought him in contact with two of his most
powerful enemies, the Earls of Ross and Buchan.
Moray, however, apparently gave him more active
help than Carrick. He was able to make a demonstration in force against Ross, sufficiently imposing to in-
duce him to consent to a truce for the winter : Ross
says himself that he had 3000 men. The Earl, probably,
was not unwilling to treat : it is possible that the disposal of the ladies whom he had captured may have
upset him somewhat, and his sympathies, though anti-
Bruce, were Scottish. He made a truce until the 1st
of June—i.e., of 1308.

Here was a very important success at once, for the
young Earl of Sutherland (who was later on to marry
King Robert's daughter) was Ross's ward, and the
truce would neutralise for the winter and spring the
whole further North, beyond Moray, and clear the

King's rear for a drive south and east, at Buchan or John of Lorne, his two strongest opponents.

Buchan could not be dealt with as peaceably as Ross. Not only was he a Comyn, with the affair of Annandale in the background : his Countess's enterprise at the coronation was not likely to endear the King to her husband. Mediaeval humour is pretty heavy-handed, and husbands have been a butt since marriage began. And on the other side, whatever the King's relations with Lady Buchan, it was hardly needful he should be her lover to feel anger at what she had been made to suffer for him.

The King marched against Buchan. And his luck, which had been rising all through the summer, seemed to desert him. He became gravely ill. The anxiety of his captains may be imagined, for Bruce, by now, was the core of the resistance. It must be understood what his life meant to it—that life jeopardised almost every hour of these years. He was not only the leader, the incomparable general : he was the King. His next heir was a girl of twelve in an English prison. With the Queen too in prison he could have no son. The next male to him was his one surviving brother, a cheerful, likeable, hard-fighting soldier, but no more than that. And Edward Bruce was unmarried : his life was as uncertain as the King's. And after him in the straight line of succession was another Maid of Norway, Queen Margaret's little half-sister Ingebjorg, daughter of Isobel Bruce and Eirik II, and then only Mary Bruce's boy Colin Campbell and the little Earl of Mar in his English prison before one came to the English baron Lord Hastings, or as possible alternative, the son of Toom Tabard.

The King's illness came on him dangerously near Comyn country, and they took him in a litter to Slioch above Strathbogie, not far from Huntly. Buchan heard of them there, and in mid-November came down on them through the snow. The King's men were strongly posted about a wood, and though Buchan's force was a good deal the larger they held these latter off through three days' skirmishing of archery. Buchan's force, however, was visibly increasing, so they put the King into his litter, surrounding him closely, and marched out in full view of Buchan's men, who liked the look of them so little, according to Barbour, that they let them go without attack . . . which suggests, one would think, that Buchan's rank and file were not enthusiastic in their cause, for Buchan himself was an angry man and no coward. But—having regard to the resistance the province Buchan was to put up later—it seems more probable, I think, on the whole, that there was some kind of strategic diversion of which Barbour's informant may have been unaware.

Strathbogie was friendly country, but probably by reason of the King's illness, they went down Donside again, to the more sheltered town of Inverurie. Buchan raised fresh troops, and with reinforcements from the South under Brechin and Moubray, marched to Oldmeldrum, which is about three miles off, arriving there the day before Christmas Eve. Apparently he intended to attack, for at dawn next morning Brechin was sent to make a reconnaissance in force, and got himself embroiled with the King's outposts. King Robert was not able to sit a horse, but claiming that the challenge had done him more good than medicine, he ordered two men to hoist him into the saddle and hold him there, assembled his force, and before Buchan could get his men in order for attack, took the offensive. Buchan had not expected such rapid action. His force gave way, and there was a running action as far as Fyvie—twelve leagues, Barbour says, but twelve miles is nearer it. It was a royal castle, held for England, which would offer a refuge to the defeated force.

The sick King must have collapsed after the battle, for he had to give over the pursuit to his brother, who followed Buchan into his own country, and is said by local tradition to have defeated him again, at a place called Aikie-Brae, not far from Old Deer. Such a victory would leave the province of Buchan open, and it is certain that Edward Bruce ravaged it with such thoroughness that the Herschip (harrying) of Buchan left a long tradition. It is too generally assumed that the business was a mere piece of mediaeval brutality : but harsh though it certainly was, it was not that. Bruce, by the testimony of his enemies, was at all times notably humane to prisoners and non-combatants. The Herschip was not a mere raid, from one point of view, or a punitive expedition, from the other : it was a fierce little local war, that lasted at least three months, from mid-winter to Easter, at a time when the time-element was growing more and more urgently important.

The situation in early 1308, in fact, was far from agreeable. 1307 had not seen the unbroken chain of disasters that had marked 1306. There had been some encouraging small successes, and at its end the—still only provisional—defeat of Buchan, the temporary and not too certain immobilising of Ross. But the definite gains were comparatively small. The whole further North was neutral, for the moment : but even if the truce should not be broken, the King might have it against him by early summer. Moray was Bruce's : it had always been strongly nationalist. But the South Highlands were divided, with the two most powerful chiefs, the Lord of the Isles and Macdougall of Lorne, against him. In the North-east at the beginning of the year, all the strongholds were garrisoned by English or pro-English troops. Below Forth, the situation was even worse. Lothian had not moved, and was well pegged down by English garrisons. Galloway was hostile. In the Middle West, nearly a year had produced no more effect than to give Douglas, left there, some chance of preventing troops from being sent north to take the King in flank.

The reduction of Buchan, and as quickly as might be, before spring opened the Highlands for campaigning, was urgently necessary from the military point of view, and still more from the political. And it was not an easy thing to do quickly. Sir Edward had to take either four or five strong castles, without artillery,

and with every chance of an attack on his rear if the
Badenoch Comyns—Red John's own vassals—should
come to the support of their Buchan kin.[1]   Urgent as
the business was, it took, as we have seen, three
months at least.

The early spring saw sporadic risings elsewhere.
The father of Gray of the *Scalacronica* was besieged
by Bickerton in Cupar-Fife.   Matters in England
tended to make the pressure of time rather easier.   At
the beginning of the year King Edward had fulfilled
his ten-years betrothal to Madame Isabelle de
France, and was engaged with his marriage and the
coronation of his twelve-year-old bride.   The latter
event took place at the end of February, but action
against Scotland was hindered by the fact that immediately afterwards his barons, already sulky, were at
loggerheads with him over his favourite the young
Gascon Gaveston, a gracefully graceless and quite tact-
less young man whom he had created Earl of Cornwall
and actually left at the head of affairs while he went to
France in January for his wedding.   Gaveston proved
as good a friend to Scotland as the worthy John Baliol
had been to England.   For the next few years, the
political situation of the two countries is reversed.

---

[1] Mr Barron makes a very suggestive comment on the different
behaviour of the districts of Buchan and Badenoch.   The Badenoch
men have always been stubborn fighters : but Red John and his
house to them were mere incomers, whereas John of Buchan represented through his grandmother Marjorie, Countess of Buchan in
her own right, the ancient earls of the province.   To anyone who
knows the Highlands—and the mediaeval North-east was Gaelic-
speaking—this is a perfectly good *vera causa*.

Instead of a united England hammering a Scotland whose leaders are as likely to fly at each other as at the enemy, there is an England whose leaders are at odds with each other, and a Scotland steadily forging into one of the few periods of real union that her distracted history has witnessed.

King Robert presumably had some sort of intelligence service that would keep him informed of the situation in England. He could not know, of course, how long Edward's troubles were to continue, though, as he knew personally most of the men concerned, he might make a good guess that England, for this summer, *might* not be capable of large-scale action. He sent Sir Edward south to help Douglas to occupy the English commanders, and went on consolidating his position in the North-east, and in early June was able to invest the castle of Aberdeen. The citizens of the ' Braif Toun ' declared for him, and tradition says its fine motto of *Bon Accord* was their rallying-cry at the storming of the castle . . . though unfortunately there is no evidence that it was used until a century later. The castle was taken, after a siege of some weeks, and destroyed, in accordance with the King's regular policy, of leaving his enemies nowhere to dig themselves in.

The successes continued. We do not know when the other castles of the North-east were taken, or how, but taken they certainly were, the royal ones of Fyvie, Kintore, and Aboyne among them. By the end of this summer of 1308 the only castle of the North-east that was still in the hands of the King's enemies was Banff, which could be provisioned from the sea. From Loch Ness to the Tay practically the whole of the great eastern 'hump' of Scotland was in his hands: and Douglas was still holding out in the South-west.

The moral success of the summer, as one may call it, shows clearly in a despatch of King Edward's, in which, by the way, the defeated Buchan is transferred to another sphere of operations, by being appointed to a command in the South-west. It speaks of truce. Edward himself will not make one in his own name, but his representatives are given authority to make truces for themselves, for as long a time as they can until the next Easter, when the regular heavy campaigning season would begin.

We do not know whether King Edward's generals did propose any sort of armistice to King Robert. It seems probable that there was some short-term suspension of hostilities, for Douglas, who had been in charge of operations in the South, was able in August to share in the King's campaign against John of Lorne, but did not return with him to the North-east in October. The King's successes northward of Forth had apparently convinced him that his best policy was to take advantage of Edward's domestic troubles and to get the whole of the north country into his hands, as a base from which to clear up the Lowlands and meet the inevitable English attack in force that he would have to expect in the coming year.

Above Forth, the East was his now, the Far North uncertain, but still maintaining its neutrality, the West divided. A success there would probably bring the Far North in on his side. He struck, therefore, at the disaffected western elements, whose chief strength lay in the Lorne and Argyll Macdougalls and the Lord of the Isles, the brother of his friend Angus Macdonald. These were by far the strongest western chiefs then, for the Campbell, Maclean, Macleod, and Mackenzie powers were small yet, though the first and fourth had been with him from the beginning, and the second came in some time before Bannockburn.

At the beginning of August he marched on Lorne, with a force that seems to have been mainly Highland. Alexander of Argyll, the Macdougall chief and the uncle of Red John Comyn, was an old man, and John of Lorne, his son, apparently acted as Captain of the Clan. The King seems to have been marching by Glenorchy. John came to meet him at the boundary of Lorne, the narrow strip between Loch Awe and Loch Etive, proposing to contest his advance below Cruachan, in the Pass of Brander. Where Cruachan goes steep to the black water of Loch Awe he ambushed his men in the heather of the pass, while he with his galleys lay in the loch below. The King either heard of the ambush from his scouts, or, with his eye for country, guessed at it. He arranged a sort of mobile counter-ambush, sending his archers, under Douglas, who had joined him, to climb the face of Cruachan and take the Macdougalls from above in flank and rear,

while he led a frontal attack on the pass itself. Douglas
put in some very competent stalking, and the two divisions struck simultaneously. John with his ships had
a pleasant view from below of the outgeneralling of his
arrangements.

The forcing of the pass left Lorne open, and before
long the King's men were in front of Macdougall's
chef-lieu, Dunstaffnage at the mouth of Loch Etive,
and had taken it. Alexander and his son had to make
peace : it did not last long, as by 1310 he and his son
appear at an English council, but at the time it relieved
the situation in the West very considerably.[1]

Dunstaffnage was garrisoned. The details of what
happened next are not very clear, but we may take it
that the next action was against Alexander Macdonald,
Lord of the Isles. Sir Edward may have been conducting a separate expedition against him, simultaneously with the operations in Lorne, for it is from him
that Alexander is said to have escaped to Castle Sweyn
on the outer shore of Knapdale, where he was captured, and sent to his brother's castle of Dundonald in
Kintyre, where he died. He certainly disappears about
this time, and his lands were conferred on his brother,
Angus Og, from whom the later Lords of the Isles
descended, till the lordship was merged at last with
the royal title, and is now held by the heir to the Scottish throne : the title of viscount of the Western Isles
is also borne by an eminent English soap-merchant.

---

[1] The old man died in Ireland in 1310, and John of Lorne, to his
death in 1317, was Edward's Admiral of the Western Isles.

The other chiefs of the West had either supported the King already or came in now, and King Robert was able to send Douglas and Sir Edward south again, while he went north himself to deal with Ross. Ross had only been half-heartedly against him, and the success of the Buchan and Lorne campaigns decided him. On the last day of October 1308, he and his vassals surrendered in very stately form at Auldearn, and did homage to King Robert, who made him Sheriff of Sutherland and his loyal follower to the end of his days : the alliance was cemented by the marriage of his heir to the King's third sister, Maude or Matilda Bruce.

In addition to the very important successes in the North, this summer of 1308 had seen some small advantage gained in the South. There was nothing that had materially altered the actual situation, but Edward Bruce had defeated the Galloway men in June, and Douglas had been able to strike as far east as the Water of Lyne, that flows into Tweed a few miles west of Peebles, and had taken a prisoner who was to be important, Bruce's young kinsman Randolph, whom he brought to the King when he joined him to march on Lorne. Young Randolph was by no means well received, as indeed he could hardly have expected to be : he had been one of those captured at Methven, but owing to his youth Edward had offered him terms : he had accepted, and for nearly two years had been in English service. Neither he nor the King was likely to be in a sweet temper when they met, and there were high words. The young man, according to Barbour, had the nerve to taunt Bruce with cowardice for his elusive tactics. He was promptly sent to prison to cool his blood, and apparently the King's personality had its common effect, for the young renegade rejoined him whole-heartedly, and became, next to Douglas, his most famous general, doing such service that at the King's death he was left Regent for the child King David.[1]

By the end of the year 1308, there had been an impressive change in the situation. At its beginning the King had been very barely master of Moray, at death-grips with Buchan, and terribly open to attack from three sides. By its end he held all Scotland above the Tay, except a few castles in the north-east Lowlands, whose commanders were wailing to England for reinforcements. It is worth remarking that all through this year, direct action against the English is subsidiary. Douglas, with later the help of Edward Bruce, held them in the South, and won a few small successes, and their considerable number of garrisons in the North-east had mostly been cleared up. But the major action is all a consequence of the death of Comyn. That Bruce should have to spend nearly a year, in the most critical juncture of his fortunes, at deathgrips with men who for a good eight years had been leaders of the previous struggle with England, shows not only how little chance there is of his having intended murder

---

[1] His daughter carried on the family tradition. All Scots have heard of Black Agnes at Dunbar.

to Red John Comyn, but also the almost ruinous effect of the Baliol-Bruce factional cleavage of over a decade. It had hampered resistance all through the first war, and delivered Scotland helpless to Edward I. Now, in the first two years of King Robert's reign, it all but delivered the country to Edward II. If he had pushed home his invasion of 1307, and got John of Lorne to take Bruce in the rear, he would almost certainly have crushed resistance, that had been slow in finding itself a footing. And if he had managed to capture or kill the two Bruces, the heirship to Scotland lay between a girl-child in one of his own prisons, a boy of no more than his early teens in France, and another girl-child of not more than twelve in Norway. It is possible, indeed, that Red John's death was, in the long run, really the saving of Scotland, since it changed the two factions from jarring mistrustful allies to open enemies who could deal with each other. But that Bruce intended this is hardly likely, for the risk was too enormous, even for him. If Edward I had lived, it would have been ruin.

As it was, the thing had turned out to his advantage. He had dealt, expensively but effectively, with the civil war, and except for Galloway, it was definitely settled. He had now two-thirds of Scotland actively for him, with the Tay for a frontier, and all the North for retreat. The centre of action henceforth shifts to the South. The North had made him King in more than name : but the whole land below Forth was still in the power of England.

CHAPTER X

SCOTLAND YET

FIVE YEARS : 1308–1313

'De l'audace, encore de l'audace, toujours de l'audace, et
[l'Écosse] est sauvée.'
Danton in 1792.

THE events of the end of 1308 are rather vague. As
often happens in this year and the next three, we have
to infer a good many of them from their known effects,
as these are reported in English, or sometimes French,
official papers. It would seem that King Robert, being
now *de facto* King of much of Scotland, thought the
time had come for a renewal of the French alliance.
The negotiations have not survived, but they would
hardly have been feasible before at least the middle of
1308 : Bruce before that was no sort of ally for any
man who was not desperate, and Philip was on fairly
good terms with Edward, who became his son-in-law
early in that year. By the latter part of 1308, however,
Philip had evidently recognised his government, though
possibly with some kind of reservation, and was inter-
vening, as he had more than once done in the previous
war, in order to smoothe down Anglo-Scottish relations, and negotiate an armistice in which some arrangement might be arrived at. At the end of November he
sent his eldest son in person to deal with Edward.
The latter had already, in the summer, let Lamberton

north on a sort of parole, apparently for some kind of *pourparler* with King Robert. Now he appointed the Earl of Angus and three others to go north as plenipotentiaries for the express purpose of arranging a truce.

King Robert, meanwhile, had moved slowly southward. Forfar and Brechin fell into his hands that winter, and by the beginning of 1309 he was in Fife, where he found many adherents. The obvious next stage in the campaign was to push his effective frontier to the Forth, and he set about this with so much success that by the middle of March he was able to hold parliament in St Andrews. So far as we know, it was the first of his reign, and its date, the 16th March of 1309, is almost exactly three years from his crowning, two years less two days from the first small success of his cause, the Douglas Larder, and eighteen years since the last free assembly of the Scots Estates had sent the unlucky invitation to Edward.

Its composition shows how far advanced was the process of national consolidation . . . as well as how far that process had yet to go. The Earl of Ross, the young Earl of Sutherland, and the Earl of Lennox were there in person. Carrick was represented by the King himself. Young Caithness was a ward of the Earl of Ross. Menteith was a child, but his uncle, who was his guardian, was with the King, and the other earldoms sent representatives of their *communitas*.[1] Edward

---

[1] The Earls of Angus, Strathearn, Athol, and Dunbar were in the English interest. Buchan had died in the previous year, and his young heir was in England.

Bruce, who by now was—nominally—Lord of Galloway, was present, Randolph, now nominally Lord of
Nithsdale, James Stewart, Douglas, Gilbert Hay the
Constable, and—a Lothian name at last—Robert Keith
the Marischal, who had newly come in. There are
also Lindsay, Wiseman, Barclay, Boyd, Neil Campbell
and his brother, old Macdougall of Argyll, more or less
as a hostage, and Alexander Fraser, Sir Simon's
brother, who was later to be King Robert's Great
Chamberlain and the second husband of Mary Bruce.
Nearly all these, as one would expect from the previous
three years' history, if not from most of its historians,
are northern.

We do not know with what domestic affairs this
parliament dealt, if any : but it is probable that its
major business was a matter that certainly was under
discussion, the armistice proposals of Philip and
Edward. Philip was apparently represented, as his
envoy Olivier des Roches was given a safe-conduct
through England a fortnight before. The terms of the
safe-conduct contain a phrase that shows what was to
wreck the negotiations : it describes the French Envoy
as going into Scotland ' to the Bishop of St Andrews
and *Robert de Brus.*'

Now, Robert was in a greatly improved position.
He could have tried for some sort of arrangement
based on the *status quo*, but with two-thirds of Scotland
now united behind him he was in better case, at any
rate, to repeat his challenge to England, and he did so.
He declined to make peace except at the price of his

full recognition by England as independent King of
Scots. Edward would treat, to make time while he
was encumbered at home : but he was not prepared
to go as far as that. After all, England, even disunited,
had many times the man-power of all Scotland, to say
nothing of her wealth : and the South Scots provinces
were still in his grip. The negotiations dragged on,
with each side, in all probability, trying to make time,
and by July they had been broken off, and Edward
was mobilising.

English relations were not the only foreign affairs
this parliament dealt with. There was France as
well. Philip had clearly made some kind of recognition
of Robert's ' belligerent status,' and had shown himself
well-intentioned generally to the new Government.
Part of the business, therefore—the only part whose
actual official record survives—was to secure his definite
recognition of Robert's sovereignty, by means of a
stately *communiqué* setting forth the acceptance by the
Three Estates of Scotland of *Dominus Robertus Dei
gratia Dominus noster rex.* The letter is probably
drawn up by a churchman, and its pious terms have a
note of deep thankfulness in them that sounds a good
deal more than merely formal.

Philip, apparently, tried to deal diplomatically with
the situation. With the Pope, and other troubles, on
his hands, he could not afford a definite breach with
England, but he would not repudiate the Scots Alliance
by refusal of recognition. He soothed both sides, and
as men are very liable to do in that case, got into trouble,

for there is a letter of Edward's the next August up-
braiding his father-in-law for double dealing : in
French *communiqués* to England King Robert is still
styled the Earl of Carrick, but the same messenger has
been found to be carrying despatches for Scotland, and
these are addressed to Robert King of Scots ! What
Philip said to this violation of the embassy post-bag is
not on record.

The parliament was followed by another assembly
that it will be logical, if not quite chronological, to
mention here. To be Philip's friend at the moment,
was to be the Pope's enemy : and the news of this
fresh Franco-Scottish *rapprochement* stirred up Clement to excommunicate the King again, for ' damnable
perseverance in iniquity.' This fired that very ' Galli-
can ' body, the Scots Church, to a fresh demonstration
of the growing national unity. On the 24th of February
1310, they held a *concilium generale* of the Bishops,
Abbots, Priors, and other clergy, in the Kirk of the
Friars Minor (Greyfriars) at Dundee,[1] and issued a
manifesto ' to all the Faithful,' that is practically a
vote of confidence in King Robert. It sums up the
general political situation, and recognises him as King,

---

[1] It was probably not convened *ad hoc*, but simply the Annual
Provincial Council established in 1225 by Honorius III, who em-
powered the Scottish Bishops to hold it under a *Conservator
statutorum* elected annually : this led to the regular holding of such
councils without the usual intervention of a Legate, and these
claimed and regularly exercised the right to manage all Scottish
ecclesiastical affairs. It is not without interest that the Episcopal
Church, driven underground by the persecutions of the eighteenth
century, should have returned to something not unlike this, having
no archbishop, but electing one of the bishops to serve as Primus.

ut Regni deformata reformet, corrigendaque corrigat, et dirigat indirecta. Lamberton probably had a hand in it, and if the vigorous trumpet-note of its Latin reached old Bishop Wishart in his English prison, it must have warmed the cockles of his heart.

These political events have carried us somewhat past the military. We left these in the early spring of 1309, when Bruce, having pushed his effective frontier to the Forth, was able to hold parliament at St Andrews. The military events of that year have not much in them that is of major importance, as the negotiations for a truce, dragging into the early summer, had caused, for the time being, rather a lull in hostilities. What action there is is again in the South-west, and is mostly rather vague.

It will be remembered that at the end of the Lorne campaign of the previous year, Edward Bruce and Douglas had gone south again. They took Rutherglen Castle on their way, and then with a force mostly of Highlanders, largely, it would seem, Macdonalds from the Isles, they marched against the last important section of the Comyn party, the Galloway Macdowalls, who had defeated the Lochryan landing early in 1307, under Thomas and Alexander Bruce. This attack was successful, for by April Lady Macdowall and her children were being given shelter in an English manor, though Macdowall remained behind to command Dumfries.

Some dozen of the smaller castles were captured, and they must have provided some lively little actions :

the greater ones—Dumfries, Dalswinton, and Caer-laverock in Nithsdale, Lochmaben in Annandale, Buittle between the Dee and the Water of Urr, and Tibbers, held out for another three years yet. We know of one famous *fait d'armes* of that time, the Defeat of the Fifteen Hundred by the Fifty. That cheerful hothead, Edward Bruce, had a small handful of cavalry, fifty or so, and with these he was carrying out a reconnaissance, apparently trying to discover the whereabouts of Aymar St John, who had been to England for reinforcements, and was moving with a force of some 1500. Edward's men came on the trail, in a thick fog, and followed it, comfortably concealed. Then—Barbour says he had the tale from Sir Alan Cathcart, who was there with Sir Edward—the fog rolled up suddenly, as it does in hills, and they found St John's detachment within bowshot. His archers unslung their bows, and began to shoot. Sir Edward, seeing them strung out in column of march, swung round his command, charged straight through St John's column from the flank, wheeled, galloped back, and repeated the manoeuvre, in a fresh place. He was wheeling to do it once more, but the English broke, and many were killed or taken in the rout, though St John, who was well mounted, got away.

The peace negotiations collapsed in the summer, and by late July King Edward was mobilising. He had got his barons and parliament somewhat soothed, and Gaveston, banished to Ireland the summer before, was back at court. Edward had taken advantage of the

partial suspension of hostilities to provision and
strengthen the castles he held in the South, which included Edinburgh, Berwick, Stirling, Linlithgow, Roxburgh, and beyond the Forth, Dundee and the strong
town of Perth. That he could do so, and the importance of these names, shows how little had yet been
effected below the Forth, in spite of three years campaigning in the South-west. The South-east, in fact,
had simply not been touched yet.

He was still, however, trying to gain time, and three
weeks after his mobilisation orders were issued, he
appointed a fresh envoy to the Scots, King Robert's
father-in-law, the Earl of Ulster. Neil Campbell and
John de Menteith came south under a safe-conduct
and met him : but nothing was done. Presumably the
question of recognition was raised again, and refused.
It was to postpone a peace for nineteen years yet, and
England, after all, still held considerably the stronger
cards.

Edward's mobilisation was slow. It was late autumn
before he could move in force. He marched two armies
to Berwick and Carlisle, and the Scots must have turned
up their sleeves for the final tussle. It did not come.
The English generals—Segrave and Hereford, Clifford
and Cromwell—evidently baulked again at the prospect
of *loca palustria et immeabilia* as a terrain for manoeuvre,
and promptly made truce till the 14th of January of
the next year, 1310. By the time it expired, Edward
was again in trouble with his barons, and was glad
enough to prolong it until March. In March he had

more to handle, the famous ' Armed Parliament.' He had to surrender, allowing the appointment of Lords Ordainers, who were practically a temporary Regency, and the truce had again to be prolonged until June.

Of Scottish events of the early part of this year we know little. The Dundee *Concilium* has already been mentioned. It shows the strengthening feeling for the King. It is to be presumed that he used the respite *deformata reformare et dirigere indirecta*, and in making preparations to meet a large-scale invasion in March, and then, as the truce was lengthened, in summer. And the situation would not be improved by the incidence of a very serious famine.

By the middle of June the looked-for invasion began to organise, in greater force than anything since the abortive one of 1307. At the beginning of August, forty-two English ports were ordered to send ships. This was growing late, but a fairly dry September and October would leave plenty of time for a deciding campaign, and King Robert's intelligence service must have had some anxious weeks. Edward, in fact, got to Berwick a little later, but wasted time by squabbling again with his barons, and it was not till the middle of September that he got himself and his army across the Tweed. The usual account of the invasion is that ' nothing happened.' In fact, if we study a large-scale contoured map in the light of the known movements of both sides, it becomes clear that a good deal happened, and of first-rate importance. This invasion, indeed, is the second great turning-point in the war,

the King's 1307 decision to go north having been the
first.

Edward reached Roxburgh on the 20th September,
and began to move cautiously west towards the Clyde
and Tweed. He reached Biggar on the 1st of October,
and lay there for a fortnight. One of his generals was
a strategist, for it is a good central position for a thrust
east or west, or one downward to the low country
between Lothian and Renfrew. He was feeling for
Bruce, as the obvious strategy was to get to grips and
smash him by sheer weight. King Robert, being
equally well aware of the fact,[1] kept very carefully out
of his way, holding, apparently, the line of the Forth,
and letting Edward's army march and grouse as it
chose, for the famine was standing his friend now, and
every move of the English towards him meant a

---

[1] A doggerel of later in the century, *King Robert's Testament*,
professes to formulate the principles of his tactics, and in fact it
accords very closely with his general practice. Modernised, so far
as rhyme permits, it goes

> On foot should be all Scottish weir,
> By hill and moss themselves to rear,
> Let woods for walls be bow and spear
> That enemies do them no deir. (harm)
> In safe places go keep all store,
> And burn the plainland them before,
> Then shall they pass away in haste
> When they shall find the land lie waste.
> With wiles and wakings of the night,
> And muckle noises made on height,
> Them shall ye turn with great affray,
> As they were chased with sword away.
> This is the counsel and intent
> Of Good King Robert's Testament.

There is a Latin version also.

lengthening drag on their lines of communication, though since they had Lothian solid on their flank, there was not much chance of being able to cut these. Someone, however—probably Douglas, who was a deacon at that kind of job—saw to it that their outposts were well harried.

Edward did get news of the Scots army at last, at Stirling, presumably keeping an eye on the bridge. He swung into Clydesdale, and marched down it to Renfrew, perhaps with some intention of turning Bruce's position by getting round on his flank by Killearn and Kippen. If he did, he changed his mind and came round on the wrong side of the Campsie Fells to Linlithgow. He spent five days there, waiting for something to happen. Nothing obliged him by doing so. It was late October, a famine, and winter coming. He decided to march back to Berwick, and wait till spring.

He marched, and King Robert promptly rolled down on his rear-guard. Edward turned at bay, and the Scots disappeared forthwith, and there was nothing left but to go to Berwick, with nothing but healthy exercise for his pains, and such amusement as could be extracted from reading the returns of assorted missing. His fleet, which was supposed to be acting in support, had suffered badly in brushes with Scots privateers, who had nipped into shelter on the Flemish coast : and he sent a very pained note to his father's old ally, the Count of Flanders.

Edward was merely waiting for better weather, and

still, apparently, kept his army on a war footing. By mid-December, however, he had word that King Robert was arranging an attack on Man, which he probably contrived himself to let Edward hear of. That drew off the English fleet from the East Coast, and since the fleet was essential for the commissariat, and even before this weakening was being well harried, he decided to negotiate again. At Christmas he sent two envoys to Robert at Selkirk : we do not know what happened, but a further discussion was arranged at Melrose. King Robert, however, never attended it. He was warned of some projected treachery, and instead proceeded to reopen hostilities, taking the initiative this time with a drive towards Galloway, very early in February, perhaps with the intention of counter-attacking England by the western march, and forcing Edward to a very awkward cross-country move to repel him.

Edward, on his part, tried to cut him off from his real base of operations, Scotland north of Forth, by sending Gaveston to Perth in February. The Lanercost Chronicler, who is pretty well informed of Border events, gives this definitely as the purpose of the move —to cut King Robert's communications and prevent his reinforcement. Edward, in fact, seems to have had a strategist on his council, for all the futile chess-play of this campaign is very well planned. The trouble, from his point of view, was the two-fold one that he had no one who could, or would, *lead* an army, and an equally good strategist was against him. Except for affairs of outposts, which were constant, and to Edward's men demoralisingly irritating, and for Bruce's attack on the English rear in November, the campaign had seen no active fighting on land. But none the less, it had been won and lost. As a campaign of manoeuvre it had been a complete success for the Scots, for Edward's great army was much the worse for wear, and Robert's was cheered by the failure of an impressive enemy demonstration in force, which was naturally an exhilarating spectacle.

Most of 1311 passed in a sort of stalemate. Edward's great force was still cantoned at Berwick, and might strike at any moment. But his barons had again begun to quarrel. He hovered at Berwick until after midsummer, when he was forced to take Gaveston, who had rejoined him after trouble with forage and the bitter cold of the spring, and go to London to meet his Parliament, who promptly exiled the favourite again.

King Robert does not seem to have been active in the spring. The country would still be weakened by the famine, and so long as Edward was in Berwick in such force, he might strike heavily, and had to be watched. None the less, he must have been working to strengthen his army, and when the first hint of opportunity came, he took it with vigour. As Edward marched down the eastern road to London, Robert flung his army across the Sark on the west, and counterattacked, raiding Gilsland and striking east down Tynedale, where he burnt Haltwhistle. It was a mere

lightning raid, that could have had little military value :
but no doubt it had a moral effect on both sides.
And the loot, even of that poorish district, would help
the commissariat a good deal : it was harvest time,
which probably had something to do with deciding
him.

The success, and perhaps the moral effect on his
men, of this first stroke made him risk another at once.
By early September he was back again, with a greater
force, striking across the Cheviots in a sweep by
Coquetdale and Redesdale, as far as the Lower Tyne.
England tasted her own medicine, and did not like it.
He spent a fortnight, this time, on English soil, and in
force enough to make the Wardens of the Marches
keep out of his way. Northumbria, indeed, sent to
beg for a truce, and offered £2000, a very large sum in
mediaeval money, for one which should last till Christmas. King Robert agreed, and later extended the time
to Candlemas. No doubt the money was useful for
his war-chest. According to the Lanercost Chronicler,
Northumbria cannily raised it by taxing Lothian,
which perhaps was economically sound, but politically
was playing for King Robert. No Lothian man, since
Lothian wore woad, has taken a tax-collector to his
bosom.

The year 1312, whose March completed the sixth of
Robert's reign, and the twenty-fourth since the death
of King Alexander, dawned with more encouragement
than unhappy Scotland had seen since the seals were
set to the Treaty of Birgham. And the steadily grow-

ing hope, strengthened immensely by the fact that the King was able at last to act on the offensive, was not belied. The next two and a half years bring, not ultimate victory, for he had to wait another fourteen for that, but triumph, the crown of his remembered achievements, and the clearing of the enemy from Scotland.

King Edward, this year, apparently took in hand to attack betimes. He got to York in early January. There he had to stop, for his troubles were behind him as well as before, and the opposition was concentrating in the person of his powerful cousin, the Earl of Lancaster, who was also cousin of the Queen of France. He had to stay at York till early April, and tried to make an armistice with King Robert, sending up Lamberton with Athol and three others. King Robert, as before, would not consider any terms but the complete recognition of Scots autonomy, and the negotiations collapsed as the others had done.

On the military side, the first half of the year was fairly quiet. The King, with Edward at York and threatening to move, had to stand by for another large-scale invasion. Edward Bruce was besieging Dundee, which was of great strategic and political importance, as not only was it the last English garrison, save Perth, to the north of Forth, but it was in position to afford a base for an attack on the King's rear when he came to deal with Lothian : and owing to its site it was easy to reinforce and provision by sea. Sir Edward, however, perhaps with the help of the above-mentioned

P

privateers, succeeded in reducing it to straits. Its commander, Montfitchet, agreed at last to surrender if he was not relieved in a given time, and reported the arrangement to King Edward at York, who was badly upset by it, Perth and Dundee and Stirling being the only bases left for an attempt to recover Northern Scotland. He ordered Montfitchet to break the agreement and hold on, clinching the order with a threat of confiscation and death if he failed. In spite of this encouragement, however, it fell sometime this spring, though we do not know when.

Edward stayed on at York until early April, then moved north at last. He got to Newcastle, but no further. In a few weeks he was back again at York, and domestic quarrels immobilised him there until June. Matters grew so warm that the unfortunate Gaveston had to bolt. He was caught at Scarborough by Edmund of Lancaster, and beheaded out of hand on the 19th of June. This was open revolt, and Edward had to deal with it. He turned south, and King Robert, relieved from the threat of invasion that had hung over him for the last six months, promptly set to work to clear up the English garrisons.

He held parliament in early July, at Ayr, which means that one of the strongest places of the South-west was now in his hands. There it was decided to use the army that had been gathered to face Edward's threatened invasion, by sending the main bulk of the troops into England under Sir Edward, while the King remained by the Solway to deal with the three great strengths of Caerlaverock and Dumfries in Lower Nithsdale, and Buittle over the march of the Stewartry. These arrangements, however, were altered before they had been put in practice. The King himself led his troops across the Border in mid-August. This time it was no mere raid, even on the scale of the last, but an invasion in force. They went by the western route, and lay at Lanercost for three days, sacking the priory lands : it is improbable that the good brothers amused their visitor with the Chronicle. Then he held down Tynedale again, burning Hexham and Corbridge, and camping near the latter with his staff, sent Sir Edward and Douglas farther south to Durham. They made a forced march, took Chester-le-Street on the way, and reached Durham. The Castle was too strong to attempt, but its garrison looked on while they burnt the town. Edward Bruce retired then on Chester-le-Street again, while Douglas swept on to the sea and sacked Hartlepool, returning with booty and a drove of prisoners, douce well-doing burghers who would pay snug ransoms.

The effect was immense. For Scots towns to be sacked was natural and proper, but that English ones should be was a crying outrage. And since the King did not help, the Scots had to be bought off, a move as useful to King Robert's empty war-chest as deplorable in its effect on English morale. £2000 was offered for a ten months' truce—that is, till next midsummer : but King Robert was in a position to make his own terms, and refused to accept unless they would add free

passage for his troops on their occasions through the
county of Durham. It is probable that the purpose
of this condition was rather political than military : to
push an invasion so far was not likely to be feasible as
yet, but apart from the threat to Yorkshire, which
would not improve that county's peace of mind,
Durham was the County Palatine, the Warden of the
North. If she caved in and gave free passage to the
invader, all England would feel that the situation was
being reversed.

In fact, the whole North of England was smitten
with panic. Northumbria offered another £2000 for
inclusion in the truce, Westmoreland, Copeland, and
Cumberland following suit. Having raised £10,000 in
indemnities, besides private ransoms and the loot of
five towns, and left England in a panic to the Trent,
the King returned. The spoil and the moral effect
were not all the results : he had built, in England
itself, a barrier against English pressure, and now, with
his flank cleared, went back to undertake what he had
waited and worked for through more than six years—
the recovery of Scotland below the Forth.

He did not go about it, in person at all events, at
once, for recovered Scotland had managed to organise
something of a national life once more, and he was not
only Commander-in-Chief, but head as well of the
civil government. He left the conduct of the war in
the South-west to his brother and Douglas, and went
north himself for a parliament at Inverness, which met
on the 29th October. It is unfortunate that we have so

little information about this meeting, as a knowledge
of the various business transacted would help us to
gauge how far the recovery had gone. All we know,
however, is that it dealt with relations with Norway,
renewing with Haakon V the treaty that Alexander III
had made with Magnus IV over the cession of Man
and the Sudreys—the treaty sealed by the marriage of
Margaret of Scotland, whose daughter had been the
little Maid of Norway. The renewal, by this time, was
in itself mere form, but it implies a recognition of
King Robert's government by a friendly Power. The
record sent to King Haakon gives us some information
as to who was there. They included Randolph, who
was now—perhaps created so at this time—Earl of
Moray, and a new name, that of the Earl of Athol, son
of the Athol who had the special gallows. At the beginning of the year he had been one of King Edward's
envoys to Scotland, and had then, apparently, been
won over by the King's personality. He stayed in
Scots service until Bannockburn, and won high favour.
King Robert made him Constable of Scotland, and
Edward Bruce was married to his sister. It was perhaps this that ruined the relation, and sent Athol, just
in the hour of victory, back to England, abandoning his
Scots lands and the King's favour to seek a pension
from the man whose father had hanged his : for Sir
Edward and his wife did not ' get on,' and he left her
for the daughter of the third Earl present at this
parliament, Ross, whose sons were his brother-in-law
and his intimate friend, and lived with her openly

until the death of his wife allowed him to marry her shortly before he was killed.

While these peaceful political matters were in progress, and the less peaceful domestic ones were brewing, the King's generals seem to have been fighting in the South. The course of events in late 1312 is obscure, but it is marked, on the 6th of December, by the first serious attempt on the South-east, an attack on Berwick, which though it was unsuccessful at the time, shows that it had now become possible to broaden the area of operations, and attack the root of the English strength in Scotland.

The Lanercost Chronicler gives a lively account : he seems to have been in Berwick himself at the time. He says that the King was there, but this is made unlikely by his known movements, though it is not certainly wrong : Bruce could move quickly. The odds, however, are on its being a confusion with Sir Edward, and the method of attack rather smacks of Douglas. The attack was made by means of scaling-ladders of uncommonly ingenious construction, made with hooks to grip the wall, and sockets in the hooks to allow of their lifting on the point of a spear. The escalading party got up to the wall, and had two of these fixed in place, when a dog barked and gave the alarm, and they had to withdraw.

Berwick, for the time, had to remain unrecovered, but the delay was made up for within the next few weeks by the winning of one of the strongest cities in Scotland, Perth, on the march between the North and the South. It was the last place untaken north of Forth.

It fell on the 8th of January 1313, the first of the four famous captures of this time. (It is worth re-marking, in the by-going, that the heroes of the four are King Robert himself, Douglas, Randolph, and a country farmer, who though his name has happily come down, may stand representative for the common soldier, the great anonymous mass of the fighting forces.) Perth took a seven weeks' siege, in the heart of winter. The King sat down before it, apparently, on his way south from the parliament of Inverness, where the attempt may have been decided. The commander of Perth was Oliphant, who as Baliol's Governor of Stirling had held off Edward I so manfully, and been last of the Comyn leaders to surrender. He had never made peace with Bruce, but thereafter had fought for England all through the war : and the siege of Stirling, and the fact that Perth had held out until now, say something for his quality as a soldier.

The King had been before the town for six weeks, without result. He was, as usual, short of siege artillery, and the town was too strongly walled and deeply moated to be carried by a storm, and too well provisioned to be starved out for months. He went scouting in person in the long dark nights about Yule, and took soundings of the moat, a job as cold as it was dangerous, till he found a place with not much over five feet of water.

That was his key to Perth. He laid his plans, and

just at the New Year he raised the siege, and the grinning garrison jeered from the walls at the besiegers packing their gear and flitting. They were given a week to enjoy their satisfaction : and if they suspected at first, suspicion died down. After all, they had held the place firmly for several years. The King spent the week in making scaling-ladders, and, choosing a suitable night, left his horses in camp (he cannot have been very far from Methven) and brought his men silently before the dark town, at the point where he knew the moat was at its lowest. He himself took a ladder and dropped, armed as he was, in the water, sounding his way with his lance in his free hand, and wading up to the neck through the icy foulness, to the great admiration, says Barbour, of a French knight who apparently was there for the fun of the thing— which, at the time, was not at all unlikely : the French, all over mediaeval Europe, were as omnipresent as the Scots themselves. The admiring Frenchman dropped after him and followed, and the rest did likewise. They got across in silence, and no dog barked. The ladders were set in place against the wall, and one man —possibly it was the Frenchman—contrived to beat the King in the race to the top.

The King divided them, the smaller part being stationed to hold the ladder-heads, for a line of retreat. It was not required. The garrison were taken by surprise before they could arm and rally, and surrendered. There were few casualties and no unnecessary slaughter, but the King made sure of the town by razing the walls and filling up the moat with the débris. Scotland was wholly clear now to the Forth.

Perth was the first of a string of like successes. On the 7th of February, just on a month later, and almost on the sixth anniversary of the Lochryan disaster, Macdowall (who had been responsible for that) had to surrender Dumfries to Edward Bruce. Caerlaverock and Dalswinton appear to have fallen much about this time, and Buittle had done so by the end of March, thus practically clearing the South-west, though Bothwell in Clydesdale was still holding for England. In May the King set out for the Isle of Man, where he took Rushen in the middle of June.[1]

The truce with England expired directly after, and the King set about preparing another invasion. The North of England begged for a longer truce, and paid a heavy indemnity again, for one till Michaelmas of the next year—that is, till the end of September 1314. The King accepted, and since there were no signs of any large-scale movements from England, he now at last could bend all his energies to deal with the South-east, and recover Lothian.

It was seven and a quarter years since his coronation. The first of these years had seen unbroken disaster, the next small indeterminate successes. By the end of the third, North Scotland, beyond the Forth, had

---

[1] At the end of the year the island was given to Randolph, who lost it to John of Lorne before the summer. It changed hands once or twice again, but was lost for good by the middle of the century.

been practically recovered. There had followed two years of fighting that had left him in case to risk an invasion of England. After two more, he had got back the South-west. But not until after near seven years of war is there even an attempt at clearing Lothian—the province which, according to Andrew Lang, and historians who innocently follow him, had borne the brunt and done all the work of the war ! In fact, through the first seven years of King Robert's reign, the whole province—more than the modern Lothian, for it included the Merse, much of Roxburghshire, and a good deal of the counties of Selkirk and Peebles—was administered, and taxed, by English officials. In June 1313 it had still eleven English garrisons, while all the rest of Scotland had only two, namely Stirling, which Edward Bruce had invested since Lent, and Bothwell, cut off and isolated in Clydesdale, where it was none the less to hold out till the next year.

Unlucky Lothian, for the last few years, had been in an extremely unpleasant position. Some of its gentry, as early as 1309, had drawn English suspicion on it by joining the King, and its defenders against him had not been conciliatory to the local population. A pitiful petition of 1313 tells a sorry tale of oppression to King Edward, that reveals the brutalities of the garrisons, who were lining their pockets while they had the chance, and arbitrarily arresting peaceful people. Gray, in fact, admits very candidly that one reason why Bruce was welcome was *moult par caus de mauves*

*gouernail dez ministres le roy (Dengleterre) qi trop
asprement lez gouernoient pur singuler profit.*

The serious attempt upon it comes, as has been
said, in the second half of the year, and just at its
beginning a considerable Scottish force was set free,
and a gauntlet was finally flung in the face of England,
by Edward Bruce's arrangement over Stirling. He
had been besieging it for three or four months, and by
all that is known of him the dull work of blockade
would not be congenial to his temperament. He contrived to set himself free for something more entertaining by rashly agreeing with its governor, Moubray,
to suspend hostilities on the latter's undertaking to
surrender if the castle were not relieved within eight
days of the next Midsummer Day, by an English army
appearing within three leagues of it.

The King's emotions over this arrangement were
probably fervent, and a good deal varied. He was no
knight-errant, fighting for his amusement, but a king
with much of a stiff job of work ahead, and Sir Edward's
light-hearted arrangement ' cowpit the creel,' for
English politics were clearly settling down. King
Edward, in fact, made peace with his chief enemies
that autumn, and the birth of an heir at the end of the
previous year had considerably strengthened his position. England had lost too much prestige already to
be able to refuse such a violent challenge : it was not
a blow to morale, like the terms of the truce with
Durham, but rather a spur to more fervent retaliation.
Barbour, and probably with a good deal of truth,

represents the King as telling Sir Edward that he was a fool, and then kindling to his brother's reckless temper, and welcoming the chance

> ' to put [his fortune] to the touch
> And gain or lose it all.'

England and Scotland set furiously to work, the English to raise the most powerful army of that generation, the Scots to make sure of Lothian while there was time. In September, Linlithgow fell, to a local farmer. Every Scots boy knows that tale [1]—how the castle, that guarded the Edinburgh-Stirling high-road, where the gaunt shell of palace stands now above the loch, was used to buy its hay, or at least to get it, from a worthy of the name of William Binnock; how Binnock grew somewhat bored with the arrangement, and promising them a load of unusual quality, kept his promise. He was ' a stout carle and a stour,' and intelligent. He raised a band of like-minded friends of his, and ambushed them, during the night, at the castle gate. At sunrise he turned up with the expected hay-cart, in charge of only himself and one of his lads. The English porter opened the gate, the waggon creaked

---

[1] One of the earliest things I remember—I know I was certainly not more than six—is my father bringing home a little blue book, whose frontispiece showed Bruce, handsomely equipped in armour of the late fifteenth century, laying out De Bohun : its contents, as I know now, were tales from Barbour. I retired with it to a space behind the piano, conveniently inaccessible to grown-ups, and the first thing I read in it was the tale of this capture. I can still remember shedding tears of excitement as the axe fell with a dunt on the waggon shaft, and being hauled out protesting by my nurse with Randolph half-way up Edinburgh Rock.

innocently between its leaves ... and then halted,
jamming them, while the lad in front pulled out an
axe from his belt and cut the traces, and Binnock himself attended to the porter, yelling the rallying-cry,
' Call all, call all ! ' The falling portcullis jammed on
the pile of hay, and before the castle soldiers could
clear the waggon the Lothian men were swarming
through the wheels, and once within, made short work
of the garrison. Some were slain, some captured, some
bolted to Edinburgh, and the castle itself, as usual,
was razed.

There was only minor action through the winter,
but the early spring of 1314 shows two of the most
famous *coups de main*. One exploit was Douglas's, the
other Randolph's. Douglas tried for Roxburgh at the
end of winter, and won it with the help of a craftsman
called Sim of the Ledhouse, who brought him cleverly
fashioned scaling-ladders. It may be Sim who planned
the attack on Berwick, for Barbour's description of
the Roxburgh ladders resembles the Lanercost one of
those used at Berwick—wooden treads slung firmly by
ropes from an iron hook, though he does not mention
the ingenious device that enabled the hook to be lifted
on a spear. Douglas chose Carnival for his attempt,
when the garrison would be full of beef and ale, and in
the dusk of a February evening he and his men, with
black gowns over their armour, crept up on all fours to
just under the castle wall. They were seen, but in the
dusk and perhaps the river mist off the Teviot they
were taken for cattle. They heard jests pass on the

wall, as to Such-a-one's celebration of Carnival, and his probable Lenten emotions the next morning when he found his oxen lifted by the Black Douglas while he was too drunk to put them in their byre.

The ladders went up, and Sim was the first to mount, but the hook had clinked on the stone as it jammed down, and the sentry came up . . . and luckily lost his head, and instead of shouting, threw himself at Sim, who, half across the wall, made a grab for him, caught his throat before he thought of making a noise, and managed to knife him and heave the body over. The others swarmed up behind, and the garrison, dancing cheerfully in the hall, heard nothing, till the shout of ' Douglas ! ' rose at their very door. There was panic, for it was a name to dread. Sir William de Fiennes, the Burgundian commandant, rallied a party, and got them into the keep and barred the gate. He held it for two days, and then, being gravely wounded by a Scots arrow, surrendered on terms, Douglas escorting him safely into England, while the King sent Sir Edward to raze the city walls.

Randolph, besieging Edinburgh Castle, heard this : there was some little rivalry between the two knights. Edinburgh Castle, before gunpowder and indeed for a long time after, was one of the strongest fortresses in Europe, and the garrison were strong and well provisioned. Its main strength lies in the height of the sheer crag : and Randolph's force, since he now was Earl of Moray, was likely to hold a good many Highlanders, lads from the Grampians, who would

climb as they fought, like wildcats. He determined to
try for it by escalade. It is one of the great tales of
mediaeval war.

He found a discreet civil soul called William Francis,
who in his youth had been much less discreet : ' sum-
dele volageous ' is the way Barbour puts it, and the
epithet, in the context, is rather pleasing. This worthy,
in his unregenerate youth, had been for a time in the
castle garrison, and had been in the habit of risking
his neck, when leave was scarce, by climbing down the
rock to visit a pretty lady in the town. The lady's
charms, and kindness, had lasted so long that he
thought he could find the lunatic road again, and get
up to where a twelve-foot scaling-ladder would get
them on the wall . . . if they could reach it unheard by
the English sentries, and if no one came a cropper in
the dark on a path that a hill goat might baulk at in
daylight. Randolph accepted the chance, picked thirty
of his wildcats and put it to them, and on a dark
March night they followed the excellent Francis and
his ladder—presumably of Sim's handy folding pattern
—with their fingers clawing in the cracks of the rock,
the March east wind growing deeper underneath, and
sudden death, without any salt of a fight, if any one of
them slipped or made metal clank : revealed on the
face of the rock, they would be quite helpless.

A hundred feet up, and no doubt sufficiently winded,
they came to a ledge that was broad enough to sit on,
and there they rested to get their breath for the top.
Then they found they were in an unhealthy spot for

repose, for immediately over their heads on the castle wall was the officer of the watch going his round, and he halted there for a little conversation. Apparently there was a trifle of ragging, for some irresponsible soul tried to scare the others by flipping over a stone with a shout of ' I see you ! ' Randolph's discipline was good. His men kept their heads, ' froze ' where they sat, and never made a sound : and the English watch, looking over, heard nothing, saw nothing move, and carried on. The Scotsmen, having got their wind again, heard the watch recede and likewise carried on, and climbed in due course up the second hundred feet. Francis got his ladder fast, and went aloft, Sir Andrew Gray next, and then Randolph himself. Someone's accoutrements rattled before they were over : the watch heard and gave the alarm, and those first on the wall had to fight desperately to hold their footing above the sheer drop. There were two hundred men in the garrison, and Randolph's scaling-party was only thirty, but—this is the Lanercost Chronicler again, for Barbour does not say so—he had timed a diversion for the castle gate. It could not have done much more than make a noise until Randolph's men could fight their way to the gate-house and deal with the guard : no doubt the resourceful Francis knew the road. But the Englishmen were confused between two attacks, and the Gascon constable, Sir Piers Lebaud, was killed almost at once.[1]

[1] So Barbour. Gray says he lived, took service with the Scots, played double, and was hanged by King Robert.

With no one to take command, the garrison broke. The castle followed the others into ruin, save for St Margaret's little oratory, and remained a ruin for many a year after.

When the other Lothian castles fell is unknown. But on the eighth anniversary of his coronation, or seven years from the landing at Turnberry, Robert Bruce was king of a united Scotland, save only for five castles. Berwick, Bothwell, Stirling, Jedburgh, and Dunbar were still in enemy hands : but only these. But the danger was not over, far from that, for the English also were united again, and determined to use the whole national resources to win back Scotland by sheer steam-roller weight, and teach it a lesson it should never forget. They taught the lesson, but not as they intended.

END OF 1308

SUMMER OF 1313

Q

CHAPTER XI

BANNOCKBURN

TWO DAYS : 1314

'When he therefore saw that the battle was begun . . . he said
unto his host, Fight this day for your brethren.'
I. Maccabees, v. 32.

THE adventures of the war will never be told, the story
of reckless attacks, of little sieges, of conflicts here and
there of forgotten leaders, of wild days in the hills, of
nameless men dying desperate or in hope. We have
the major outlines, and here and there episodes stand
clear, like Randolph's escalade, by the chance that
Gray or Barbour, Froissart or Fordun, happened to
come across old men who had been there. The
'official' history that King Robert had made disappeared in later wars, or the Reformation : the men
who shattered the King's splendid tomb would not
have much regard for what he did. But of the chief
adventure of the war, save perhaps for the coronation
that began it (since all adventure begins, and is most,
in the will)—for the Midsummer Day of the year 1314,
it so happens that after a long and careless confusion,
in which what the nineteenth century thought likely
overrode more and more the testimony of men who had
spoken to eyewitnesses, we do know a great deal more
than the bare outline. The patient research of Dr

Mackay Mackenzie has so pieced together the contemporary or almost contemporary records that we know
as much of its movements as we do of those of Waterloo.
Only in his setting of the movements upon their terrain
he has been misled by the modern changes in its surface
and by the almost classic confusion of historians over
Gray's *fosse* and the *Vita Edwardi's fovea*. Mr Miller's
study of the fourteenth century condition of the
ground makes it clear that Dr Mackenzie's map of the
battle will not hold : and in any case it is topographi-
cally incorrect, for it puts the Borestone on the wrong
side of the road, which does not matter much,
and, what does matter, almost ignores—his account
does quite ignore—a natural feature which by all
the accounts played a most formidable part in the
action.

The situation, early in 1314, was that Scotland had
been almost entirely won back. One castle in Clydesdale, one on the Forth, one on the Lothian coast, one
at Tweedmouth, and one between Tweed and the
Cheviot Hills, were all that remained in foreign occupation. The country was united, triumphant with success, under a brilliant leader whose generals were devoted to him and to their cause, and well accustomed
to co-operation : on the other hand, at all events south
of the line Inverness-Loch Linnhe, it was devastated,
and some eighteen years of intermittent war, punc-
tuated by nine large-scale invasions, meant a serious
drainage to the man-power of a country whose total
population, of both sexes and all ages, could not be

more than at most four hundred thousand. The Pope was no longer an ally. King Philip, though friendly, was in difficulties himself, and could not afford to quarrel with his son-in-law. England had suffered very little material damage, beyond a considerable waste of money : only her northern extremity had been touched. Supposing her actual casualty-list equal to the Scots one, it represented a fifth, at the very most, of the loss in proportion. She had been hampered by political disagreements, including a trifle of fighting : but Scotland also had suffered the cross-purposes of faction, and added to these a bloody civil war.

It is clear enough therefore that though Scotland, so far, had won, the issue was not by any means decided. England, now united once more, was aware of this, and strained her resources to settle the matter in one smashing blow. Scotland set her teeth, and mustered what means she could to stand up to it. Victory, it seemed certain, would give her peace now, defeat meant the loss of all that had been gained.

Edward's preparations were set in hand very early in the year, since the immediate objective of the invasion was the relief of Stirling by midsummer. Early in May an embargo was put on the export of English foodstuffs, and waggons were commandeered from twenty-one sheriffdoms—106 four-horse and 110 eight-ox ones. The actual number of soldiers ordered in the levy is as usual much less than the traditional figures : it comes to 21,540 English and Welsh (which in practice means less) with 4000 archers from Ireland, an uncertain number of men from the French provinces, and an unknown but by this time probably small contingent of persistently anti-Bruce Scots. In addition to these were the heavy cavalry, the fully armed men on heavy barded horses, who were the shock-troops. Dr Mackay Mackenzie and Mr Barron agree, after detailed argument as to the data, in counting about 2500 heavy cavalry, and 20,000, more or less, of the other arm : I should say rather more than less myself.[1]

King Robert could only raise a fraction of this. Even admitting his presumable power to get a larger proportion of the population under arms, he cannot have had, at the outside, more than 7000 foot. He had no foreign auxiliaries at all, and a serious weakness in the cavalry arm. What he had there was only a contingent of not more than 500 light cavalry, men in mail on light unarmoured horses, very mobile, useful in pursuit or in a charge on broken ranks, but useless as shock-troops and quite unable to stand up to anything like their own number—let alone five times their number—on barded destriers. The mounted infantryman or hobeler, whom Bruce was to use so brilliantly thereafter, does not appear, and in fact was not called for in the circumstances.

[1] Sir James Ramsay makes the figures a good deal smaller on both sides of the battle, but in much the same relative proportion. Sir Charles Oman, still keeping the proportion, however, makes them much larger.

The discrepancy was thus not short of enormous, and on any estimate the odds were severe. They were not, however, quite as bad as they looked upon the face of it. In the first place, Scotland, even at the time of his unquestioned ascendance everywhere else, had never relied entirely on the mounted knight. The Scots gentleman did not consider that he *dérogeait* by fighting on foot in the ranks of his own men : nor did he think of these men as mere stuffing for a gap, mere lance-fodder. Besides this, in a fight of infantry against cavalry and superior missile armament, position is of very great importance : and the King, within certain wide limits, could choose his position, and get himself into it before Edward arrived. As another element, there was the moral factor, and by this time it was as much on the side of the Scots as eight years before it had been on the other. And finally, very closely linked with this, there was discipline. It does not seem to have been remarked on, even by Dr Mackenzie, that sheer drill clearly played a large part in the victory. Scots armies have commonly suffered from lack of discipline. In the list of our defeats in pitched actions its lack is, I think with only two exceptions, Falkirk and Flodden,[1] the deciding factor. Bannockburn did not suffer from this lack. King Robert showed himself a brilliant strategist and tactician : but neither quality would have led to such results if he had not been able to handle his men *as*

[1] Both decided on armament : the discipline at both seems to have been excellent.

formations. We speak of ' soldiers' battles ' and of ' generals'.' Bannockburn was both : but it may also be called a company officer's. To bring a mediaeval army to the pitch of drill that is revealed in the fighting is an immense, an almost incredible achievement. (The Swiss did it later, and are considered pioneers.) To get a Scots mediaeval—or later one—there, and especially one with a large Highland element, implies a miracle of sheer personality. Nothing else overcomes the worst weakness of the Scot, his inability to co-operate.

We know that even as early as March, King Robert was mustering his forces in the Torwood : and it is more than possible that the time between then and the beginning of June, when there was no fighting to speak of, was mainly spent in sheer drill. All his tried generals were with him, and a new one, a lad who in his short life was to prove himself a brilliant soldier, and become the father of a most tragic line of kings— Walter Stewart, son of James Stewart (who was dead now) and cousin of both Douglas and the Queen.[1] Randolph had the men of his earldom of Moray, and with them, probably, a contingent from Nithsdale. Edward Bruce led those of the Galloway men who would fight,[2] and those of Aberdeen and the South-east Highlands. Douglas and young Stewart were to-

---

[1] His mother was the Queen's aunt on the father's side, his father Douglas's uncle, on the mother's.

[2] This clause is not an aspersion upon their courage. But Baliol's old province did not love the Bruces.

gether, the latter in command of the men of Renfrew, the former with his tried followers of the long campaigns of the South-west. The King himself, besides his own Carrick men, had those of the West Highlands and the Isles, a considerable body, as a full score of Highland chiefs were present. In addition there were the cavalry under Keith the Marischal, and outwith these fully-armed and disciplined troops of the line, another and probably rather large assembly of lightly armed undisciplined infantry, good fighting stuff as individuals, but not to be relied on to keep formation. These are the famous ' camp-followers ' of our youthful schoolbooks. Barbour, who lived a trifle nearer the battle than writers of text-books of the eighteen-nineties, calls them ' the yeomen, swains, and poor folk,' and in another reference, ' small folk,' a term which its other uses make clear. They played a part, and a useful one, in the battle : but they did not come into it as organised and drilled troops of the line.[1]

---

[1] The 1318 statute, *De Armaturis pro guerra*, makes the division clear, though its meaning in quotation is sometimes obscured by the obstinate habit of our historians, of copying each other's mistranslations, in this case taking the *lawit man* of the English text to mean landed man, when a glance at the adjacent Latin would have shown them *quilibet homo laicus*. Every layman possessing £10 in goods must, under penalty of the loss of the said goods, provide himself for national defence with a padded leather jerkin, steel helmet, and gloves of plate, or alternatively, if he likes to go to the greater expense, with the more modern breast-plate over a hooded mail-coat, an ' iron hat ' (so in English text) and gloves of plate. (The *chapel de fer* was not unlike the ' tin hat ' of present-day equipment.) These are the heavy infantry, corresponding to the Bannockburn troops of the line. The ' small folk,' ' having in goods the value of a cow,' are not obliged to have body armour, but must have ' a good spear or a good bow with a

Preparations thus made, the English moved with the coming of full summer. The muster was at Wark on the 10th June, Edward and his staff reaching Berwick a week later. Crossing the Tweed, they marched unopposed by the Roman road down Lauderdale, reached Edinburgh on the 21st, and were suffered to lie there for the night unmolested. Next day, which was Saturday, the King's scouts brought him word that they were moving. Sir Edward's agreement with Moubray had ensured that if they were allowed to march unopposed their objective would necessarily be Stirling, and the King's dispositions were already made. At the end of May, before the English muster, he had moved from his training-ground in the Torwood, and encamped on high wooded land to the south of Stirling, the New Park, where he could guard the Roman road to the town.

With the enemy a matter of two days' march off, and coming definitely from the east, he had plenty of time for his final dispositions, and he arranged them to make full use of the ground. The large-scale map, opposite page 272, gives the terrain of the subsequent actions not as it is now but as it was in the Middle Ages.[1] It may save the reader confusion to remark

sheaf of twenty-four arrows,' inexpensive weapons that could be made at home with the heads fashioned by the local smith. Those poorer still are tacitly exempted from service.

[1] The Reverend Thomas Miller has made a very careful study of all evidence bearing on its condition at that time, and applied to it a lifelong knowledge of the whole area, at first hand. For the detail of his various topographical data, see his *The Site of the Battle of Bannockburn*, Historical Association, 1931. Between two writings

that the area given on the Ordnance map as the site of
the action quite certainly saw no fighting until after
the battle had been won and lost. The English, as a
force in being, never came near it. The true position
lies east, not west, of the Borestone, but (unlike that
given by Dr Mackenzie) in much the same latitude.
The traditional association of the Borestone with the
battle is in fact borne out by all the evidence.

This position—see map—lies between the present
village of St Ninians, to the south of Stirling, and that
of Bannockburn, further south again, and is bounded
on the east by the low haughland, now arable, of the
Forth, and on the west by the wood of the New Park,
whose eastern edge corresponded roughly to the
modern St Ninians-Glasgow road, as far as the cross-
road leading to Whins of Milton schoolhouse, which
latter road marks almost exactly, down to the burn,
what was the southern boundary of the wood. The
southern boundary of the relevant area (I must use
the points of the compass rather loosely, but the map
elucidates their sense in the text) was the Bannock
Burn, which runs roughly east and west, south of the
New Park, till it reaches a deep, rather narrow, and
extremely steep-sided glen, like a huge trench, wherein
was (as much of it still is) the village called by the

of this chapter I have walked, or occasionally crawled or scrambled,
over every part of the ground; and the mediaeval accounts of both
movements and terrain, including those parts to which he does
not himself refer, fit precisely the position he suggests: certain
peculiarities in the terrain, invisible even on a six-inch map,
exactly account for one or two points in the movements which seem
odd when one reads of them, not knowing the ground.

name of the burn : then it turns north-east to flow
across then boggy haughland to the Forth. The burn
itself is no great obstacle : until it reaches the carse it
is only some ten feet wide with a hard bottom, and in
a dry April (the battle was fought in a dry midsummer)
is no more than mid-leg deep : [1] a man on horseback
would hardly notice it. None the less, if the burn is,
as has often been remarked, no obstacle, *the place
where it flows* is a most formidable one. Cavalry, even
infantry, in formation, can cross only in one short
section. West of the crossing, its banks are high and
steep. East of that, it flows through the deep S-shaped
gorge, with banks over twice the height of a three-storey
house, very steep, and often, in spite of the slope, bad
ground : [2] *this glen, not the burn itself,* is what the
Lanercost Chronicler means by the *fovea* (pit or trench),
the *Vita Edwardi* by the *fossa* (the technical word for
a trench or moat) and Gray by the *fosse,* of Bannockburn. (Gray's Norman-French is written without
accents, and the word is probably equivalent to Modern
French *fossé* rather than *fosse*—i.e., to the word that
means a castle moat.) The English equivalent of any
of these words is one that would naturally occur to
any modern man, even a civilian, trying to describe

---

[1] To this fact, often remarked, should however be added that
there is a good deal of water going down the present mill-lade.
Before that existed the burn may well have been bigger.

[2] Exploring it after a long drought, I had a laced shoe dragged off
my foot by the adhesive mud near the *top* of the gorge : and there
is, and probably was, an exceedingly rich crop of briars and
brambles.

the place to someone who had not seen it. It is, in fact, a *ditch* on the giant scale. Barbour speaks of it as ' Bannokburn betuix the brais,' which clearly indicates which part of the course he means : and his very editor, in his account of the battle, has ignored that most illuminating phrase. A single light horseman, with perfect confidence between himself and his mount, might possibly get up and down some parts in safety, though I should not care to make the attempt myself. A body of cavalry, even light horse, let alone mediaeval men-at-arms, could no more do it than they could cross the Minch. And below the gorge the burn then flowed through peat-bog, until becoming tidal (at possibly a higher point then than now) it reached the Forth.

Now, the Roman road to Stirling forded the burn in the short stretch where such a crossing was practicable, and struck north by west just within, and parallel with, the eastern rim of the New Park. To the east of this rim of woodland (this is important) lay a sort of shelf of gently undulating table-land, firm ground, whose edge is marked by a very definite slope, steepish in parts, that drops a matter of some fifty feet : below this slope lies, between it and the tidal Forth, a broad stretch of what is now firm arable land but was then the peat-bog of the Burgh of Stirling—bad mossy ground in itself, spongy and full of pools, and made worse by deep peat-hags, some of them over a century old, with fresh moss, as dangerous as quicksand, forming below several feet of water : this ' carse-land ' also was to play its part. West of the road and well northward of the burn, the firm ground rises gently : it was all woodland then. The Borestone, high ground at the rim of the wood, commanding a view towards the crossing, is the end of a long gentle sagging rise, running parallel with the road and swelling at its northern end to the gentle eminence of Coxet Hill, some thirty feet higher than the Borestone, but not more, at the summit, than at most 130 feet above the shelf of table-land I have mentioned. West of this ridge is a dip—it is scarcely a valley—and then the ground rises again, still very gently, to the still wooded Gillies Hill, a foothill of the Campsie Fells, whose summit is 450 feet above the plateau.

I apologise for a so detailed description, but so much of what has been written of the battle is nonsense because the writer has tried to force the descriptions into a wrong conception of the ground, often rejecting them when they did not fit that, and inventing manoeuvres as ' what must have happened.' We can see the process as early as Fordun, who casually gives *foveae* in the plural, as indeed one might fairly speak of the S-shaped gorge, though it is probably merely a blunder, very likely of Bower's who worked up Fordun's notes much later on : and Skene in his translation renders *pitfalls*, with superb results to the work of other historians. I found that even a good many hours spent kneeling over a six-inch Ordnance map had left me with an inadequate conception of essential features : and a smaller map would be actively misleading.

Now, the natural approach for an enemy in force, in heavy marching order, was by the road. It was conceivable, though improbable, that they might try to advance to the west of the road, through the wood, or to the east of it, over the table-land of firm ground lying outside the selvage of the wood. The western deviation was easily provided against by blocking the forest tracks, which was duly done. The eastern was improbable, since it meant exposing Edward's flank, in column of march, to an enemy under cover on higher ground. The King clearly assumed, and was justified in assuming, that Edward's push on Stirling would come by the road, though he did not overlook the other possibilities. The fourth possibility, the thing that actually happened, was something that he could not have foreseen, though he took brilliant advantage of it when it came. The precise details of his original dispositions are impossible to determine, since they were not those of the battle as it was fought. We know the essentials, however, and they were these. Within the southern margin of the wood, between the Borestone and the road, he placed his own division, probably facing the crossing of the burn and astride the road, which goes down from a point a little east of the Borestone exactly along the west wall of the present schoolhouse garden at Whins of Milton. Between his front and the ford, west of the road, was a stretch of bad ground, Milton Bog : he extended this ' badness ' to the other side of the road by causing his men to dig, where the ground rises, a large number of small knee-

deep holes or 'pots,' a foot across, and to cover
them over with their own turf on sticks, his idea
being obviously, as at Loudoun Hill, to force the
enemy to attack on a narrow front. These pots play
an enormous part in history : in the actual battle they
played none at all, unless to get some fugitives into
trouble.[1]

The King's position at this point is known for certain, and Randolph's whereabouts is also known : he
was ' beside the kirk to keep the way '—holding the
road, that is, at a second line, rather more than a
half-mile in from the King's extreme front, where the
road rises on the slope of Coxet Hill, about the level
of St Ninians Kirk. His position was roughly that of the
present St Ninians recreation-ground, whose upper
wall is on the line of the road. He was only just within
the eastern and northern rim of the wood, and from
later events seems to have been intended to watch the
plateau outside it. We do not know exactly how he
faced, but the idea seems to have been that if the enemy
refused the road and attempted to march by the plateau,
Randolph would be able to move and engage them in
front, while the King and the other divisions fell on
flank and rear. For the other two, our information is
not precise : we know that they were *between* Randolph

---

[1] The famous calthrops seem to be pure myth. Barbour describes
the pots in careful detail (the English never knew anything about
them) but has not a word of calthrops. The only thing that ap-
proaches contemporary mention is a casual reference in the poem
of Edward's clerical laureate Baston . . . who seems, like some later
Special Correspondents, to have written his description before the
event, and merely altered the conclusion *ad hoc*.

and the King, with Sir Edward, apparently, the nearer to his brother, as at the feint of engagement that opened the action of the day on which the battle was expected, he is known to have moved to support him. We shall not be far out in putting Douglas about the site of the present new hospital since the road crosses under the detached superintendent's house, and Sir Edward somewhere between that and the Borestone : but we do not know how either faced. Nor does it matter. As I have said already, the actual battle ran on lines unforeseen, and of the original dispositions only the King's and Randolph's—both certainly known—are of importance. Where Keith and his cavalry were meant to be is quite unknown, and equally unimportant. The odds are on Robert's right flank : but it does not matter. The whereabouts of one further division is known. Those mentioned already, except Keith's light horse, were all troops of the line. The light irregular foot, the ' yeomen and poueraille,' the school-book camp-followers, had been sent with the baggage and commissariat to the dip between Coxet Hill and the Gillies Hill, which it is customary to call a valley, though the word in fact is rather over-emphatic. Their orders were clearly to stay there for the time, for everything we know about the battle suggests the King's reliance on *formation*, on being able to move his men in closely formed units, a point which contributed vitally to the result, and of which Barbour makes him speak with much emphasis.

Things stood thus, then, early on a blazing morning of summer, before the great rampart of hills beyond the Forth, rising coloured from the flat carse with its fantastic loops of the broad river. It was win or lose all now : those morning hours of inaction would be long.

Edward's great host had bivouacked at Falkirk, after a hot forced march of twenty miles from Edinburgh. At this dawn they were within half that distance of Stirling, and both Robert and Moubray, the Governor of Stirling, were equally anxious to know just how they were coming. Both attempted to find out. The King sent out Keith and Douglas to reconnoitre, with a cavalry detachment.

> And soyn the gret host haf thai seyn,
> Quhar scheldis schynand war so scheyne,
> And basnetis weill burnyst bricht,
> That gaf agane the sonne gret licht.
> Thai saw so fele (*many*) browdyn baneiris,
> Standartis, penownys, and speris,
> And so fele knychtis apon stedis,
> All flawamand into thair wedis,
> And so feill battalis (*divisions*) and so braid.

The great host moved through the summer morning in all its glitter of steel and heraldic colour, and the Scots captains rode back with the news. It must have been even worse than they had looked for, for they told it privately to the King, and he bade them conceal it, and carried on, apparently undisturbed.

The glittering masses advanced through the wood on the south, with the fate of Scotland on the points of their lances. No King of England had led a more splendid army. A few miles from the crossing of the

R

Bannock they were met by Moubray, who had ridden from Stirling Castle round the Scots flank. His intelligence service seems to have been good, for he was able to warn Edward that the forest tracks were blocked, and the road held. He considered himself to be technically relieved, as the English were within the agreed three leagues and he in touch with them : and it would seem he advised them to go no farther. At all events, their main body certainly halted, and decided that before, or instead of, a general engagement, they would attempt to effect the relief of the castle, by throwing into it a detachment of picked cavalry under Sir Robert Clifford and Sir Henry Beaumont. Clearly, these could not attempt to go by the road, and the first blunder of the day was made. They should have gone by Moubray's route round the back of the Gillies Hill : instead, someone whose local topography was better than his sense of strategy pointed out a shorter one. *Below* the Bannockburn Gorge a bridle-track, still extant as a foot-path and right of way, crosses the burn and follows the *bottom* rim of the slope that falls from the plateau, till it reaches a point more or less under St Ninians Kirk, where it rises on to the plateau and makes for the road : it would be the common way from Stirling to Bannockburn village, and until it rises by the Kirk men riding on it would be invisible from all but the edge of the plateau itself, much more from the wood.

Beaumont's detachment, then, swung out to the east, came out from the wood near this lower ford over the

burn, and found themselves looking straight across the
carse at Stirling Castle in the morning sun.   Seen
thence—from the present Bannockburn Sewage Works
—it stands astounding : one sees the rock of it from
the narrow side, sheer, like a tower itself with the castle
for crown, poising higher, it seems, than the mountains
that spread beyond it, like some incredible illumination
in the border of an Arthurian romance.   It was there
in plain sight and sun, challenging England, straight
before them over two miles of level ground, with not
a sign of any Scottish army.   And if they had blundered in choosing their road thus, a counter-blunder,
as often happens in war, brought them very near to
success, in spite of that.

Not quite, though.   They jingled peacefully along
under the slope, and Randolph, who should have been
moving to intercept them, had clearly bungled the
posting of his scouts, for he never knew they were
there till they all but passed him.   The King was aware
of them, though,[1] and when there was no sound of
movement behind him, sent a caustic message informing his general that he looked very like wrecking his
reputation—that ' a rose had fallen from his chaplet.'
In fact it was, like Waterloo, ' a d——d near thing.'
But Randolph rose very handsomely to the occasion.

He took a detachment—Barbour says five hundred,
so it was probably less—and hurled them out of the

[1] From about the Borestone they *might* have been seen for a
moment as they passed the gully that holds Broomridge Farm,
rather more than half-way from the ford to the level of the Kirk.
It is difficult to be sure because of buildings.

wood, across Beaumont's advance. Where they met is
quite impossible to determine : it may have been the
present ' Randolph's Field ' but that name is on no map
before 1780. It was probably somewhat to the south
of that. Wherever he halted, he drew them up in the
schiltrom. What followed we know from Gray, whose
father was in the front rank of the English force.

Beaumont, according to Gray, was for swinging
round their flank, which seems on the face of it sensible
enough, since his job was clearly to get his men into
Stirling. Gray's father told him he was too late, and
there was tough work coming. (Why *too late* is not
very easy to make out, and Gray does not explain : the
area is so built now one cannot decide, but there may
have been bog on their flank. Old Gray had seen many
years of Scots service, and possibly knew the ground.)
Beaumont lost his temper and jeered at him for a
coward, whereat Gray spurred between him and
D'Eyncourt, who was leading, and charged, with the
others after him at the gallop.

They crashed on the spears. D'Eyncourt was killed
at the onset : Gray, his horse killed under him, fell
and was taken prisoner. The charge did not break the
ring. Beaumont and Clifford drew off, charging at a
fresh place, wheeling their command about the unbroken circle, and flinging it again and again at the
spears. It was wild work, and hot in every sense :
they fought sweating under the sun of midsummer
noon, the dust rising like smoke from the dry trampled
ground. Again and again Beaumont sought to break

the ring, and still the impenetrable spears held good,
till his men took to flinging their maces and even their
swords at their opponents, in hopes to make a breach.
Some of the Scots rear rank must have carried bows,
for Barbour tells how they shot from within the schiltrom, and at that short range brought down both men
and horses.[1]

It went on and on. Douglas, in command of the
next division, grew worried, and with some difficulty
got the King's leave to lead down a reinforcement of
his own men. They plunged out of the wood, their
eyes on the fight, and as they drew near they saw that
the English were wavering, and Douglas, like the great
gentleman he was, shouted orders to halt, for it was
Randolph's fight and he was winning, and the fame of
the exploit should be fully his. The mere sight of
Douglas's detachment had worked, though. The
English, already weakening, fell into confusion, some
of them, no doubt, trying to wheel about. Foot, by all
the laws of tactics, cannot charge cavalry : but Highland
infantry have been known to do it, and this was one
of the times . . . and it succeeded. Randolph flung
his men, still in schiltrom, at the wavering English
knights, and drove right through them. What had
been the flower of King Edward's knighthood fled,
losing all formation, one part galloping past the Scots
foot towards the castle, the rest by the road they had

[1] Both Mr Barron and Dr Mackenzie take *schutis* to mean *leap out*.
I am no soldier, but even a training with the foil makes it clear that
men who did so would be ridden down at once, besides leaving a
disastrous breach. And we are definitely told that there was none.

come, to their own main body. Foot may break
cavalry, but they cannot chase them. Randolph's men
pulled off their helmets, mopped their sweat, and—
though that detail is one that Barbour omits—undoubtedly thought with affection about beer. The
Quatre Bras of the battle was won and lost.

So indeed was the main action, in great measure,
before the opposing armies were fairly in touch. A
victory, as Napoleon wisely said, and as Bruce and
James Douglas knew very well in their day, depends
not on the number of killed but on that of the fright-
ened. And the moral effect of the action was immense :
the chroniclers, of both sides, make that quite certain.
The gilt-edged cavalry ought to have ridden over foot
as if they were furrows : and the footmen had not
merely held their own—Randolph's casualties, apparently, were minute—but had charged the cavalry and
broken it. It was not decent. It was against all rules.
The English knights, with their tails between their
legs, were neither popular nor exhilarating when what
was left of them got back to King Edward. If those
devils in the wood could break mailed knights, the outlook for the mere private was not at all pleasant.
Randolph's detachment, and their waiting comrades,
took, naturally, another point of view. They had been
resolute : now they were exultant. And, at the other
side of the position, events had occurred that were
anything but likely to dash their mood.

On the arrival of Moubray, as has been said, the
main body of the English army had halted, some dis-

tance short of the exit from the wood at the Roman
ford. Moubray, however, must have struck their line
of march behind their advance-guard, who went on
unchecked : or perhaps (I think myself this is more
likely) on learning the road was held the higher command ordered the advance-guard forward to reconnoitre the alternative route, that would avoid an attack
on the Scots prepared positions : one must remember
that many of the English officers would have known
that country and road from former campaigns.

The advance-guard moved on, at any rate : they
were heavy cavalry, under Gloucester, King Edward's
young nephew, and Hereford, the Constable of England. What follows depends on a shaping of the
ground impossible to give even on a large-scale map.
They debouched from the wood and went on across
the burn : if they did not take the road, they were
very near it, for just westward of this point, and on the
east not much more than a couple of hundred yards
off, the crossing becomes impracticable for a long distance. There, Bruce on his horse at the Borestone
could just have seen them, but the upward roll of the
ground north of the burn would mask them, and the
Scots army, from each other.

Before them, to their right, was an inviting gentle
slope of good ground, with the tops of the New Park
trees above its skyline. But the tree-tops would cease
almost in front of them.[1] They swung their men,

---

[1] This point of the trees is necessarily conjectural, as there are
none there now. The Borestone flagstaff offers something to go by.

therefore, to the right, rode up the slope, and found two most relevant pieces of information. On their right front, as they topped the gentle rise, was a long advance of open champaign country, raised above the wet carse, perfect ground for cavalry, and stretching straight before them like a broad road—it looks so from that place—to the dramatic upthrust of Stirling Castle : one would not be surprised if there was some cheering. On their left front the wood edge of the New Park swept gently upward, and visible in the trees was a force of Scots moving, apparently in flight —King Robert's men, being marshalled ready for action.

Hereford's nephew, a knight called Henry de Bohun, was leading. He rode out ahead to make sure just what was doing, and realising the Scots were not in flight, he signalled to his force to fall back on the ford. Then he saw something that made him unsling his lance. A man had ridden out from the Scots position, in full armour but riding only a little grey hack : and there was a crown instead of a crest on his helmet. King Robert himself had been marshalling his men, and had ridden forward to watch the English movements.

De Bohun was fully armed, on a barded horse. He saw his chance to end the war at a stroke, dropped his lance to the rest, struck in his spurs, and charged. The

One has to allow for the higher eye-level of a mounted man, for in ground of that nature even a few feet of extra height make a difference.

King had no lance, but only a light axe : he held his ground and let De Bohun charge him full, and then— it would need the most consummate timing—just short of the impact swung round his little hack, rose in the stirrups, and as De Bohun thundered past, brought the axe down in one crashing blow on his helmet. The axe shaft broke, but the blade went through steel and bone.[1]

It was the St Ninians affair on the single scale. The English advance-guard wavered as they saw it, and the Scots that the King had been marshalling advanced, Edward Bruce apparently moving up in support. They did make contact, and there was some fighting, in which De Bohun's squire, standing gallantly by his master's body, was killed. But the English gave ground and fell back across the burn, and since they were mounted and his own cavalry scarce, the King held back his men from the pursuit. His officers came about him with reproach that he had taken the very serious risk of standing up to De Bohun at such odds of equipment : but all that they got out of their commander was ' I am sorry my good axe is broken.'

By this time the day was growing well advanced. The initiative, up to this stage of affairs, had been with the English, but their use of it had so far been rather worse than ineffective. The reason why Edward did not attempt to push on—there must have been several hours of daylight yet—seems less the

---

[1] Between Whins of Milton School and the burn is the place, about where the by-road bridge goes over the lade.

result of an eight-mile march in hot weather than the condition of his men's morale. We know, from their own disgusted historians, that it was decidedly the worse for wear. And the long march of the day before would not help matters.

Edward's staff decided, then, to bivouac for the night, where they could find water, and bring the Scots to action in the morning . . . provided these latter did not attack in the night. It is likely that water had much to do with what followed. They had over 3000 horses besides the men, and at least the better part of a thousand oxen : and the weather was scorching, even apart from the dust of such an army on ill-made roads.

Now the standard assumption of historians, who are too often given to seeing men as words walking, and therefore to ignoring such things as this multiple thirst, is that the English army did try the road, or, crossing the Bannock Burn by the Roman ford, deployed by the *left*, to the west, on a broad front, and attacked on the battlefield marked on the Ordnance map. I have a battle-map in my possession, in one of the standard historical atlases, which shows them so doing, in nine neat divisions. Now (apart from thirst and the local configuration) this looks very neat and rational on paper. But all the fourteenth-century accounts agree in contradicting it point blank. Gray's description of the battle, those of the Lanercost Chronicler, the Monk of Malmesbury (*Vita Edwardi*) and Barbour, are clearly independent of each other ; but they all fit into each

other, and the ground. Gray's father was present,
the Monk may have been, and he and the Chronicler,
who says definitely that he had his story from a trust-
worthy eyewitness, are both contemporary. Barbour
clearly had talked it over with men who had been
there. And their joint testimony, *when one looks at the
ground*, is both coherent and intelligible. It is with
Fordun that the assumptions begin, and they have
accumulated ever since.

One must remember that neither side had guns.
The plateau reconnoitred in the morning, the ' hard
field ' east of the wood, looked excellent for advance
if the Scots would not stand, and no less excellent for
cavalry evolutions if they would. Edward's staff
decided to halt by the nearest water within reach of it,
and, apparently, either to beat the wood or to advance
along the edge of it : we do not know which, as they
were not in fact allowed to do either.

They swung right from the ford, and found the
fovea—the Bannock Gorge—across their path. They
could not get down to water until it ended, just where
the plateau sinks to the low carse. The slope is possible
there even for waggons, if the skids are on, and there
was plenty of water, and with the peats, which by Midsummer Day would be cut and stacked for carting,
any amount of good fuel for cooking supper. They
flooded down the slope, then, to the water, just above
where Skeoch steading stands to-day, and the railway
bridge goes over the Bannock Burn. Then they found
themselves floundering on rotten ground—*vn mauueis*

parfound ruscelle marras Gray calls it, cut up with
sykes, pools, and peat-hags, and squelching with moss.
They unroofed some houses, presumably from Bannockburn village,[1] and used the beams and thatch to
bridge the worst, and apparently a party got to the
castle under cover of dark, and brought back doors
and shutters. Their position for access to the ' hard
field,' the plateau along the wood, was fairly good.
Edward's staff, from the brae-face above the camp,
to the south of the burn—or to the north of it either—
could see over the plain : and the slope from the plain
to the carse is for some half a mile from the end of the
gorge (along the present Balquhiderock Wood, that is)
quite possible for cavalry at a walk.

It is to be hoped they found the fact consoling, for
that, and a meal, was all the comfort they had. They
lay very miserably through the night. They had food,
they had water—very much too much water—but they
dared not unarm, or even unbit their horses : and
small doubt but the midges and clegs improved the
occasion. And the day's events had done nothing to
help their morale. There was grousing, and worse.
Someone sent heralds round to address the men, in a
desperate attempt to raise their spirits, but no addresses
would get over the fact that they were horribly un-
comfortable and that their crack cavalry had been cut
up that morning by a —— lot of —— Scots *infantry,*

---

[1] It is odd that it does not seem to occur to anyone that the traditional name of the battle bears out this site. The *burn*, it is agreed,
is not big enough to have played any important part in the battle :

who might be down on them any time during the
darkness. In fact, *durement avoient pardu countenance,
et estoit de trop mal covyne pur la iournee passe.*

Meanwhile, the Scots had to make up their minds
what to do with the unforeseen situation. The expected major action had not come off. The success
of such fighting as the day had seen had been, and very
brilliantly, with the Scots, but the King knew that
the real issue was not decided. Man for man, and at
longer odds, his men were proved, but he had word
now of the full weight against them, and it seems to
have been more than he had expected, from his care
in concealing from the army at large (who knew well
enough they were in for something big) the result of
Keith's and Douglas's reconnaissance. Another Falkirk would mean the end of Scotland. The prudent
course was to draw off to the Lennox, as he could now
without damage to morale, and trust to another campaign of manoeuvre and harassing guerilla tactics on
the lines that had been so successful in 1310. In that
direction lay almost certain success : but such a success, won before, had proved inconclusive. The alternative (and he had to decide this at once) was to stake
everything on a conclusion, take advantage of a strong
position, the initial moral success, and Edward's
blunder in delaying attack, and fight the thing to a
finish, then and there. A victory might well mean the

but if the site of Edward's camp was close to the *village* (instead of a
mile from it, to the west of the road, or a couple of miles off in the
carse at Muirton) the name is understandable enough : we know
that the main action was close to the camp.

end of the war. A defeat would certainly end it, and
Scotland as well.

We know what he chose. The accounts of Gray
and Barbour, as to how the choice was arrived at, are
different, but there is no reason why both should not
be true. Gray's story is that the matter was hanging
in doubt, with an inclination to the more prudent
course, when Alexander Seton, who may have been
some kin to Christina's husband, deserted from the
English and coming to Bruce informed him of their
demoralised condition. Barbour says the army surrounded Randolph to cheer him as he came in, and
the King addressed them, and put the question to
them, Fight or move. That he should put such a
question to the army is so improbable, in mediaeval
war, that it seems unlikely to be mere invention :
fiction has to be much more probable than fact. If it
were put, it is eloquent of the relation between the
King and his men, and of the latter's attitude to the
war. The point against Barbour is whether the army
would have been allowed to break rank to that extent
with the enemy so near. We know that the original
positions were spread over something like three-
quarters of a mile. The most likely solution would
seem to be that the King spoke in turn to each division,
and Barbour, to save repetition, ran the speeches in
one : it is a most stirring speech. Or he may have put
the issue to a council of officers, and Barbour, perhaps
getting the points of both from the same informant,
telescoped what he said with a later address to the

troops. It is worth remarking that what Barbour makes him say is not the rhetoric of an epic poem : it is so full of a practical grip of the immediate situation that either Barbour was a first-rate novelist with a good deal of military training, or it represents a lively recollection of what King Robert actually said, derived from a man who had heard, and as he well might, remembered the main points, even some of the phrasing.

The decision was made to stand, at all events, and they lay on their arms in the wood for the short summer night, with the English camp-fires gleaming on the carse, and those of Midsummer here and there on the hills that walled the low country, *champ clos* for opposing nations, with Scotland's very existence staked on the morning.

Even so far south, it would scarcely be dark three hours. At the first note of dawn, the priests with the army said mass. The day was the festival of St John Baptist, and the Lesson for the mass is the great fortieth chapter of Isaiah, ' Comfort ye, comfort ye, my people. . . . Speak ye comfortably to Jerusalem, and cry unto her that her warfare is accomplished,' while the Gospel breaks in its midst into the triumph of the *Benedictus*—' that we should be saved from our enemies, and from the hand of all that hate us . . .' and the praise of God's mercy, that gives light to them that sit in darkness and the shadow of death. Some of the priests, in arms below their vestments, must have felt their voices shake at the great words. Mass went over,

and the Abbot of Inchaffray blessed the army. Then
the rations were issued, and in accordance with the
custom before an important engagement, the King
made knights. Young Walter Stewart was one, and
another James Douglas, which seems rather strange :
by now he had won spurs enough for a squadron. But
it may be that he had some kind of vow to abstain from
knighthood till the final issue : it would accord with
the temper of the time. Or perhaps the record is
only intended to mean a raising to banneret, which by
tradition was always effected on the field of battle.
Barbour's phrase, that they were made ' ilk ane in thair
degree,' suggests that some changed the pennon for
the square banner.

King Robert had recast his dispositions. The
English had chosen that beautiful cavalry ground . . .
and his eye for country promptly took in its weakness,
and saw how he could make them sorry for it. He
broke every conceivable orthodox law of tactics, but
by breaking them, as and in the place he did, he immobilised a great mass of the English army. The
fundamental idea of the battle is really not at all unlike
Stirling Bridge. He got part of the enemy immobilised,
and wedged their active part into a loop, with the carse
and the gorge instead of the bend of the Forth, so that
their own number became their impediment, and their
own weight was turned back on them to destroy them.

Having conceived a flaming audacity, of throwing
away his cover and his high ground, and marching foot
against heavy cavalry, he went about it with long-

headed caution. His own division he held back in his
hand, keeping them under cover still by the Borestone :
the English accounts all agree as to *three* Scots 'battles,'
while we know there were four, and this is the reason
why : three were all they saw as the Scots moved to
attack. Bruce had sacrificed the cover of the wood :
but he saw the possibility it held for ' moral attack,'
and used that with great effect, as we shall see.

Sir Edward's division, Douglas's, and Randolph's,
marched out of the wood, then, with their banners
flying : the King had asked for a brave show of these,
for knowing men he knew how imagination, and resolution, are stimulated by a material sign. They came
down from the wood in an inverted wedge, Douglas
between but a little behind the others.[1] The English
trumpets sounded the alarm. Edward's men mounted
in haste and some confusion : it was vital they should
get up from the carse, and their confusion would not
be amended by the fact that they had looked for a night
raid, and the dawn would just have made them feel
safe from attack, and convinced them the Scots were
going to keep the defensive.

Edward was in a post whence he saw the advance—
on the slope at the mouth of the gorge, very probably—
and they say that he cried out to Umfraville, ' What,

---

[1] The formation seems odd, but the Lanercost Chronicle mentions
it categorically, and Barbour's account of the order in which the
divisions made contact is only explicable by such an arrangement,
unless we are to assume that two divisions went through the clumsy
and pointless evolution of changing place with each other during
the night.

S

will these Scots fight ? ' perplexed, perhaps, that footmen should challenge knights, and mocking at such a
contemptible little army. Umfraville, who was a
Baliol Scot, knew they meant business, and said so,
advising Edward to fall back and adopt the old tactic
of a feigned retreat. Edward would not—from arro-
gance, Barbour says, and may be right : but in any
case, his position being what it was, it would have been
difficult to take the advice.

The Scots came down on the plain between wood
and carse, and there they halted, dropped on their
knees, and said a Paternoster.[1] Edward mistook the
gesture, and cried out joyfully, ' They are asking
mercy,' and Umfraville, who was a Scot after all, told
him curtly, ' True enough. But not of you. I tell
you certainly, those men will win or perish.'

The English, as many as could, swarmed up the
slope, but between the haste and the ground, the
pressure of those behind, and the latter's difficulty in
seeing what was happening, their deployment was
clearly confused : and the confusion was rapidly made
worse. Someone had got the archers into action, posting them, probably, strung out along the north side of
the gorge, where they poured a hot fire on the advancing
Scots schiltroms and incidentally sprinkled their own
front ranks as well, which would not cheer these, since

[1] Some historians deny this, as unlikely. But it was before the
day when many Scots preferred to address their Maker sitting down,
and the evidence is not only Barbour but the Lanercost Chronicler,
who makes Scots out no more pious than he can help—to put his
attitude very mildly indeed.

to find oneself under the fire of one's own side
does not strengthen confidence in one's higher
command.

The archers were a grave danger to the Scots. The
whole battle depended on the unbroken schiltrom.
King Robert, remembering Falkirk, was ready for
them, and sent Keith and the cavalry out by his right.
The rise where the St Ninians-Bannockburn road runs
now would conceal them almost until the moment of
impact. They drove down on the flank of the English
archers, who could not have seen them in time to make
a stand, and who were not armed to meet horsemen at
close quarters. The archers broke, flying to the deploy-
ing English line, and causing further confusion and
shock to morale, while some of them were struck down
by their own comrades.

The advancing schiltroms narrowed the ' hard
ground,' cramping the English, who were cramped still
more by the rushing pressure of their own advancing
rear, who, remember, would many of them be unable
to see precisely what was happening on their front,
though they could hear the sounds of beginning action.
Someone ordered a countercharge of cavalry : it was
probably this that caught the archers' fire, since the
first moves of the general engagement were of course
going on simultaneously with Keith's attack. It might
have held up the Scots advance a little, and given the
English time and room to deploy. But the chance was
missed. Gloucester and Hereford quarrelled over who
was to lead it. Hereford held to his rights, as Con-

stable, and young Gloucester, losing his temper, flung
alone at the Scots, before his own five hundred men
could follow, and was killed at once, to King Robert's
great regret.   The English van, under Hereford,
charged after, and crashed against Edward Bruce's
advancing schiltrom, the Scots right.   The English
right seems to have tried to charge too, for to break
the schiltroms, get the ground clear to form for an
attack in mass, was their obvious counter, and King
Robert had seen that the night before, when he im-
plored the schiltroms to keep formation and not to
break their ranks whatever happened.   Randolph, well
away to Sir Edward's left, met them full, let them
shatter against his front like a wave on a rock, and drove
on into the confused mass of the English, 'as ... plungit
in the se:' and into the gap between the two Scottish
wings came Stewart and Douglas, closing the moving
wall.

The whole note of the orders is ' Press, press.'   The
gorge pinned the English helpless on their left.   Their
right and rear were held up by their own front :   many
men never struck a blow that day, and two hundred
knights never even drew their swords, not for cowardice—the panic came much later—but simply because
they never had the chance.

The eddying confusion in middle and rear grew
worse as remorseless pressure drove in the front, and
the Scots archers, from the slope behind their own
line, poured in a short-range fire above the schiltroms.
Their arrows would go down too in the mass on the

carse, of men and horses struggling to reach the
plateau, and not able to see what they could hear in
front. Then, out from the wood, the King led in his
reserve. It seems to have struck in upon the flank,
alongside the rest, pinning the English wing and
buckling their line still further. It was probably under
the stress of this new impact that an appalling thing
happened. The muddled men and the maddened
horses broke : the steady pressure drove them left on
the gorge, whose bank goes down steep and suddenly
from the plain, and a flood of men and squealing, kick-
ing stallions poured over the edge, where *chescun
cheoit sur autre*—mailed men and their crazy beasts in
one awful confusion, helpless. No wonder that Bannockburn ' was in English mouths for many years
thereafter,' because of that horror. To look at the place,
and think of it, makes one sick. And yet one can see
exactly how it would happen.

Panic spread, and now a shout rose from the schiltroms, ' On them ! They fail ! ' The pressure grew
fiercer yet : and then there was more shouting from a
fresh quarter, and from the dark obscurity of the wood
there appeared another division of the Scots. It was
the ' small folk,' from behind Coxet Hill. Schoolbook
tradition says they came of themselves. It is much
more likely that they were part of the plan, for—Mr
Barron has made the point before me—no discipline
could keep Highlanders out of a fight unless they were
given a clear strategic reason . . . and a general who
tackles a force three times his own will certainly want

every able-bodied man, though not necessarily, if some are ill-drilled, for shock-troops.

They came pouring from the wood, in rough formation, and remembering the King's words overnight, they had made banners out of the camp blankets. The sight of them struck on the broken English nerves : there was no knowing what more the wood might hold, on top of the devils it had let loose already. There was excuse, for King Edward's staff threw their hand in, and tried to get their master clear of the field, making for Beaumont's and Clifford's track by the slope. The sight of the royal banner in visible flight, with a new force advancing yelling from the wood, completed the demoralisation of the English. They broke hideously, in a tangled fleeing mob without formation, while here and there men more stubborn than the rest fought on singly or in small groups till they went down. They fled all ways. Many of them were caught in the hell of the gorge—*ecce, quaedam fossa multos absorbuit.* Some got across, perhaps higher up, and dismounted : some—they were a considerable number—streamed after King Edward, by the bridle-path to Stirling. The bulk, it would seem, poured back through their own lines, breaking up their rear and carrying away its ranks in the flood of their own panic across the carse—no ground for fleeing men and heavy horses. Many were drowned or trodden into the marsh, or the mossy lower reaches of the burn, of which some, even with the carse drained, are dangerous yet. Even Forth, a mile off, seems to have taken its toll with its broad strong current : the winding ' links ' twist unexpectedly with their low banks, a trap for men flying blindly, perhaps seeking some half-known ford at the wrong tide : there are vague suggestions that the tide played a part : it would have risen, too, in the sykes of the carse.

King Edward's staff and bodyguard cut their way out, some hundreds of them, still in some kind of formation. Edward was a fool, but no coward, and he would have stayed : he was forced by Pembroke and Sir Giles de Argentine at either rein, laying about him with his mace. It took some bitter fighting to get him clear, for Edward was the major prize of the action. The Scots knights, on foot, flung themselves at his horse's housings and clung there, but his party were well mounted and got clear, galloping for the castle. When they were out, Argentine loosed his master's rein, and said, as both Scots and English testify, ' I am not used to flee, and I will not now,' swung his horse round, struck spurs, and charged the Scots, fighting among the mellay until he died. He was counted to be the third best knight of his day, after Bruce himself and Henry of Luxembourg whom he had served ; and if he could not lead as could these others, he was a brave man, and his death, though useless, is one of the things that are perhaps less useless than they appear when weighed in the grocer's scales.

Pembroke and Edward had clearly lost their heads.

and Moubray, who had reached the castle before
them (he had been fighting in the English ranks) had
unluckily the sense to tell them so, pointing out that
by the terms of his agreement he would have to hand
over the castle to King Robert.   So, being well
mounted, they made off again, got round the Scots
rear by the back of the Gillies Hill, and headed east
for Dunbar.   Someone saw them, and reported, and
Douglas flung himself into the saddle, scraped together
what cavalry he could lay hands on—they were probably pretty scattered by now in pursuit—and went
after full pelt.   He had too few men, however, to cut
them off, though he hung on their rear and chivvied
them all the way, and King Edward got safely within
the red walls of Dunbar, whence he could fly by sea
to Bamborough.   He founded Oriel College as thank-
offering.   It was the best thing England got out of that
war, and it is pleasant to be able to note that the tombstone of a Provost of Oriel now adorns the belfry of
St Ninians Kirk.

   The other fugitives who had swarmed to Stirling
were also refused admission to the castle.   They took
up a position on the crag of the rock, and it took an
attack in force to break them up : they surrendered
at discretion almost at once, but according to Barbour
their action saved King Edward, as we are told there
were so many of them that King Robert had to keep
his men still in formation, in case of a counter-attack
if they should scatter.   This rally undoubtedly saved
many fugitives, and if it had been a little more firmly

handled would have saved many more, since it led the King's force to the north, while the bulk of the English, of course, were flying southward.

Hereford, Angus, Umfraville, and some others (the latter two were kinsmen and Baliol Scots) rallied a sizable body, and tried for Carlisle : but on the way the chief of them took shelter in Bothwell Castle, whose governor surrendered, refugees and all, to the Scots. Pembroke fled on foot with some Welsh, and got away, to the great saving of his tenants' pockets : his ransom, after Methven, might not have been light.[1] The keepers of Edward's seal and shield were taken : he had to make proclamation about the seal, and King Robert, hearing of it, politely returned the missing property. Twenge, the hero of Stirling Bridge, hid his arms in a bush, and surrendered the next morning to Robert in person, who received him kindly, and let him go without ransom. The Englishman Trokelowe, in fact, says that the King treated the prisoners with so much courtesy that many after felt grateful affection for him. The most entertaining of the captives was an English clerical poet, one Baston by name, who had come provided with an exciting account of what he thought he was about to witness : his lavish descriptions of King Edward's great victory not unnaturally gave ribald joy to the Scots, who let him go on condition he brought his epic up to date. The good Baston, a true

[1] He was caught later by a Burgundian while on his way to Rome, and carried into Imperial territory, and it cost him £20,000 to get home.

journalist, obliged, and adapted the praises neatly for King Robert.

The English casualties were, for a mediaeval battle, very high, not only in the fighting but in the rout. Bruce's cavalry were too scarce for effective pursuit of such a great force flying in all directions, but the fugitives were a long way from the Border, and though the King's own treatment of prisoners was kindly, much of the country had long scores to pay. Many starving men were rounded up and killed or taken by the country-folk, even the women joining in the chase. The spoils also were huge. The English had come splendidly equipped : we hear of the gold plate and ' vermeil '—silver-gilt—dishes that their gentlemen had brought as camp-furniture, and they lost the whole of their luxurious baggage, to the tune of a couple of hundred thousand pounds of mediaeval money. Some five hundred prisoners of rank were held to ransom, or exchanged : Hereford's wife was given fifteen Scots prisoners of importance to offer for her husband : they included the Queen, Princess Marjorie, Christina Bruce and her son the young Earl of Mar, and old Bishop Wishart, now blind, who thus came home after eight years of prison. There is no sign anywhere of Lady Buchan, and it seems as if she had died a prisoner.

The Scots losses are said to have been very small. Few men of note fell, and none of the greater leaders, while the casualties of the ' other ranks ' were slight. Indeed, so long as it remained unbroken, the schiltrom formation meant a very low butcher's bill for the troops that used it. In short, the victory was as complete as could be.[1]

It was victory, but it was not success yet. The war was to drag for another fourteen years. But the terms of it, after that Midsummer Day, were different. Scotland was cleared. The remaining castles surrendered, all but Berwick, and Stirling was razed. Better, Scotland was now united. There was no doubting now who was her king, and no King of Scots has ever been more beloved. The material odds, for the rest of the war, were great still, but the moral ones now were enormously with the Scots. Bannockburn did in fact exact its payment, for the tactics used there were foolishly used again by men who copied them mechanically when they would have been very much wiser to rely on those of *King Robert's Testament* : they cost us Dupplin Moor and Halidon Hill, while on the defeated side Edward's grandson and great-great-grandson learned from them how to win Poitiers and Agincourt. Yet, none the less, the memory of that day was like a flag in men's minds, above any defeat. In the blackest of the weary Three Hundred Years War that begins with the Sack of Berwick in 1296, men recalled, in the words of the gallant old English poet, ' *That* was got over, therefore so may this be,' set

[1] Edward Bruce's great friend, Sir Walter de Ross, was killed, to his deep grief : and apparently the feud between him and his brother-in-law Athol, over Sir Walter's sister, came to a head at this time, for Athol, in the night before the battle, cut up a Scots convoy under Herth at Cambuskenneth, presumably on its way across the ferry : Stirling Bridge, of course, was commanded by the castle.

their teeth and saw through what looked like final disaster . . . and held firm till it proved not final after all. A man may be defeated when he is dead. A nation is not till it accepts defeat. And a nation with Bannockburn as a living remembrance would not make that admission while one man could stand.

IV

THE WAR FOR PEACE

FOURTEEN YEARS: 1314–1328

' Carduus et spinis surgit . . . acutis.'

Virgil, *Eclogues*.

CHAPTER XII

THE WAR CONTINUES

SIX YEARS : 1314–1320

'Les Escossois sont durs et hardis et fort travailleurs en armes et en guerre, et à ce temps là ils aimoient et prisoient assez peu les Anglois.'

J. Froissart, xxxiv.

THE English army had been completely crushed in the open field, and save for Berwick, Scotland was practically clear of the enemy. King Robert, apparently, waited for two or three weeks to see if any move were made towards peace. There was none. For another thirteen years, in fact, the English authorities, in the phrase Miss Daviot gives to Richard II after the collapse of another such attempt at the annexation of a neighbouring kingdom, ' wasted men and money in a futile struggle, and when someone ' (like the luckless Andrew Harclay) ' suggested it would be sensible to stop the silly business, they talked about prestige, and were shocked and furious.'

If peace were not granted, it would have to be forced : and Scotland was in better case to force it than she had been for the last quarter-century. In fact, for the whole of this last phase of the struggle, very little actual fighting is on Scots soil. Having received no proposals, King Robert decided on a demonstration in force, sending troops south in early August, under

Douglas and Sir Edward, to sweep through Northumberland. Durham paid ransom, and they went on past it as far as Teesdale, and marched home by the west, burning Appleby as they passed. He then wrote to King Edward, offering peace, and appointing as commissioners the Constable and the Marischal, Hay and Keith, with his brother-in-law Neil Campbell, and Kirkpatrick. Edward called a parliament at York, and the terms were discussed. Commissioners were appointed to meet the Scots at Dumfries, while Pembroke was made Guardian of England North of Trent.

The negotiations came to nothing. England was willing enough for an armistice, but—perhaps encouraged by John of Lorne's recapture of Man—would not yet recognise the autonomy of Scotland, nor grant the royal title to King Robert : and the King knew that bitter as must be the prolongation of the war, any lower terms would make all that was won ineffective. The business had to be carried through to a finish. In the winter he invaded England again, and Cumberland bought a truce until Midsummer.

The King was now turned forty, and the four and a half years of his second marriage (leaving out the Queen's imprisonment, it is no more) had produced no heir. Something had to be done to determine the succession, and prevent his death from producing a repetition of 1290. In the latter part of April 1315, Parliament met at Ayr, and settled the question. Princess Marjorie was by now a young woman of about twenty, and her marriage arranged, to young

Walter Stewart, who had greatly distinguished himself at Bannockburn : but in the circumstances it was decided to postpone her rights, with her own consent, to those of her uncle Edward, now Earl of Carrick, whom the act describes as *vir strenuus et in artibus bellicis pro defensione iuris et libertatis Regni Scotiae expertus*, a clause which explains the avoidance of a queen. His heirs male were to follow, then Marjorie and her heirs, and if the King succeeding were a minor, Randolph was to be Regent. Should these fail, Randolph was still to be Regent until the barons should determine the succession.[1]

Sir Edward, thus brought close to the Scots throne, was approaching even more closely to another. Sometime in the winter or early spring after Bannockburn, the O'Neills of Ulster, pricked on no doubt by the example of Scotland, decided to break loose from the English dominion, and considered that a suitable leader for the attempt would be King Robert's brother. They approached him therefore, and offered to make him King over all Ireland. He, having helped King Robert, very loyally and devotedly, to a crown, had no objection to winning one for himself, and his brother

[1] After Edward and Marjorie, who had neither of them at this time any heir of their bodies, Edward's two sons being illegitimate, the male line of the Bruces would be extinct, since the other three brothers had all died unmarried. Isobel Bruce, the King's eldest sister, had only a daughter, Princess Ingebjorg of Norway : but Mary, Lady Campbell of Lochow, Christina, Countess Dowager of Mar, and Maude, Countess of Ross, who came after in that order, all had sons, while Margaret, the youngest but one, was also married.

T

could hardly refuse him his assistance. Moreover, a
free Ireland, under a king close kin to the royal house,
should promise an invaluable ally, lying as she did
upon the flank of England, who already had a Scots ally
to her rear. Indeed, had Sir Edward been able to
found a dynasty, the history not only of Ireland but of
Europe might have been very different from what it is.
It is hard to conceive a change in Irish history that
would not have had to be one for the better : and there
would certainly have been no Hundred Years War.

That was not to be, but the chance was one to be
taken. On the 26th of May, Edward landed at Carrickfergus in Ulster, with a Scots army, and a number of
the best Scots knights, among them Randolph, John
Stewart, cousin of Sir Walter, Soulis, Menteith, Sir
Philip Moubray, lately King Edward's Governor of
Stirling, and Ramsay of Auchterhouse, whose father,
Sir John, had been a friend of Wallace. The course of
the Irish War need not greatly concern us, though it
was a lively one. As Gray says of it (*ceo*) *seroit vn
graunt romaunce a rementynir tout*, and space presses.
I shall speak of it only as, in the next two years, it
comes into contact with affairs in Scotland.

Meanwhile the King, with young Stewart, had sailed
to the Isles, where he received the homage of the
chiefs. The Comyn blood-feud apart, he ' got on '
admirably with the Highlanders : when a force of any
size is under arms, the West Highlanders and Islesmen
are always in his division, and the Middle Highlands
rose for him before Carrick itself. By the time he

returned, the truces with the North of England had expired, and at the end of June Douglas raided Durham, occupying Hartlepool, while a few weeks later the King led an expedition by the western march, and sat down before Carlisle. He was better equipped than usual with siege artillery, but Carlisle was a very strong town under a fighting governor, Sir Andrew Harclay. The siege engines failed. A storm was attempted, under Douglas, who had joined the King : it all but succeeded, but was beaten back after very hot fighting, and Douglas himself was very nearly taken. An English relieving force came up, and the King, whose available man-power was seriously depleted by the Irish expedition, had to retire. It was the first English success for a number of years, and Harclay received 1000 marks from King Edward—well earned, for he had made a most gallant defence.

Early in January—that is, of 1316—the King and Douglas made an attempt on Berwick, and were again unsuccessful. They made a night attack on the land and sea sides simultaneously, and the moon came out at the wrong time, and showed them. The place, however, was still in a precarious situation, for the Scots fleet was cutting off supplies, and we have some desperate letters of the next months, complaining that even the horses have been eaten. By February the garrison were driven to mutiny by sheer starvation, and a party of Gascons, against orders, made a sortie to forage. They ran into Douglas, and there was a fierce little action near Coldstream. They lost twenty men-at-arms, including their commander, and sixty foot : but Douglas, according to Barbour, is said to have thought it his hottest minor action. It is worth noting, by the way, that they tried the Scottish tactic of the schiltrom.

In the early part of the year, King Robert was left childless. On the 2nd of March, Princess Marjorie, with child and near her time, was thrown from her horse. The shock killed her. The surgeons, desperate for the succession, delivered a living child from her dead body, who bore through his life the marks of that grim birth. Fifty-four years later he became King of Scots as Robert II, the sad father of a brilliant tragic line, shadowed among the royal houses of Europe.

Two months after Marjorie's death—that is, early in May—Edward Bruce was crowned King of Ireland, after more than a year of fierce successful war, of which Barbour gives a spirited description. He had defeated the Earl of Ulster (brother to Queen Elizabeth) at Connor in Antrim the previous September, Roger Mortimer at Kenliss about Christmas, and a few weeks later the Justiciar of Ireland, Edmund Butler, at Arscoll : and thereafter he laid siege to Carrickfergus, which arranged a truce. Relieving troops under Lord Mandeville broke the truce, and there was a fierce action, in which Mandeville was defeated and killed. The city had to surrender in the summer. Randolph, who had added to his fame by some distinguished service in this war, had been back in Scotland to see about reinforcements, and early in autumn King

Robert, leaving Douglas and Walter Stewart to act as
Regents, sailed from Lochryan with an expeditionary
force, and joined his brother at Carrickfergus.

The Irish war proved a disappointing sideshow.
King Robert appears to have suffered some kind of
defeat at the hands of his old enemy, Bisset of the
Glens of Antrim, who had sought to capture him nine
years before. The circumstances, even the date, are
obscure, but it cannot have been a serious disaster, as
the King's force was still in good case for further operations. Sir Edward, in spite of his coronation, was
master only of the North of Ireland, with a somewhat
uncertain hold even of that. The whole of the campaign is very obscure, but in the spring they advanced
by Louth, on the south-east march of Ulster, and
moved on Dublin. It was too strong for them, and
they marched south-west across Leinster and as far
into Munster, the southernmost of the Four Quarters,
as Limerick. We know little of what happened beyond
that it was a ghastly march through a country so
famine-stricken that there are rumours of cannibalism
among the native Irish. One small incident survives
—that King Robert, about to abandon a dangerous
position, learned that a camp-woman was taken in
labour, and since the poor soul was in no case to be
moved, halted rather than leave her to the enemy. It
would not, as soldiering, please Frederick the Great :
but it was recalled and valued as a lesson in manhood.

The campaign, for all its hideous hardships, proved
barren of results. Southern Ireland refused to make

cause with the new king, who after all was as much a foreign baron as any Plunkett or Mortimer from the Pale. A large English force had arrived, and under Edmund Butler and Richard de Clare, was based on Kilkenny in Leinster. Why they did not cut the Bruces off from Ulster is rather mysterious : if they made any sort of attempt to do so, it was unsuccessful, but the Bruces, with a strong force on their flank and rear, were compelled to fall back to the North and get above Butler, and probably decided also to adopt King Robert's policy of the Scots war, and make sure of the North before trying to push further.

In March 1317, King Robert, having spent the winter in Ireland, returned to his kingdom. Nothing had happened of very great importance. Scotland still held the upper hand. King Edward had attempted to mobilise, mustering at Lancaster. The muster was deferred and deferred again until October, and when the army was more or less ready to move Edward quarrelled again with his cousin the Earl of Lancaster, and either would not or could not take command, and the army was disbanded. The Scots had thereupon invaded England, striking as far south as Richmond in Yorkshire and then right across to Furness on the west coast, returning in safety with great store of iron, a necessary commodity for war, and as yet not extensively worked in Scotland.

1317 itself shows little military action. There were a couple of attempts to take advantage of the King's absence. A fair-sized force under the Earl of Arundel

tried for Jedburgh Forest. Their aim was to cut down
the forest, which afforded excellent cover for a Scots
muster, and the men had been equipped with felling-
axes. Happily for the bonny trees of Jeddart, he ran
into Douglas, who was spending the spring weather
—it was April—in building a hunting-lodge at Lintalee. Douglas had only his little personal guard, but
knowing the country he blocked Arundel's route and
ambuscaded him, with complete success. A little later
he had equal success in an incident characteristic of
the age. An English knight stationed at Berwick, Sir
Robert Neville, whose by-name was the Peacock of
the North, boasted that he would tackle Douglas
whenever he should see his banner. Douglas, hearing
of this as he did of most things, very promptly marched
to Berwick, and displayed it. Neville came out with a
party, kept his word, and was killed by Douglas himself, his men scattered, and his brothers taken prisoner,
and Douglas rode back, having pretty well paid for the
building of Lintalee by so convenient a clutch of
ransoms.

Another little episode of the time has the fighting
Bishop of Dunkeld for hero. Sometime this spring a
number of ships from the Humber set ashore a strong
landing party near Inverkeithing, perhaps intending a
raid upon Dunfermline, where the Queen of Scots
was very likely to be. The Earl of Fife (the brother of
Lady Buchan) tried to hold them, and was beaten.
His men broke and there were the makings, if not
worse, of a rout, when they crossed the bows of

Bishop Sinclair and his guards. He raked Lord Fife and his men with a caustic tongue, threw off his episcopal chimere, and being, like a wise traveller, armed beneath, rode straight for the English. Fife's men rallied and followed, and the Englishmen were driven back to their boats. One stubborn Yorkshireman (Barbour tells the story) decided that he was not going empty-handed : he caught a Scots assailant by the wrists, flung him over his shoulder, and carried him captive away. One rather hopes the ransom was not disappointing. There was a lively action on the shore : a good many Englishmen were killed or drowned, and the rest got back to their ships, up-anchored, and made the most of a fair wind. The Bishop's performance so delighted King Robert that he called him ' his own bishop ' from that day on.

This affair, and Sir John Soulis's capture of Sir Andrew Harclay, the gallant Governor of Carlisle, were of no great importance. Randolph's recovery of Man in the autumn was of more, but the main events of the year are diplomatic.

Edward had been invoking the Pope's assistance. His father's ally, Clement, had died soon after Bannockburn. There was so much trouble over the next election that a new Pope was not appointed until the August of 1316. John XXII was, like his predecessor, a Frenchman from King Edward's fiefs of Guyenne. He came from Cahors, and—the more since he had inherited Clement's Italian troubles and was threatened with being drawn into the disputes of the anti-

Emperors, Frederick and Lewis—was anxious to keep
on good terms with England, and play her off against
France, where the son and grandson [1] of Scotland's old
ally Philip IV had ended brief reigns of some eighteen
months between them, and the king was now Philip's
second son, Philip V, who was the brother-in-law of
Edward II. He therefore, at the very beginning of the
year, issued the bull *Vocatis nobis*, commanding a two
years' truce between Scotland and England.

Tactfully done, it might have been of service to both
countries. But Pope John had not been tactful in the
least, for the terms in which he addresses the two
monarchs were well adapted to put up Scottish backs.
Edward is the Pope's *carissimus in Christo filius Edwar-
dus Rex Angliae Illustris*, while Robert is only *dilectus
filius nobilis vir Robertus de Brus gerens se pro Rege
Scotiae*,[2] and they are referred to all through as *Rex*
and *Gerens* respectively.

Cardinals Guacchini and Luca were sent as Legates,
with power to absolve Robert's subjects from allegiance.
They sent envoys to the Scots court in September, the
Bishop of Corban and the Archdeacon of Perpignan.
These found they had to deal with a diplomat as well
as a soldier. The King received them with perfect
courtesy, and told them, which was no doubt very
true, that he greatly desired a good and lasting peace.

---

[1] Louis X and John I. The latter, born King, lived a week, and
his sister was passed over for her uncle, the first application of ' the
Salic Law.'

[2] Our dearest son in Christ, Edward, illustrious King of England :
our dear son the noble Robert Bruce, acting as King of Scots.

He allowed the Pope's open letters to be read, and listened to them, in spite of their terms of address, with the greatest deference. Then, having put the threatening envoys in an awkward position by such impeccably correct behaviour, he blandly refused to take the slightest notice of the sealed letters addressed to Robert Bruce, informing the bearers, still with the same politeness, that there were various gentlemen of that name, and the letters might possibly be for one of the others.

The unfortunate envoys tried to argue the point, in terms as conciliatory as they could manage. The Pope could not address Robert as King of Scots, as the matter was still at issue, and he could not prejudice it by taking one side or the other. Robert pointed out sweetly—*laeta facie et amicabili vultu*—that in fact he had prejudiced it, by this public refusal of the royal title. The envoys slid tactfully off to the truce. The King would be delighted to make a truce . . . if, of course, his parliament would consent to do so : and he added a very broad hint that they would not, unless King Edward would make a final peace, on terms that they considered satisfactory. Then he handed the envoys over to his Council, who gave them, one gathers, a more forcible version of the same opinions.

The Legates, baffled, did what they had to do, and proceeded to have the Papal Truce proclaimed. The moment they chose was rather inauspicious. King Edward was stopping all jousts in preparation for fresh war, and King Robert, on his part, was moving on Berwick. The envoy they sent was the Superior of the Berwick Franciscans. He went to Robert, who asked if his message were to the King of Scots. It was not, so the King of Scots could not find any reason to receive the poor man, who had to make the best of his way home. On the road he was waylaid, robbed of his diplomatic papers and even of his clothes, and went back like a forked radish, without the Bull. This was not Bruce's method of dealing with such affairs, though of course he got the blame of it at Avignon : the rank and file of the army were less restrained, and a Border expert at lifting a herd of cattle would have small compunction over a Papal Bull that so far forgot itself as to be rude to King Robert.

Edward, baulked of the spiritual arm, took secular measures. He had been preparing to mobilise in October, but King Robert took the field before he was ready, and at the end of March Berwick, the last of unrecovered Scotland, was taken, with the co-operation of its own townsfolk, who had had enough of the English governor, Horsley.[1] The castle held, and Horsley, sallying while the Scots were scattered, nearly re-took the place and would have done so if

[1] Some English correspondence of the previous year suggests a very dishevelled state of affairs. Someone who wants to farm the garrison's pay and undercut the gentleman who is doing so says that many are drawing cavalry pay who are only knights' servants or peaceful burgesses, and can't even ride, while the infantry claim it on the strength of having bought garrons they can't ride either, and many who call themselves crossbowmen can't shoot. The evidence comes from a frankly dubious source : but one has heard of such arrangements in later wars.

young Keith of Galston had not rounded up some men and driven him in. Walter Stewart was given the command of the town—no sinecure, for the castle held out for another eleven weeks—and meanwhile a Scots army had gone past it to Newcastle, taking Wark, Harbottle, and Mitford. A second invasion in May pushed further, into Yorkshire as far as Skipton, burning Northallerton, Boroughbridge, and Knaresborough. This was coming far south, for Knaresborough is only some fifteen miles from York itself, and about a hundred and twenty from Coldstream Ford. Yorkshire disliked the situation extremely, but the Scots, with a heavy booty, got safely home, followed by the excommunication of the Archbishop of York, which probably did not worry them very much, as they were getting too used to it by now to recognise at any rate the imported article.

The Pope also threatened the same to King Robert himself, who took precisely the same amount of notice, and King Edward assembled an army at York in June. They effected no more than the Archbishop, however, as the curse of the Baliol wars had by now moved south, and their generals quarrelled themselves into immobility, until the army had to be disbanded without even making an effort against the Scots.

In October, Scotland lost one of her best generals, and, what was even worse, the heir to the throne. Edward Bruce was killed in action at Dundalk. His wife had died a little while before, and he had married his mistress, Isobel de Ross, the daughter of the Earl, but he had left no legitimate son,[1] and still Queen Elizabeth had borne no children. In December Parliament assembled at Scone, and passed a fresh Act of Succession, settling the Crown now, unless *heres proximior et legitimus* should be born, on Robert Stewart, the King's infant grandson, with Randolph again to be Regent and after him Douglas.

This parliament did much other work as well. Scotland by now was more or less settling down—' it hadna been burnt this year or more,' at least—and required a good deal of new legislation to be made for ' the honour of God and Holy Mother Church, the amending of the land, and the defence of the people.' There are statutes for the protection of the Church, for equality of legal administration as between rich and poor, several controlling legal procedure, a Fishing Law regulating tackle and close seasons, the Arming Act referred to on page 248, and several statutes dealing with men ' called up ', and protecting both them and the places through which they pass. Lords joining the army are to bring adequate provision for their men, or the money to pay for it, and not to commandeer without payment—a law which a good deal surprised some French knights in the next generation, who found the Scots farmer, standing on his rights, a novel and disconcerting phenomenon. Another statute that is of some importance is one enacting that no goods or

---

[1] He had two by Isobel, but as they were adulterine, his subsequent marriage to their mother did not legitimate them. After David II's accession the Regent Randolph gave the elder of them their father's earldom of Carrick.

money were to go out of the kingdom : this, on the face of it, looks hard on trade, but in fact it was a temporary political measure, intended to deal with those Scottish landowners who were still fighting for Edward without permanently alienating them from King Robert's government. Their lands and goods were not forfeited, but their effectual possession of them was suspended, while they were still left free, if they chose, to regain their full privileges as Scottish subjects, by assuming the responsibilities of the position. It marks the end of the old international caste.

In the spring of 1319 Edward effected some kind of reconciliation with Lancaster, and began to make lavish preparations for a move. The Pope sent him a subsidy of £2500 from the Crusading Fund, and before the end of July he assembled an army of over 12,000 at Newcastle. (The figures are from the pay-roll, not the chronicles.) His captains included the Baliol diehards, Umfraville and his kinsman Angus, who were now almost the last of the old Baliol faction to put party feeling before national, and with them the hard-fighting Harclay, now free again, and the chronically unfortunate Pembroke. A fleet of some strength was raised from the Cinque Ports to act in support, and the immediate objective was to be Berwick.

The defence of Berwick is one of the great exploits of the war, and Barbour's account of it is exciting reading. Edward brought up all the siege engines stored at York, and the English army dug itself in round Berwick, entrenching itself firmly, for Edward had heard that Bruce had vowed to relieve the town by a given date : he gleefully told the Archbishop of York that his spies kept him fully informed of the Scottish movements.

On the 7th of September, the army attacked in concert with the fleet, and tried to storm the town by sheer weight of assault. The attack had been very carefully thought out, even to the detailing of snipers to deal with the individual crenelles and make the garrison keep under cover while the ladders were placed. A ship provided with a falling bridge came alongside the Brighouse and tried to make fast, and was barely held off till she grounded on the ebb and was set on fire by a desperate sally from the town. There was a fierce action on all sides of the city, but the Englishmen were beaten off at last, with the capture of one of their best engineers, and for five days they lay about the town, working at a very formidable engine, a ' sow,' which is somewhat on the principle of the tank, but worked, of course, by man-power. Stewart, however, had a Flemish engineer, a resourceful soul (he was also a privateer) of the name of John Craib or Crab, who got wind of these preparations and made his own, evolving a ' crane ' or catapult, apparently with original improvements, that could be shifted from place to place on the walls.

At dawn on the 13th the attack came in force, with the Sow advancing dangerously near the wall. Craib was told firmly that if he failed to smash her he would hang : the technical branches, in the Middle Ages, were not always treated with very much politeness. He rose to the occasion, neatly bracketed her with a couple of trial shots, and having got the range, sent a great boulder crashing through her roof, and followed it with piles of blazing faggots. Meanwhile, the fighting was going on fiercely elsewhere. Another ship tried to land a ' boarding party,' but the crane was rushed round, and the excellent John Craib managed to hit her mast at the first shot : the fighting-top carried away, and the men on it,

' Some dede, some dozened, cam doun wyndland,'

and her rigging fouled so that she was out of control.

It was hot work yet, in spite of these successes. The women, the very children, turned out to help, gathering spent arrows and running with them under fire to their men on the walls, and Walter Stewart galloped from place to place where the fight was thickest, taking such order as he could to beat off the assailants. These stormed the outworks of the Marygate, burning loose the drawbridge (with fire-arrows, probably) so that it fell and let them up under the wall, where they fired the gate. Someone brought word of the danger to Sir Walter : he could spare no men from the fighting on the walls, but he called out all the garrison of the castle, which was the last defence if the walls were taken, and flinging open the burning gate from within, broke out through the fire in so stout a counter-attack that it was held until night, when the English withdrew.

It was the last attempt, for King Robert relieved
the town as he had promised. As usual, he did not do
the expected thing, and attack King Edward's beautiful
entrenchments. He sent Douglas and Randolph south
by the Western March. An English historian says their
direct objective was to capture Queen Isabella, then
at York, and hold her as hostage for Berwick. They
certainly did march on York, at any rate, and the
Archbishop got together what men he could raise,
priests and monks as well as laymen, and met them at
Mytton, about twelve miles from York, where the
Swale joins the Ouse. Douglas and Randolph cut his
force to pieces : because of the number of clerics that
it contained the Scots later called the action ' the
Chapter of Mytton.' The unfortunate Archbishop lost
all his plate, a lesson for him as to luxury in camp, and
so much else that he had to raise funds from no fewer
than thirty-one religious houses.

The Scots were not in force to tackle York, but the
raid had done what it was intended to do. The whole
North of England was wailing for protection, and
Edward had to raise the siege of Berwick and go after
Douglas and Randolph, who slipped round his army
with their usual neatness. He had to disband his army
and content himself with an attempt to damage the
recovering Scots trade, by getting the ports of Flanders
closed to the Scots. He was politely but very firmly
snubbed, as a letter from the Burgomaster and échevins
of Bruges (then one of the greatest trading cities in
Europe) informs him that the Count of Flanders has

U

forbidden intercourse between his subjects and 'pirates who pretend to be Scots ' (one would like to know the story behind that phrase) but cannot prevent peaceful merchants of any country from coming to Flanders on their lawful occasions, while another epistle, from the Count himself, tells Edward politely that if he *should* catch John Craib committing piracy, he will of course have him broken on the wheel, but he knows nothing of any ships sailing from the Swin with munitions for Scotland. He will of course forbid any such breach of neutrality, but to the best of his knowledge all the Flemish ships that have cleared for Scottish ports are innocent peaceful traders, and he cannot do anything to hinder their movements. It all sounds very like a more recent war.[1]

At the onset of winter, Edward decided to try for a truce, sending up the Bishop of Ely, his own favourite Despenser, Pembroke, and another. William Soulis, Keith, Kirkpatrick, and two other Scots met them at Berwick, and they managed to agree this time on the terms. The truce was to last two years. King Edward promised to destroy or else hand over Harbottle Castle (it was destroyed) and King Robert undertook that while the truce lasted he would build no castles on the Marches, a clause that would save King Edward's

---

[1] John Craib was not the only Flemish sea captain in Robert's service. Gray mentions that his father killed a Fleming of the name of Cryn, *vn amirail de la mer, vn robbour*, who was Robert's *grand meistre*—i.e., presumably in command of the Scots fleet. As has been said, there were numbers of Flemish merchants and sailors in Scotland.

face a little, and cost him nothing, as his constant policy was not to build castles, but to destroy them.

This agreement was signed on the 22nd December. It was not peace yet, of course, but an armistice, a *soeffrance et triewe* in contemporary phrase,[1] that left the main point at issue still undecided. Diplomatic pressure was still being brought to bear, in King Edward's favour, by Pope John, who had not yet embroiled himself, as he soon was to do, with both the Franciscan Order and the Empire. He intervened once more in January (1320), summoning the King and the Scots prelates to appear at Avignon and answer for their misdeeds. The terms of address this time show a slight improvement : the King is *nobilis vir Robertus de Brus, regnum Scotiae gubernans,* which is at least politer than *se pro Rege gerens.* But it was not enough, and the King declined to take any notice of the summons. The Pope ordered the Bishops of London and Carlisle to carry out the excommunication which he had several times threatened. A little later, Bishop Lamberton, Bishop Sinclair of Dunkeld, the Bishop of Moray and the Bishop of Aberdeen, received the same treatment.[2]

These diplomatic and spiritual exercises did nothing to change the practical situation. Their only effect was to draw from a parliament held at Arbroath on the 6th of April 1320 what ought to be one of the classic

---

[1] *Sufferentia et treuga guerrae* is the Latin equivalent.

[2] Dante, in a passage written much about this time, has a caustic reference to these political excommunications, and it is worth noting that a few lines before it he refers to this war.

statements of the right of a nation to govern its own affairs as a free country. The Second and Third Estates—the clergy, though they certainly approved, could hardly take a formal share in it—sent a note to Avignon. It is a piece of stately calligraphy, with a fringe of ribboned seals in scarlet and green wax, some of great beauty. One wishes the name of the man who drafted it were known. In the name of eight earls, thirty-one barons, and *tota Communitas*, it reminds the Pope, in very courteous terms, of his responsibility as Father of Christendom and God's Vicegerent, who should do equal justice to all nations. It promises all due and right submission to spiritual authority justly used, and deals a warning, the sterner for the courtesy of its terms, against partial and interested intervention, by which John will come to share in the guilt of the war, and calls him to work for peace among Christian princes, so that Christendom may be held against the heathen, who are breaking through the gates while the kings whose duty it is to stand in defence are concerned to overthrow their neighbour's landmark.

Two passages of the address ring out like trumpets. One is the end, the note of sober faith in a righteous cause, that appeals past the Pope to the Master he represents. The other is what it has to say of King Robert. It speaks of the horrors of the annexation, and then the grave Latin words seem to break into flame. ' Through the grace of him who woundeth and maketh whole, we have been freed from so many and so great evils by the valour of our Lord and Sovereign,

Robert. Like Judas Maccabeus or Joshua, he gladly endured toil, pain, the extremity of want and every danger to save his people and kingdom from their enemies. By reason of his desert as of his rights, the Providence of God, the lawful succession which we will maintain with our lives, and our common and just consent have made him our King, because through him our salvation has been wrought. If he should give up our cause and yield us to England, we would cast him out as the enemy of us all, and choose another king who should defend us, for so long as only a hundred of us stand, we will never yield to the dominion of England. We fight not for glory nor for wealth nor for honour, but for that freedom which no good man surrenders but with his life.'

The Hammer of the Scots had forged something in Scotland.

CHAPTER XIII

TOWARDS PEACE AT LAST

SEVEN YEARS : 1320–1327

'Excogitavit quod melius foret pro communitate utriusque regni
quod uterque rex suum regnum libere et pacifice possideret sine
homagio aliquo, quam quod tot homicidia et incendia, captiva-
tiones, spoliationes, et depredationes fierent omni anno.'
Chronicon de Lanercost (of Harclay).

IT was probably sometime in this year, 1320, that
King Robert, at last, came to have hopes of an heir.
After something like nine years of marriage, the Queen
was with child. The child was born, and lived, but
proved a girl, who was christened Maude, and the
settlement of the succession appears to have been left
where it was, upon Robert Stewart, by this time four
years old. The heirship all but became of acute importance, as this year saw a conspiracy against the King
which was meant to bring about probably his death
and certainly his deposition. It is thought (the circumstances are obscure) that the conspiracy, which certainly
existed, was intended to place on the throne Sir William
de Soulis, who seems to have been a son or grandson
of the Nicholas de Soulis who had been one of the
Claimants of '92, his claim being based on the (con-
tested) legitimation of his grandmother Marjorie,
illegitimate half-sister of Alexander III, so that by
blood alone, without counting legitimacy, he was the

senior of the candidates. The plot was a wild one, for
by this present year any man who had succeeded in
murdering Bruce would have found the Scots throne
a good deal too hot to hold him.

The whole working of the business is very obscure,
but it seems that Soulis had some English backing,
presumably in return for accepting Baliol's position as
vassal of England. He had been in King Robert's
service and was treated by him with consideration,
having been one of the Commissioners appointed the
previous year to treat for a truce. (It is possible that
he was tampered with at this time.) Involved in the
affair were three or four others, headed by the Countess
of Strathearn, whose husband had been one of Baliol's
commissioners in the Succession Case, had sided with
Edward in the Comyn War, joined Bruce soon after
his coronation, and returned to the English side again
after Methven.[1] With her were Sir Roger de Moubray,
Sir Gilbert de Maleherbe, and to the general regret,
Sir David de Brechin, a nephew of Comyn of Buchan,
who had been called the Flower of Chivalry. He had
fought gallantly on the Scots side in the Comyn War,
sharing with Bruce in the attack on Lochmaben in
1299, and thereafter, being a Baliol man, had fought
for England until some time after the fall of Dundee in
1312. Barbour says the matter was revealed ' by a
lady,' and Fordun specifies her as Lady Strathearn :
but as the latter was given a sentence of life-imprison-

---

[1] After her death he married King Robert's niece, Maude de
Ross, but this did not prevent him from backing Edward Baliol.

ment the identification is probably incorrect, unless
she let something slip through sheer indiscretion.
Gray assigns the revelation to one Murdoch de Menteith, who had been in English service through most
of Bruce's wars. He may possibly have gone into the
business in English interests, and been won over by
the King's personality, for he certainly remained in
Scots service after, and was killed in it in the war after
Bruce's death.

The conspiracy struck general horror. A parliament,
called later ' the Black Parliament ' was called at
Scone in August to deal with it ; Soulis and Lady
Strathearn were imprisoned for life. Maleherbe and
two more were hanged and five others charged with
them were acquitted of complicity. Roger de Moubray,
concerned with them, had died, but his body, like
Huntly's in 1563, was brought to trial, and received
the same sentence, which the King, however, forbade
to be carried out. Brechin was in a peculiar position.
He declared that the conspirators had sworn him to
silence, then revealed the plot, and that he would
neither join them nor break his oath. He received the
same sentence as Maleherbe and Logie, which seems
severe, when one considers Soulis. (Most people
at all events—I do not agree—consider that a sentence
of life-imprisonment is a more merciful one than a
sentence of death.) His condemnation had a sequel.
Ingelram de Umfraville, taken at Bannockburn, was
still in Scotland. He had been a Baliol man, and had
fought as such against England till 1304, and thereafter,

until his capture, against Bruce. Now he was clearly
inclining to Bruce's side : he was in possession of his
Scottish estates, and his name appears on the Arbroath
Manifesto in the spring of this year. Brechin, however, was his friend, and at his death he denounced his
new fealty to Robert, who allowed him, characteristically, to go free, to give burial to his friend's body, and
to sell his Scots lands before he departed for England,
where Edward restored to him his English estates, on
the polite fiction that he had never really left his
English allegiance. The whole unhappy affair of the
conspiracy seems really to be the last boiling-up of
the Bruce-Comyn feud : the Bruce-Baliol one was to
recur, no less dangerously, again, but not until after
King Robert himself was dead.

The Arbroath Manifesto would seem to have set
Pope John to thinking. After receiving it, he wrote
to King Edward, and there is a perceptible change of
tone : Robert is not yet described as *Rex Scotorum*, but
he has become *Regens regni Scotiae*, which is at least an
advance upon *Se pro rege gerens*. He was still hedging,
however, for when King Robert sent ambassadors to
the Holy See to establish friendly relations by asking for
the removal of the ban, they were not received.

In September, when half the truce was nearly gone,
Edward did take some steps towards definite peace.
A commission of four, headed by the Archbishop of
York, met a Scottish one at Carlisle, and discussed
the terms for a *pees finale*, but with no more than the
familiar result.

In February, Pope John came down definitely on the English side again, sending Edward no fewer than six bulls against the Scots, excommunicating all invaders of England, directing the Archbishop of York and the Bishop of Durham to excommunicate once more the much-cursed King Robert, which no doubt they did with a hearty sincerity, and citing the Scots bishops to appear at Avignon. On the strength of these, Edward tried an odd subterranean expedient, directing Athol, Harclay, and some others to receive to his peace *as secretly as might be* those Scots who were troubled by their excommunication, who being so received were to have the ban lifted. A few did come over, one of them Alexander de Moubray, whose kinsman had been executed over the Soulis Conspiracy, but the spiritual bribe had very little effect.

The negotiations for a settled peace dragged on all through 1321, but as might be expected with these testimonies of Edward's frame of mind, to small effect, foundering as usual on the old snag. King Robert could not afford to compromise, and King Edward would not agree to do anything else. The truce was to end at Christmas of that year, and both sides prepared for a renewal of the war. It was staved off for a little by a fresh quarrel between Edward and his cousin Lancaster. The latter took up arms, with the definite intention of deposing Edward and succeeding to the English throne. In order to achieve this he sought Scottish backing, offering a settled peace, full recognition of Scottish independence, and a guarantee of his own neutrality on condition that the King of Scots with Randolph and Douglas would assist him without claiming a share of his conquests : in order to save the Franco-Scottish alliance, the assistance was definitely limited to action in England, Wales, or Scotland. These terms are from the papers taken on the body of Hereford, who was killed in March. It is not known whether the agreement had actually been ratified, but there seems to have been some discussion with Randolph in January, as he had a safe-conduct then to meet Lancaster ; and there was certainly some sort of understanding with Douglas a little later, as at the end of January Lancaster was writing to him. We do not know what was in the letter, but Douglas's answer, addressing him as King Arthur, shows that it had arrived ten days overdue. It arranges a meeting for discussion (*parlance*), but any possibility of using the affair to make peace came to an end a few weeks after that, for at Boroughbridge on the 15th of March, Lancaster was defeated and captured by Harclay, and he was executed a week later.

The riddance of his dangerous cousin put Edward in high spirits. He wrote cheerfully to the Pope that he had no need now to worry about a peace, and resolved to settle Scotland once for all, on his own terms, by the sheer weight of an overwhelming invasion. It was the third time he had made that resolution : but this was to be *la revanche* for Bannockburn. He appointed a muster at Newcastle for the 24th of July, and before that time the Scots had come south again

by the Western March, got as far as Preston, and after
a short and unsuccessful siege of Harclay in Carlisle
(he was now its earl, as reward for Boroughbridge) got
safely home with a large amount of booty, recrossing
the Sark on the day before that appointed for Edward's
march, and moving to deal with the imminent invasion.

The campaign turned out another 1310, only rather
more so. At the beginning of August, Edward's great
force rolled across Tweed, without opposition. It
rolled on by the Lothian coast, still without opposition.
And it soon began to feel extremely unhappy. King
Robert could not afford to risk his army without
necessity. What he did was to leave the attack to
General Famine. He evacuated the whole non-
combatant population of the province, with their
goods and gear and above all their provisions, then
moved his army north of Forth, and sat tight : the
strategy came hard on a district just beginning to
recover from years of war, but the people were bound
to suffer, whatever happened, and as it turned out
brilliantly effective, it probably spared them most in
the long run.

The English found Lothian bare as a washed slate.
All they could raise in the province was one lame cow,
that De Warrenne called the dearest beef he had seen.
The weather too seems to have fought for King Robert
as consistently as it fought against his descendants,
for the autumn westerly winds arrived strong and
early, and Edward's store-ships could not get up the
Firth. By the time they had been a week on this side

of Tweed, the English were starving and going down
with disease, and all the fighting they had achieved so
far was the murder of a few sick monks at Melrose,
and the killing of some others, left to guard them, who
had tried to defend the Host from profanation. They
sacked the Abbey, and that of Holyrood, and burnt
Dryburgh : but it was difficult to eat silver plate, and
vestments and painted books were no more nutritious.
After lying three dismal days at Edinburgh, they had
to turn and go home, *rebukes e mesharnys de guerre.*
Douglas swooped after them and cut up their light
cavalry near Melrose, but this seems to have been no
more than a parting salute, for the King's main army
was already marching westward. On the 1st of October,
eight weeks after Edward's cheerful march out of Newcastle, Robert crossed the Sark, raided the Eden
valley, and headed east for Durham. Other divisions
invested Norham and Bamborough. Horsley, the
unpopular ex-governor of Berwick, was commanding
the latter, and chose to ransom it, and Edward, whose
sense of humour was not his strong point, dressed him
down for the dishonour of having surrendered ' when
he had a larger force.'

The King was not content with merely operating
behind Edward's rear. He evidently decided that
after the complete *débâcle* of the campaign, the enemy
would be demoralised enough for it to be worth the
risk of a pitched action. Edward, his force still in
being, was moving south, presumably to disband or
canton them at York. King Robert called up his various

divided forces, and came up with him on the 14th of October, about a day's march from the city. Edward lay, with his staff, at Byland Abbey, on the side of the Cleveland Hills that looks across the Plain of York to the Pennines.

The English, under John of Brittany, were strongly posted on a ridge between Byland and Rivaulx. Their advance-guard, under Uchtred and Cobham, commanded a narrow pass that led to the Abbey, with the main body behind them, out of sight. Douglas was ordered to take the ridge, and made a frontal attack, Randolph going with him, apparently for the fun of the thing. The ridge was held firmly : Cobham was called the best English knight of his day, he had the upper ground, and his men were able to roll down great stones, which played havoc among the Scots, while his archers had the cover of the skyline. Things were looking ill for Douglas's command, so the King detached his Highlanders, whom as usual he was commanding himself, and sent them to climb the rocks on Cobham's flanks and attack him from behind, with the old tactic of the Pass of Brander. When they reached the top they had an unpleasant surprise—John of Brittany marching up with reinforcements. The Highlanders, in spite of the climb, did not halt, but flung themselves against the new enemy, who promptly broke, and, says Gray disgustedly, ' fled like hares before greyhounds.' Their panic apparently infected Cobham's men, in whose rear the new developments were taking place. They broke too, and meanwhile

King Edward was flying to York, leaving his baggage. Walter Stewart chased him to the gate of the city, and not being so well mounted, arrived in time to find it locked and bolted in his face. He withdrew out of bowshot and waited until night, in the hope that someone would come out and fight him : but no one did, so he went back to Byland, where the army was in a very cheerful key, dividing the gorgeous loot of Edward's camp. John of Brittany had been taken, and received an unfriendly greeting from the King, of whom, it appears, he had spoken insultingly. The speech Barbour gives King Robert is not very clear, but the point seems to be that he would have called John out (as a later age would say) had the latter not been too much of a knave for him to fight. John apologised for whatever it was he had said : but he had to pay twenty thousand of a ransom.

A number of French knights had been captured also, among them the Marshal of Brittany and Henri de Sully, King Philip's ambassador, who may have been some sort of distant kin to the King, whose uncle had married a lady of that name. Their greeting was different. Although they had actually been taken in arms, he treated them as neutrals, and friendly neutrals. They were there for amusement, not as enemies, so he made them not his prisoners but his guests, and sent them home free of ransom, with rich gifts. Three of them, and their squires, had surrendered to Douglas, and owed him ransom, by the law of war. Not to be generous at another's expense, Robert

bought them from Douglas with an emerald ring and
a handsome gift of lands, whose sasine was long known
as the Emerald Charter. He had not enough men for
an attack on York to be worth while, so he swept
further south and east, as far as Beverley, six miles
from Hull, and withdrew unopposed, returning about
Christmas.

King Edward's great invasion had cost him dear in
men and money and the loss of a useful general : and
since it had achieved exactly nothing beyond the
burning of a single Scots abbey, it apparently set some
Englishmen to thinking more sanely. It was by now
eight years since Bannockburn, and throughout that
time the main weight of the war had fallen on England.
To be sure her rich provinces were all well south, but
the Scots had practically reached the Humber. York,
the capital of the North, was in the front now. The
question of the feudal superiority was worth the devastation of Scotland, but not that of what looked like
being, very soon, at least half England. The failure
of the invasion of '22 is the turning-point of this final
phase of the war.

The first move for real peace, unless one counts
Lancaster's, was unofficial, and ruined the man who
made it. Harclay, a brave man, and one of the few
soldiers who could stand up to King Robert, had
before the invasion of Scotland been made Earl of
Carlisle and Warden of the Western March, as reward
for the defeat of Lancaster. He took his duty as
Warden seriously, and evidently came to the conclusion

that something was to be said at all events for Lancaster's effort towards peace with the Scots. His motive is clear. The prosperity of Cumberland was his business : he was, quite certainly, no sort of a coward, but he had had enough of devastation, and since Edward would neither protect the March nor make peace, he decided to act on his own responsibility. On the 3rd January of the next year, 1323, he met Randolph at Lochmaben. They drafted a treaty. It agreed that each country was to have its own independent King. Harclay and his party—it is clear that he was not without support—were to aid King Robert against all enemies, and they were to appoint six members apiece of a joint commission of twelve, in order to settle any disputed points. If King Edward consented to the arrangement within a year, King Robert would pay an indemnity of 40,000 marks, and marry his heir-male to a lady of the English Blood Royal, chosen by King Edward. The terms, as Hailes remarks, are decidedly odd : we may wonder how far the copy sent to King Edward, clearly by no friendly hand, represents the original, and how far it is a summing of popular gossip. The Lanercost Chronicler, who is markedly sympathetic towards Harclay, repeats them, but he seems to have been present at Harclay's trial and would have heard the indictment based on the paper, and we do not know how much that might have been cooked. Burton has made the suggestion that the arrangements may have been intended to lead up to the cession of England north of the Humber. The Scots were in a

x

position that would have made this a possibility, and Edward's council may have feared some such aim on their part. But there is no trace of it in what is known, and Robert never seems to have wished for any sort of annexation of territory : he had in fact seen enough of the consequences of any such attempt to be a lesson to an intelligent statesman.

Harclay made no secret of the negotiations. All the chief men in his earldom concurred in them, and the move was popular. Edward heard of it within a week, and was furious. Poor Harclay was arrested the following month, through a trick played on him by his own close friend, and tried and executed a few days later : he was degraded from his earldom and knighthood, hanged and drawn at Haribee, and his quarters sent as far as Bristol and Dover, where they remained for five years, until after the peace, when his sister was given leave to have them buried. He died like a brave man. What he had done was technically treason, and certainly inexcusable in a high official : but it is quite clear that it was not for his own profit, but an honest attempt to end the futile torment of the war.

Other men agreed with his aim if not with his means, and some pressure must have been brought to bear on King Edward. On the 20th March, less than three weeks after Harclay's execution, he sent an envoy to King Robert at Berwick, choosing, rather oddly, the French ambassador, Henri de Sully, one of the knights who had been set free after Byland. Sully was *persona grata* at the Scots court, and King Robert received him with much friendliness : but the despatch he carried was less tactful than the choice of the messenger. In fact, it made King Robert sufficiently angry to send Sully a copy of it with a covering letter, saying drily that he could not have known what he was carrying. Edward, badly as he needed an armistice, had shown the old truculence in applying for it. Instead of giving Robert his royal title, or even, as he had previously done, admitting the existence of at least a *de facto* government, he had calmly ignored him altogether, and offered a cessation of hostilities not to the King but to 'those Scots who were in arms against him.' As Robert says quietly, in his comments to Sully, 'This phrasing seems rather odd.' (*La quele manieré de Parler nous est anques estrange.*) As he points out contemptuously in very stately French, the mistake may not be as innocent as it looks—(*cest maniere de parler*) '*n'est forsque si simple come elle poet estre*'—since the breaking of a truce made in these terms would leave him with no more right to a complaint than any individual subject in his kingdom. It was impossible to assent to such an offer : but none the less, if the regular diplomatic forms were employed, he was perfectly willing to consider an armistice. The letter, a personal one to a man he knew, was either written or dictated by Robert himself, and is full of character.

Edward's council were not pleased, but they had none the less to mend their manners, and a truce was concluded on the 30th May, and ratified eight days later by Robert at Berwick. It was to last for a term of thirteen years, and its expressed purpose is the conclusion of a final peace, while various clauses tend to better the immediate relations of the two countries. The March Laws are to be as during time of peace, Edward undertakes to do nothing to hinder Robert and his subjects from making peace with the Pope, and there are arrangements for the safeguarding of wrecks, ships putting into port through stress of weather, and foreign trade. It is possible that there were mental reservations, at any rate on the English side. Barbour says categorically that Umfraville advised the unusual length of the truce on the grounds that the Scots yeomen, who had proved that each of them was ' worth a knycht ' should be given time to lose their warlike habits and to let ' thair arming wax ald ' and be ' rottyn, distroyit, or sald,' while in such a long time many veterans would die off, and a new generation would grow up untrained.

The real issue was still left undecided. For the next few years, till hostilities broke out again, both sides were feeling for a settlement. Robert had to make sure of Scots autonomy, or twenty-seven years struggle would go for nothing. England badly needed to put an end to a war that had meant a run of disaster now for sixteen years, but she was still trying to ' muddle through ' on some compromise that would leave her a legal loophole for annexing Scotland if the chance should recur. By the end of the truce, the King would be sixty-two, if he still lived, and his heir only twenty :

and they probably hoped, if they held on long enough,
to see a repetition of 1286.[1]

Edward, in spite of the terms of the armistice, tried
a little more intriguing with the Pope. Could John
not, somehow, embroider the excommunication ? John
pointed out, a trifle painedly, that having consigned
the whole Scottish nation to hell, he had really done
as much as could be expected, and that the clause
which grieved Edward, that the Scots might get
absolution *if they could*, was one that even a political
pope could hardly omit. (He did not put it quite in
those terms, of course.) Edward then tried to get him
to refuse to sanction the election of a Scot to any Scots
bishopric, and was plainly told that this would not do
at all. His stock in Avignon, in fact, was depreciated.

King Robert took advantage of the change of wind.
He and his subjects had been undeterred by an excommunication they, clergy and all, considered unjustified.
But the Church had played a most gallant part in the
struggle, and they wished to be on decent terms with
its head. In the autumn the King sent Randolph to
Avignon, with Sully as chaperon. He arrived at the
New Year, and we have John's own account of the
interview. Randolph's mission was, officially, un-

---

[1] Another daughter had been born to Robert by this time, and
christened Margaret. She afterwards married the Earl of Sutherland, and had no children. Maude, brought up motherless at her
brother's somewhat raffish court, made a misalliance with an incon-
spicuous esquire, one Thomas Ysack, and he and she disappear
from history. All that is known of them is that they had two
daughters, of whom the elder married John of Lorne—not, of
course, the gentleman who had played such a lively part in 1306.

official : he proposed a journey to the Holy Land, and asked for the usual *licentia et indulgentia*. John politely reminded him that as he was, in the first place, excommunicated, and in the second, without an army, the journey would have very little effect on the state of either Palestine or his soul.[1] If Randolph, however, would try to make a proper peace (*concordia*) with England, he would see what he could do. Randolph, who was a quick thinker, apparently improved the occasion by professing to misunderstand, and promising with polite responsiveness that ambassadors for reconciliation with the *Church* would gladly be sent as soon as His Holiness would oblige with the necessary safe-conduct. This was rather more than John was quite ready for, since it meant a recognition of the Scots government : he compromised by promising to send Letters Apostolic to the princes through whose territories they would pass, asking for *their* safe-conduct for Scots envoys. Randolph then played his trump, an offer from King Robert to arrange a joint crusade with Charles IV of France (who had succeeded his brother the previous year) or, if Charles would not join, to go himself, or send Randolph. The Pope, of course, made the expected reply, that neither of them could engage in a holy war until he had reconciled himself with the Church. This was just where Ran-

---

[1] It has to be remembered that although the last Crusade had ended in 1270 and the last foothold of the Crusaders in Palestine went in 1291, the idea of another was not abandoned yet, and—of sheer necessity—the crusading spirit recurs in Eastern Europe at any rate until well on in the seventeenth century.

dolph had been trying to arrive. He pointed out meekly that King Robert asked nothing better than to be a dutiful son to the Holy See, but owing to a small technical error in procedure the Pope's no doubt most fatherly letters to him had never arrived. If His Holiness should ensure their future delivery by addressing them correctly—in other words, to Robert King of Scots—they were sure of the King's most filial consideration.

The whole interview must have been entertaining to Sully, who appears to have been present, and who certainly carried the Pope's official account of it to Edward. John was driven into a corner, and had to yield, and needed all his tact to explain away the yielding to King Edward, though by this time he had grown less careful of that monarch's feelings : apparently Randolph had managed to convince him that the Scots were the better bargain of the two. He informed Edward that his yielding was not prejudicial to English interests . . . which, looked at broadly, was really true enough. But in spite of John's wish that his royal circumspection would accept the situation without disturbance (*velit Regia Circumspectio aequanimiter tolerare*), Edward could only see in it a surrender of the point that cut the whole grounds of the war from under his feet, and his reply to Pope John was furious. He considers the yielding a scandal to the Church, and remarks that Scotland has been his for a long time— *Scotiam per tempora non modica tenuimus.* His reply, by the way, is dated the 1st April.

The Pope's change of tone, being equivalent to the recognition of a government by the League of Nations, was a sizable diplomatic victory, all the more as John had hitherto been almost blatantly Edward's ally. Edward's counter to it, by way of enhancing the improved relation that the truce had been supposed to bring about, was to send to Picardy for Edward Baliol, who had lived quietly there since his father's death.

The Scots rejoicings had been a good deal increased by what seemed at the time a piece of good fortune— the birth, at long last, of a Prince of Scotland. Queen Elizabeth bore a son on the 5th of March. The Prince's future career was happily veiled : they christened him after the great King David his ancestor, and the succession seemed definitely assured.

In spite of Edward's fury with the Pope, negotiations for peace were once more undertaken. A Scots commission, headed by Randolph and Lamberton, met an English one headed by Edward's favourites, the Despensers, at York. Again there was the old heartbreaking stalemate. The Scots would only make peace on one condition, and that was the one that Edward would not yield.

Through the next year and the next—1325 and 1326 —King Robert was busy with affairs at home. Scottish social and economic life was recovering : except for the invasion of 1322, the country had now been clear for a number of years,[1] and there are various signs of a

---

[1] The building of Tarbet Castle in 1326 suggests a change of policy that is significant.

trade revival.   It is significant of the changing times
that the King could even allow himself some leisure.
He built a country-house at Cardross, near Dumbarton,
a pleasant place with painted chambers and the modern
luxury of glazed windows, and had time for hunting
and yachting on the Firth.   During this time the Queen
bore another son, who was christened, rather surprisingly, John, and died almost at once.   On the 9th of
April, 1326, the King had another loss.   Walter Stewart,
his son-in-law and the Queen's cousin, and one of the
most distinguished of his commanders, died, still a
young man, at Bathgate—a sore loss to Scotland.

The social recovery shows in the fact that it was
becoming possible to pay attention to fiscal and constitutional reform.   A parliament held at Cambuskenneth on the 15th July 1326 is apparently the first
occasion on which representatives of the burghs appear
as such, a suggestion that the merchant class were increasing in influence.   Their presence here is no
doubt connected with the fact that the main business
of this parliament was a regularising of taxation, in
order to pay off the cost of the war.   The Estates passed
a resolution in loyal terms, acknowledging all that the
King had done and suffered to secure the restoration of
liberty, and granted him a tenth of all rents and profits
for his lifetime, providing, however, that the revenue
was not to be diverted to other purposes than that for
which it was raised.   No irregular imposts were to be
enforced, the feudal dues were definitely limited, and
arrangements were made for an equitable distribution

of the heavy burden of war-time taxation. The other business included a new Act of Settlement, whose record, lost and recovered again in the seventeenth century, was in one of the eighty-one hogsheads of Cromwell's documentary loot that were lost at sea while they were being returned in 1740, to the cursing of Scots historians ever since. We therefore do not know its terms exactly, but presumably they put Prince David before his nephew.

The most notable foreign event of these few years was a formal renewal of the French alliance, in the shape of the Treaty of Corbeil, negotiated in 1326 by Randolph, the Archdeacon of St Andrews, and two Scots lawyers. The treaty is definitely a defensive alliance against England : any peace between France and England is to determine in the event of an English attack on Scotland, while conversely, if England should attack France, Robert promises to send an army over the Border.[1]

At the end of 1326 the political situation was complicated once more by serious disturbances in England. Civil war broke out again, and this time the barons were led by King Edward's queen and her lover Mortimer. They had as figure-head the young Prince

[1] The treaty had an unofficial supplement, of some social importance : the Bishop of Moray celebrated the renewed alliance by establishing a college for the Scottish students of the University of Paris, to supply the place of Devorgilla Baliol's Scots college at Paris's then recently founded daughter of Oxford. The foundation of a university in Scotland itself was postponed by these wars and their wretched renewal in the succeeding reign until Bishop Wardlaw's foundation of 1411, at St Andrews.

of Wales, a boy of fifteen, and having captured Edward and hanged his favourite as high as Haman, proceeded to settle the quarrel once for all. Queen Isabel, acting as regent for her son, summoned a parliament, which met at Westminster on the 24th January, deposed King Edward, and elected the Prince, who was crowned, as Edward III, a fortnight later.

Before very long this revolution proved to have made for peace, but at the moment it produced, or at least synchronised with, fresh disturbance. The English historian I have just consulted for the date of this coronation remarks that ' some fighting took place in the North, where the youthful king showed courage in repelling a Scotch inroad.' Edward III, certainly, never lacked for courage, but in fact it was not quite so simple as all that.

The English began by an attempt to maintain the truce, King Edward confirming it on the 6th of March. Very soon, however, it had been broken again, and as is usual in such cases, each side accuses the other of the breach. Barbour's statement is that King Robert had protested time and again against the depredations of English pirates, and as his remonstrances produced no result, announced that he considered the truce had been broken, and proceeded to mobilise. This is likely enough in the unsettled state of affairs in England : and it is borne out by contemporary English records, which in the autumn of 1326 refer to four cases of English piracy or to the arrest of Scottish subjects in defiance of the clause in the armistice conditions re-

ferred to on page 324.   In one case thirty-eight Scots
passengers, thirteen of them women, were murdered
and a cargo valued at £2000 was stolen, while in another
a party of Scots merchants and students who had put
into Scarborough for shelter from pirates had been
arrested and clapped into prison.   Inquiries were certainly ordered in these four cases, but as in one it is
stated in the order that the victims had already been
in prison for a couple of years, it is clear that King
Robert had some cause for complaint.

In spring he began to move troops towards the
Border, and King Edward, or rather the Regents,
prepared for war.   By early summer they had raised a
great army.   Froissart gives it as 30,000, with 8000
heavy cavalry, and though this is certainly an exaggeration, it is clear that they intended an invasion in force.
Queen Isabel's friend and ally, Sir John of Hainault,
whose niece was to marry the young English king,
appears in command of 2500 crack cavalry from
Flanders and the Empire, whose pay cost the English
Treasury £14,000.   There was even that spectacular
new weapon, ' crakkis of war,' (i.e., cannon) which
according to Barbour the Scots regarded with as much
interest as they did another novelty in equipment,
helmet crests of carved wood instead of the old *cuir
bouilli*, which they very much admired as ' of gret
bewte.'

The court moved slowly north to begin operations.
Queen Isabel and an *escadron volant* of sixty fair ladies
held a great feast at York on the way up, in honour of

Sir John and his Flemish knights, and it led to trouble between the English and Flemish rank and file, that assumed the proportions of a nasty riot.

This bad beginning was not improved upon. Matters ran what for years now had been their usual course. Froissart gives an exceedingly lively account of the campaign. King Robert sent an army across the Border : Froissart's reason for his not leading it in person is that his mortal sickness had come on him, but in fact he was still able for a campaign, as he was to show a few months later on. Randolph, *un moult gentil prince et vaillant en armes*, and Douglas, *le chevalier le plus hardi et le plus entreprenant des deux pays*, crossed the Sark on the 15th of June, marched across to Weardale, back towards Appleby, and then east again. King Edward moved too about the end of the month, but his army was too big to be easily mobile, and he could not cope with the rapid marches of Robert's mounted infantry. Someone seems to have realised this, and tried to deal with the problem by taking the army off north in light marching order, tackling the problem of commissariat by making the men strap loaves behind their saddles, where the sweat of the horses flavoured them rather richly. Where they were heading for is not very clear. They seem to have been trying to cut off the Scots, for they certainly did get between them and the Border, though it is not very clear whether it was by intention or by chance. By this achievement, however, they also severed their own lines of communication, which, for a reason Froissart gives with some candour, mattered much more to them than it did to the Scots.[1]

They got to Haydon Bridge on the South Tyne, half a dozen miles west of Hexham, and there they stuck. The Scots were in Weardale again, to the south of them, and Douglas's foragers could be relied on to make sure that the English convoys never arrived. Edward's army lost touch with its base and its commissariat, and succeeded before very long in losing itself. They were short of food, forage, and stores of every kind, and reduced to cold water : there was plenty of that, as to improve things it poured with rain for a week. The sodden saddles rotted and galled the horses, the girths gave, shoes were cast and could not be replaced, and the men were as unhappy as their mounts. They were soaked to the bone, and could not get dry, since they had nothing but green wood for fires : and naturally there was *grande murmuration*, which may be translated as 'no end of grousing.' When they found a little village that had been burnt, those lucky enough to get billets in the ruins thought it was heaven, though they dared not remove their armour for the night, and slept with their horses' reins about their wrists.

It was not the kind of war the boy King had hoped for. Edward III, like most of the Plantagenets, was a fighter by temperament, and even at that age the soldier he became must have known that the only

[1] See Appendix III for Froissart's description of the Scots hobeler.

thing that would save his sodden army from going to pieces was to get them in action as soon as possible. He offered knighthood and a landed estate to anyone who would guide him where he could fall upon the Scots on decent ground—*en lieu dur et secke*—and there was hot, if somewhat damp, competition for the reward. The rain took off at last, and he managed to get over the Tyne at Haltwhistle, further up, with a certain number of drowned and *assez de baignés*, and marched through the hills. At Blanchland he met a drenched and excited squire, one Thomas Rokeby, who promptly put in a claim for the reward. He had been scouting, been captured by the Scots, and being of a forthcoming disposition, had told them ruefully what he had been after, whereon Douglas characteristically turned him loose and bade him run away and earn his knighthood by telling King Edward the Scots were waiting for him.

The three weeks that follow saw some stirring adventures. It was to be almost Douglas's last campaign, and it is probable that he enjoyed it. The whole business, both in Barbour and in Froissart, has an odd sort of half-daft lightheartedness, on the Scottish side of it at all events. The English army heard mass, made its soul, and moved, and Rokeby led them up to the position where the Scots army was waiting according to promise. Their recovering cheerfulness was somewhat dashed when they saw it. The Scots lay on *deux croupes de montagne*, two rounded promontories of a hill, with the swift strong river Wear running beneath, in spate after the rains. The English knights looked at the place, and took their spurs off.

Affairs proceeded with extreme politeness. Edward sent a herald, the mediaeval equivalent for a white flag, to invite the Scots to come down and cross the river, or to let him cross, either side to be unmolested during the crossing. Douglas and Randolph were as chivalrous as any man, but they were fighting a war, not a tournament. Edward had very much the larger force, and since they were in an excellent position they had not the slightest intention of giving it up, and declined to move. Edward's commanders looked at the terrain, and decided that a blockade was the best they could do : one would have expected them to try the *crakkis of war*, but these do not seem to have been used here at all : probably after the deluge the powder was spoilt.

For a few days the two forces faced each other, and there was ' a certain liveliness ' now and then. Edward sent out a thousand archers, with cavalry in support, to get round the Scots flank. Douglas, seeing them move off, promptly posted his own cavalry in ambush, under his younger brother and young Mar, threw a cloak on his surcoat with the silver stars, and rode out as bait. They saw him, and gave chase : he rode on, at just the right speed to encourage them, and led them neatly towards his ambuscade. A squire called Ogle recognised him somehow—the cloak may have blown away from the blue and silver, which by now was one of the best-known blazons in Europe—and yelled a warning. The mere name of Douglas was enough by this time, and the English pulled up, but too late : the ambushed cavalry swept out and through them . . . and young William Erskine, who had been knighted that morning, rode so far ahead of his men that he was made prisoner.

The next English attempt very nearly had better luck. They ambushed a large force in the wood *behind* Randolph, and made a feint attack on him in front. He was moving against that, and would have been done for had Douglas's intelligence been less active. Word was brought to him of the concentration in the rear, and he just succeeded in holding back the Scots from advancing and leaving their camp. They stayed where they were : the attack was not pushed home, and in the night they left their fires alight, slipped between the two jaws of the pincers, and moved off in silence, digging themselves in in a stronger position yet, on a handy wooded height a couple of miles off. There was nothing left for the baulked King Edward to do but to break his own camp and go and sit down before them.

He did not sit quietly. On his first night there, Douglas picked two hundred carefully chosen horse, rode out by his own rear and fetched a compass, crossed the Wear and rode openly up to the far side of the English camp. A sentry challenged him, and he replied by giving the man a dressing-down for slackness, which, garnished with an oath or two by St George, carried so much conviction he was passed through.

Y

He rode up to the camp, where the English had just settled to their first sleep, and took his two hundred into it at the gallop, slashing right and left at the tent-ropes and raising a hurricane of noise and confusion in the very middle of the sleeping army. They cut their way through it to the King's pavilion, and all but succeeded in taking him prisoner : his servants very gallantly gave their lives, and managed to save the boy somehow or other. The whole army by now was like a disturbed wasps' nest, and Douglas, rallying his small band with his bugle, drew them off and got clear with hardly a casualty, though it was a near thing—they had to swim the river, and Douglas, riding last, was nearly taken.

Randolph, it seems, was annoyed at being left out. He had so far had none of the sport, and was growing bored, so he tried to get Douglas to agree to a battle. That long-headed gentleman had other views. He did not mind a risk, as he had just proved, but he had no intention of running up the sort of butcher's bill involved in throwing away their good position—of presenting Edward, in fact, with another Dunbar. He wanted his command for further service. According to Barbour, he swore his pet oath, by St Bride, told Randolph a highly immoral fabliau, of how a fox tricked an unfortunate fisherman, and pointed out its present application. Randolph agreed, and they and their chuckling staff turned in for the night, and spent the next day in busy preparation, enlivened by watching the English burial-parties dispose of the casualties from

the night before. Towards evening a Scot blundered
into the English outposts, was roped in, and promptly
taken to be questioned. After a due and proper amount
of reluctance he permitted himself to inform the
English staff that Randolph had ordered a stand-to
for sunset. The English, of course, prepared to receive
another night attack, in more force this time. Cursing
and yawning, they lay on their arms, watching the
Scottish camp-fires on the hill, and hearing the bugles
blow the regular calls. The night went on and on,
and still they stood to, and still the Scots fires burnt :
and nothing happened.

   In the morning a couple of buglers walked into camp,
and announced that they were all the Scottish army,
at least as far as Weardale was concerned. The
English simply would not believe them at first, but they
sent out scouts, and these found that it was true.
The Scots had quietly marched out in the night, crossed
an apparently hopeless bog behind them, by laying
fascines which the rear-guard—a muddy job it must
have been—had picked up behind them, cutting off
pursuit, and were cheerfully marching north with all
their booty. What King Edward's staff remarked has
not been preserved, but the King, who after all was
only sixteen, burst into tears. He had to go back to
York and disband his great army, which had effected
exactly nothing at all ; and he probably wept again
when he saw the bill. The beautiful and expensive
Flemish horse had hardly a beast left sound to carry
them.

Meanwhile, though the evidence is very scanty, it would appear that King Robert had gone to Ireland. We know that he was there in that July, at the time when Douglas and Randolph were in Weardale, and made truce with the English Seneschal of Ulster, on condition of being supplied with corn for his troops. What brought about the expedition, or what happened on it, is not known. It was very brief, and presumably unsuccessful. If there had been much in the way of hostilities we should probably have had more of a record, so we may assume either that he was trying to get Ulster to rise again, and it would not, or that some-one had brought him over by promising a rising, and the powder, when it came to be fired, was damp.

Randolph and Douglas would have got home about the middle of August, just when young King Edward was disbanding his army. The King turned them and rode with them back to the English side, by the middle of September at the latest, just before the time (it was the 21st) when the luckless Edward II was murdered, at his wife's orders, in Berkeley Castle.

The campaign was a very brief one, and his last. It has the same note, of something almost like frivolity, that is in Douglas's Weardale exploits before it, as if both men had a touch of feyness on them. Douglas saw only one battle after that, in a strange land, though he had three years to live yet. King Robert was never to ride to war again.

One part of their force besieged Norham, another Alnwick. The latter affair was less like a siege than a tournament, for they held set jousts, says Gray, *par couenant taille*, under formal rules. The King went hunting in Northumberland, as he might have done in his own parks in Scotland, till that luckless province bought the usual truce, to last until Whitsuntide of the next year.

Henry Percy, the English Warden of the Marches, tried to divert them by raiding Teviotdale, and Douglas went after him and cut him up. The Percy-and-Douglas clash is the last of the war. At the end of September, while these affairs were in progress, the English Parliament had met at Lincoln, to take in hand the financing of further war. They struck : they had had enough. The bill for those Flemings may have turned the scale. King Robert had joined the besiegers of Norham Castle, and there, where thirty-five years and four months before King Edward had thrown off the mask and challenged Scotland, an English envoy arrived with proposals for peace, for a definite and final agreement at last.

CHAPTER XIV

CORONATUR OPUS

SEVEN MONTHS : 1327–1328

'God hes schawen sic fauoir to zour foirbearis, throcht the
quhilk thai hef venqueist thair enemes, and brocht the realme, be
visdom and manheid, in sykkyr pace.'

The Compleynt of Scotland.

THE guarantee for the peace was offered at once : the
marriage of King Edward's younger sister, Joan of the
Tower, to David, Prince of Scotland. England, this
time, was in earnest, and meant business. The King,
seeing the consummation of his work, received the
envoy, William de Denoun, very favourably. Hostilities were suspended. Denoun returned to Edward at
Nottingham, and on the 9th of October, he and Percy
were sent north again to discuss the precise terms of a
treaty of peace.

Queen Elizabeth lived to see this, and no more. On
the 26th of the month she died at Cullen. Her body
was embalmed, the entrails being ' erdit ' in the Lady
Kirk there, and borne to await her husband at Dunfermline, the resting-place, since the time of Malcolm
and Margaret, of the Scots kings.

The negotiations lasted through the winter. Travel-
ling, especially at that season, was slow, and although
the Scots were willing to make any amount of conces-

sions over non-essentials, their past experience had determined them to make very sure of a water-tight agreement on the main point. The English commission were appointed at Pomfret on the 23rd of November, the Archbishop of York being their head, but it was not until the 25th January that the Scottish one which was to meet them was given its safe-conducts. Matters moved a little more rapidly after that. In February the English Parliament assembled at York, and on the 1st of March it assented to a sort of preliminary protocol, embodying the terms offered for a peace. These yield the main issue as fully as possible : from the terms, the document would seem to have been drafted in Scotland, and merely presented to the English Parliament for acceptance as a necessary preliminary to further discussion. One would seem, indeed, to see Lamberton's hand in it. Edward, by common consent of his prelates, earls, barons, and the *communitas* of England in Parliament assembled, and in the name of his heirs and successors in perpetuity, guarantees that the Kingdoms of Scotland and of England shall be divided by their right boundaries as recognised in the reign of King Alexander III of pious memory—*per suas rectas Marchias prout temporibus bonae memoriae Alexandri, Regis Scotiae ultimo defuncti fuerunt habitae et servatae.* The lawful ruler of the former country is the Magnificent Prince Lord Robert, by the grace of God illustrious King of Scots, whose kingdom is to be free, whole, and quit in perpetuity—*integrum, liberum, et quittum remaneat in perpetuum*—without any subjection, servitude, claim, or demand. Edward formally renounces all claims to superiority put forward by his predecessors, and declares invalid any such claims in future : all obligations, agreements, and pacts of any kind which imply any sovereignty of England over Scotland are cancelled, and all documents which record them are null and void.

The main point being thus satisfactorily disposed of, there was nothing left but to discuss the details, and the Scots were quite ready to be conciliatory over those. Conciliatory, indeed, they were : there is no claim for any cession of territory—an uncommon wisdom in treaties even much later—or even for reparations : King Robert did not so much as demand, as he very well might have done, the return of his own estates, and he even went so far as to offer, perhaps a little contemptuously, reparations for damage done in the North of England. The Scots had decided to make very clear the truth of their claim to the Pope in 1320, that they fought for their country's freedom and nothing else, and no peace treaty in European history has ever been less vindictive to the vanquished.

The Scots Parliament met at Edinburgh on the 17th of March, and arranged with an English embassy the final conditions of *vne bone pees finale et perpetuele*. (The record is in two parts, and one, unusually, is not in Latin, the common language of diplomacy, but in a very stately and formal French.) The Latin document incorporates a good deal of the preliminary protocol signed at York : the clauses about autonomy repeat it verbatim. As for other points, the rights of the Church in both countries are defined. The Treaty of Corbeil is safeguarded by a clause to the effect that if Scottish forces operate in support of France in a war between that country and England, the King of England shall be within his rights in invading Scotland : but that such operations by either, in such a contingency, shall not be considered as abrogating the treaty. Robert agrees not to help Edward's Irish enemies, while Edward makes a similar agreement not to help Man or the Isles against the Scots crown. England will help to forward a peace with the Pope. The March Laws are to be maintained as before the war. All the cancelled documents which bear on the question of the supremacy are to be delivered to the King of Scots. In consideration of these things, Robert will pay reparations for damage done in England, to the amount of £100,000, payable before Michaelmas of 1338 . . . one of the few occasions when a victorious country has paid damages to an aggressor power she has beaten. The guarantee for the treaty is the marriage of the Prince of Scotland to Princess Joan of England, or, if she should die before this can take place, to a suitable princess of the English blood royal. Robert settles on her the sum of £2000 a year, secured on lands and rents according to a new, post-war, valuation, and agrees that if she is left a widow she is to be free to return to England if she wishes, unless she is pregnant, when she may not do so without the permission of the Scots king and barons.

This practically concluded the discussion, though it would seem that some minor points were added semi-officially, as apparently the Coronation Stone was to have been returned, since it is later recorded that the citizens of London refused to implement a promise to that effect. The English Parliament met at Northampton at the end of April : on the 3rd of May, in accordance with the terms of the agreement, letters were despatched to the Pope and the Cardinals, announcing the conclusion of peace, and a request was made to His Paternity to withdraw his *processus* against the Scots king and his subjects. Robert has now become ' The Magnificent Prince, Robert King of Scots,' and it is possible that John, remembering some past correspondence, may have suppressed a discreet diplomatic smile. On the next day, the 4th of May 1328, Edward, ' for ourselves, for our heirs and successors, and for our subjects,' set his seal to two documents, one French and the other Latin, reproducing those ratified at Edinburgh. A definitive peace was thus concluded at last, and the long desperate wasteful business was over. It was forty-two years since the death of King Alexander, thirty-seven since Edward I had launched his ultimatum, twenty-two since Robert had been crowned at Scone, and almost fourteen since Bannockburn had virtually completed the clearing of Scotland. Dates mean little on paper, but it may help imagination to recall that the French Revolution and the whole wars of Napoleon, from the first meeting of the Estates General to Waterloo, come in a few weeks over twenty-six years : the last Great War covered four years and fourteen weeks, and those who remember it will not forget the sense that it had gone on since time began, and that life before it was distant and mythical.

The Scots had won everything that they had fought for. The country was an economic wreck, her whole cultural development had been thrown back, and her tiny population, combatant and non-combatant alike, was seriously depleted by war and famine : she had won, however, not only her own freedom but the fullest possible acknowledgment of her right to it, in the most explicit terms, from her aggressor. England might, and did, tear up the treaty as soon as that was convenient : but her assault could never be repeated under the cover of any legal fiction. Such complete success, against so formidable an assailant, immensely increased the country's European prestige. Her stock fell somewhat towards the end of the century, for David II was a worthless weakling, and his two immediate successors not much better : but the Stewarts raised it again, and until the Reformation, and even for a generation after, Scotland held the key to the balance of power in the North. In the fifteenth century, it was her intervention that saved the national existence of France. In the sixteenth the English diplomatic correspondence that leads up to the Treaty of Câteau Cambrésis, one of the landmarks of European history, is full of such phrases as ' nothing shall satisfy us if we have not peace with Scotland ' and urgent in-

junctions that it is better not to have peace with
France (and England was urgently in need of that)
than to let France make it and leave Scotland out.

England's gains by her war were much less considerable. Economically, she had suffered a good deal
less. Invasions from either country had, as it happened, penetrated almost exactly the same distance
into the other : from Inverness and from Beverley to
the nearest point of the Border is very much the same
number of miles. But the major economic strength of
England then lay well beyond the invaded area, while
that of Scotland lay almost wholly within it. English
casualties for the war were probably, in actual numbers,
greater than Scottish : but the discrepancy of the two
populations made them, in proportion, relatively less.
As set-off, she had poured out men and money for a
generation, financing no fewer than twelve large-scale
invasions with formidable armies (not counting those
that had never crossed the Border) and something like
fifteen years of a costly military occupation of invaded
territory : and had gained by it nothing more than the
devastation of her own northern provinces, a very
serious blow to her prestige, and the changing of a
close and useful friendship to a bitter and expensive
enmity. Edward I's attempt on Scotland cost her
France.

The war had wrecked the relations of the two countries. And the peace, though it is difficult to see on
what milder terms, short of a Scottish surrender of
nationhood, it could have been made, did little to

improve them. The terms, as we have seen, had been
notably gentle : the Scots took an acknowledgment of
their liberty, and no more, and England was not asked
to foot the bill for the war that she had made, or to surrender a square yard of ground. None the less, the
victory was not forgiven. The attempt on Scotland
was repeated again and again for two and a half centuries after this peace. A little more than four years
after the treaty, Edward was backing a Baliol pretender,
and Robert's son had ceased in English official documents to be ' David by the grace of God King of
Scots ' and become ' David de Brus, commanding our
enemies in Scotland.' There had been no Scots
aggression : the breach of the treaty was the sequel to
a *putsch* carried out by subjects of Edward who had
lost Scots estates. Edward's attitude at first had been
correct, but when the affair seemed likely to succeed,
he tore up the scrap of paper he had signed, and came
in against his ally and brother-in-law. The next
definite peace was not made until 1423—to be ratified,
oddly enough, by the marriage of another English
Joan. Fortunately, the two English attempts on
France ran exactly the same course as that on Scotland
—an initial success against a distracted country, and
then an ignominious expulsion : and these, and the
War of the Roses that followed them, gave Scotland
time to breathe between attacks. All England gained
by the Three Hundred Years War was the town of
Berwick, by then a mere frontier post, and the Isle of
Man. It does not seem very much.

Is it worth while recalling these memories of old strife ? Courage is always worth one's while to recall, for there is no greater help to its possession (and without it no other virtue begins to be) than to remember it. That is why the convention of modern letters, their assumption that the weakling and the coward are more worthy of interest than the man of valour, is far more of a racial poison than mere dirt would be.

To point a deliberate moral nowadays is a proceeding to shock the most broad-minded. Yet no intelligent man can contemplate conduct—and conduct is the substance of history—without some sense at any rate of its values, and if it be conduct that affects himself, of the question of his own reaction to it. What I at any rate am most conscious of in looking back at this story I have recorded, is this. Robert Bruce knew Scotland, knew every class of her people, as no man who ruled her before or since has done. It was he who asked of her a miracle : and she accomplished it. In the present year, his kingdom, like the rest of civilisation, is not in much better case than in 1306. The disaster, it is true, is a different one—not fetters, but darkness, and poison of the mind. But if courage and resolution are the same yet, is there any more reason why one impossible thing should not be achieved, after all, than there was for the other ?

EPILOGUE

PEACE

THIRTEEN MONTHS: 1328–1329

English Friend (with an Oxford First). What are you doing just now ?

Myself. I've been working at a life of Robert Bruce.

E. F. Robert Bruce ? Oh, the spider man ! Whatever for ?

Myself. Well . . . I thought I'd like to have a shot at it.

E. F. I shouldn't have thought he was worth writing a life of. He didn't do anything very important, did he ?

Actual dialogue in the British Museum.

EPILOGUE

PEACE

1328–1329

' Morz est Rollanz, Deus en ailt lanme es cielz.'
La Chanson de Roland.

PEACE was signed, and Scotland could go about her business, resume her interrupted national life. But the great King who had led her to victory was not, and to her everlasting loss, to lead her through a time of consolidation. And Bishop Lamberton, who had stood by him in the darkest years, had kept him, perhaps, from giving up an apparently hopeless attempt in a young man's sick disgust at human folly, died in the year of the peace. He had lived to see it come, though, and must have been ready for his *Nunc Dimittis*.

As earnest of peace, the Scottish lands of certain English nobles were returned to them. No reciprocal restitutions were made, however, except for some owned by Douglas in Northumberland, which—possibly with a certain irony—were given back, though not till the next year. Preparations were put in hand for the royal wedding that was to be the final ratification, and much material was purchased for feasting and finery. Prince David had been created Earl of Carrick, and a household was formed at Turnberry for the

z   353

young pair—a Steward, a Treasurer, nine ladies, five knights, thirty-eight squires and a page, and nine priests and clerks for their chapel, with a clerk of audit, a clerk of the wardrobe, and appropriate servitors and garrison.

On the 19th of July 1328, the young prince, who was four years and four months old, was married to six-year-old Joan Make-peace at Berwick, whither her mother and Mortimer had conveyed her. Neither King was present, King Edward apparently for reasons that one can understand and pardon in a spirited lad of no more than seventeen, and King Robert because his mortal sickness was on him.

They say it was leprosy. This has been disputed, and the grounds commonly assumed are two. One is that neither Barbour, Froissart, nor Fordun calls it anything but—in one language or the other—'the great sickness.' But Gray says categorically *mort estoit de lepre*, and the Lanercost Chronicler *mortuus est leprosus*. The other contention is not stated as a rule, but there seems to be an idea among certain historians that a king could not be a leper. Yet he could. Poor young Baldwin of Jerusalem had been one : no bacillus was ever a respecter of persons. And leprosy, throughout the Middle Ages, was cruelly common.

None the less, though the orthodox arguments are weak, there are stronger reasons for suggesting the King's disease may not have been what we mean by leprosy. According to Sir Leonard Rogers, leprosy, even in its most virulent form, takes eight or ten years to kill, on an average. Now, it must be remembered that the Middle Ages had a horror of leprosy which they extended to no other disease. A discovered leper was put through a solemn ceremony of expulsion from the living community. He was warned of his situation by the priest, and given a chance to make his last confession. Then he heard mass, kneeling beneath a black cloth hung over two trestles, as if he were already in his coffin.

' That is the last time he will be with his fellow men. After this mass he rises, and folded in the black cloth, he is led out into the churchyard as one dead. After he has been comforted by the priest, the earth from the churchyard is cast over his feet, with the words " Be thou dead to men, but alive to God," and all may pray for him even as he asks. Then the leper is led out into the open field, and left alone.'

Thenceforward he had no company but with lepers. He was forbidden to go about without his black cowl, his overshoes, and his gloves, and he must always carry and sound his wooden clapper. He might not touch anything unless with his stick, or even answer if he were spoken to, unless he were up wind from the man who spoke. These things give the measure of his segregation.

Now, in the case of a king, and a king as deeply beloved as Robert Bruce, there would be some mitigation of this rigour. So much may be granted at once. But there is no sign of any sort of segregation at all, until at most a few months before his death, and there are signs that until at earliest three months before it, he was, though he had been seriously ill, and was still in bad health, not treated as a leper. He was fit for a campaign in the autumn of 1327 : there was not much fighting, but Barbour declares that he hunted, and a leper, even a king, would not be permitted, if he would permit himself, to handle horse-furniture others must touch and clean. Well on in 1328 he apparently expected to be at his son's wedding, as a chain and jewel were bought for him to wear. He was undoubtedly too ill to go : Barbour says this malady was caused by a chill. He must have recovered to a certain extent, for so late as the latter part of March 1329 he had been able to go on a progress into Galloway, through the country where as a lad he had ridden to war. Whatever it was that they took for leprosy had not, it seems fairly clear, come to him then.

It seems probable, then, that what did happen was this. An illness, probably a severe one, in summer (Barbour's phrase suggests pleurisy or pneumonia) on top of the strain and hardships of his life, had weakened a man who by now was well over fifty : and in spring, after a winter of the spiced and salted and doubtfully cured food that was inevitable, some violent skin disease had broken out, that to primitive mediaeval diagnostics might easily pass for a form of leprosy ; and the poisoning of his system of which it was symptom was too much for him in the failure of his strength.

After all, it does not matter now what he died of. He did die, most unhappily for Scotland, though not,

at least, until he had set her free. In October of 1328
he had made peace with the Pope, and been released
from his excommunication on no more difficult
penance than that he should not break the peace by
invading England. He saw Scotland victorious, ac-
knowledged once more as a sovereign state by all
Europe, at peace with the Church and with all her
enemies. When he came back from his last journey, to
the home that he had made for himself at Cardross, he
knew all that, and that he was a dying man. He set his
affairs in order, saw his lords do homage to the son
who was to succeed him, and passed to his rest on the
7th day of June 1329, at the age of fifty-four years and
eleven months.

They embalmed his body and carried it across
Scotland, by Loch Lomond foot, Dunipace, and Cam-
buskenneth, that looks on the field of his greatest
victory, and so to the tombs of the Kings of Scots in
Dunfermline, beside the shrine of his ancestress St
Margaret. Only his heart did not go with the body.
That was with Douglas, casketed in silver, and on the
road to the last of their adventures.

Froissart tells the story, and Barbour : they differ a
little, but only in detail that does not matter much.
Since Barbour is verse it is not easy to modernise the
spelling and leave the cadence : but one can do that
for Lord Berners' English version of the Fleming, in
the lovely prose of the fifteenth century.

' It fortuned that King Robert of Scotland was right
sore aged and feeble : for he was greatly charged with

the great sickness, so that there was no way for him but death. And when he felt that his end drew near, he sent for such barons and lords of his realm that he trusted best, and showed them how there was no remedy for him, but he must needs leave this transitory life. Commanding them on the faith and troth that they owed him truly to keep the realm, and aid the young prince David his son, and that when he was of age they should obey him and crown him king . . . he called to him the gentle knight Sir James Douglas, and said before all the lords, Sir James, my dear friend, ye know well that I have had much ado in my day to uphold and sustain the right of this realm, and when I had most ado I made a solemn vow, the which as yet I have not accomplished, whereat I am right sorry. The which was if I might achieve and make an end of all my wars, so that I might once have brought this realm in rest and peace, that I promised in my mind to have gone and warred on Christ's enemies, adversaries to our holy Christian faith. To this purpose my mind hath ever intended, but Our Lord would not consent thereto, for I have had so much ado in my days, and now in my last enterprise I have taken such a malady that I cannot escape. And sith it is so that my body cannot go nor achieve that my heart desireth, I will send the heart instead of the body to accomplish mine avow instead of myself: and by cause I know not in all my realm no knight more valiant than ye be, nor of body so well furnished to accomplish mine avow instead of myself, therefore I require you, mine own dear and special friend, that ye will take on you this voyage for the love of me, and to acquit my soul against my Lord God. For I trust so much in your nobleness and truth, that an ye will take on you, I doubt not but ye shall achieve it, and then shall I die in more ease and quiet : so that it shall be done in such manner as I shall declare unto you. I will that as soon as I am trespassed out of this world that ye take the heart out of my body and embalm it, and take of my treasure, as ye shall think sufficient for that enterprise, both for yourself and such company as ye will take with you, and present my heart to the Holy Sepulchre where Our Lord lay, seeing my body cannot come there. And take with you such company and purveyance as shall be appertaining to your estate. And wheresoever ye come let it be known that you carry with you the heart of Robert King of Scotland, at his instance and desire, to be presented to the Holy Sepulchre.

' Then all the lords that heard these words wept for pity. And when this knight Sir James Douglas might speak for weeping he said, Ah, gentle and noble king, a hundred times I thank your grace of the great honour that ye do to me, sith of so noble and great treasure ye give me in charge. And, sir, I shall do with a glad heart all that ye have commanded me to the best of my true power, howbeit I am not worthy nor sufficient to achieve such a noble enterprise. Then the King said, Ah, gentle knight, I thank you so that you will promise to do it. Sir, said the knight, I will do it undoubtedly, by the faith that I owe to God and the order of knight-

hood. Then I thank you, said the King, for now I
shall die in more ease of my mind, sith that I know
that the most worthy and sufficient knight of my realm
shall achieve for me that which I never could attain
unto. And then soon after this the noble Robert de
Brus King of Scotland trespassed out of this uncertain
world and his heart taken out of his body and embalmed, and honourably he was interred in the Abbey
of Dunfermline, in the year of our Lord God
MCCCXXIX, the vii day of the month of November.

' And when the springing time began, then Sir
James Douglas purveyed him of that which appertained
to his enterprise, and took his ship at the port of Montrose in Scotland, and sailed into Flanders to Sluys,
to hear tidings, to know if there were any noble man
in that country that would go to Jerusalem, to the
intent to have more company, and he lay at Sluys the
space of twelve days or he departed, but he would
never come aland but kept with his ship, and kept
always his port and behaviour with great triumph, as
though he had been King of Scots himself, and in his
company there was a knight banneret and seven other
knights of the realm of Scotland, and twenty-six young
squires and gentlemen to serve him, and all his vessel
was of gold and silver, pots, basins, ewers, dishes,
flagons, barrels, cups, and all other things. And all
such as would come and see him, they were well served
with two manner of wine and divers manner of spices,
all manner of people according to their degrees. And
when he had tarried there the space of twelve days, he

heard reported that Alfonso King of Spain made war
against a Saracen King of Granada. Then he thought
to draw to that party, thinking he could not bestow his
time more nobly than to war against God's enemies,
and, that enterprise done, then he thought to go forth
to Jerusalem and to achieve that he was charged with.
And so he departed and took the sea towards Spain,
and arrived at the port of Valencia the great. Then he
went straight to the King of Spain, who held his host
against the King of Granada Saracen, and they were
near together on the frontiers of his land : and within
a while after that this knight Sir James Douglas was
come to the King of Spain, on a day the King issued
out into the field to approach near to his enemies.
And the King of Granada issued out likewise on his
part, so that each king might see the other with all
their banners displayed. Then they arranged their
battles each against other. Then Sir James Douglas
drew out on the one side with all his company, to the
intent to show their prowess the better.

' And when he saw these battles thus ranged on both
parties, and saw that the battle of the King of Spain
began somewhat to advance towards their enemies, he
thought then verily that they should assemble together
to fight at handstrokes, and then he thought rather to
be with the foremost than with the hindmost, and
struck his horse with the spurs, and all his company
also, and dashed into the battle of the King of Granada,
crying Douglas ! Douglas ! weening to him that the
King of Spain and his host had followed, but they did

not, wherefore he was deceived, for the Spanish host stood still. And so this gentle knight was enclosed and all his company with the Saracens, whereas he did marvels in arms but finally he could not endure, so that he and all his company were slain. The which was great damage that the Spaniards would not rescue them.'

William Keith, kept out of the fight by a broken arm, embalmed his comrade's body, and took it back to Scotland, and the Heart also. Douglas lies in the Kirk of St Bride in Douglasdale, and the Heart in the Abbey of Melrose that Bruce had loved. The child David had been crowned as King of Scots, and Randolph was Regent. He also, bitterly to Scotland's loss, was to die in three years time, and in his bed, on his way to repel the first invasion of new and bitter war. Of the King and his four chief captains, only two, Sir Edward and Douglas, came to their end in the field.

APPENDIX I

THE Case of the Scottish Succession did much to establish the principle of strict primogeniture, but the two most famous succession cases of the next generation, in which Edward's grandson, aided by English lawyers, acted in the one case as self-appointed, in the other as invited arbitrator, were *not* decided on this principle. These were the French Succession after Charles IV's death in 1328 and the Breton Succession after that of John III in 1340. Edward III, in the former case (though not till 1337, at his convenience) advanced a claim to the throne as the son of Charles IV's sister Isabelle, against Philip VI, who was son of Charles's uncle, and therefore in a fully male line—and to whom, by the way, he had already done homage for Guyenne. This asserts seniority through a female descent as superior to a junior but entirely male line—i.e., the Baliol principle . . . though it conveniently overlooks the fact that on that principle there were two other heirs with a better claim.

Edward's own decision in the Breton case three years later exactly reverses this. John III's contesting heirs were the younger of his two brothers and the daughter of the elder, with her husband. And Edward, in this case, decided for the younger but male line, for John de Montfort instead of for his elder brother's daughter . . . as it might be for Bruce instead of for the heir of Devorgilla.

Scottish Case of 1290.

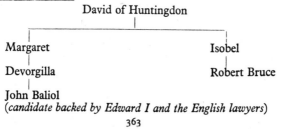

David of Huntingdon

Margaret		Isobel
Devorgilla		Robert Bruce
John Baliol		

(*candidate backed by Edward I and the English lawyers*)

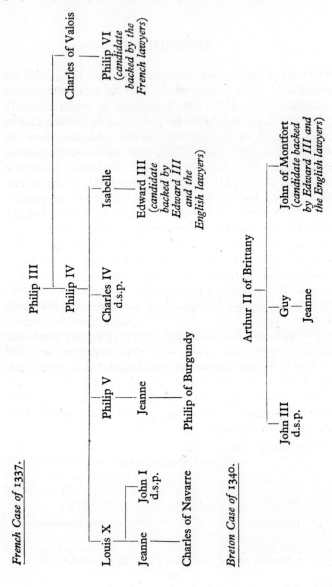

French Case of 1337.

Philip III

Philip IV — Charles of Valois

Louis X — Philip V — Charles IV d.s.p. — Isabelle — Philip VI *(candidate backed by the French lawyers)*

Jeanne — John I d.s.p.

Jeanne — Philip of Burgundy

Charles of Navarre

Edward III *(candidate backed by Edward III and the English lawyers)*

Breton Case of 1340.

Arthur II of Brittany

Guy — John of Montfort *(candidate backed by Edward III and the English lawyers)*

John III d.s.p. — Jeanne

APPENDIX II

IT has been said that Bruce was at Falkirk, on the English side, and imaginative historians have devoted a considerable amount of very interesting speculation as to his mental processes during and after the battle. But the evidence, as it happens, is for the description of his movements given in the text. Hemingburgh, one of the soberest and best informed of the English chroniclers, says categorically that he was in command of the Scottish Army of the West : and his account of Edward's brief Carrick campaign, which includes this fact, is borne out in detail by the known itinerary of the march. The documents on whose authority Sir Herbert Maxwell and, more surprisingly, Lang, rely in contradicting Hemingburgh, are two. One is the *undated* letter already referred to, from Edward to Bruce, with orders to raise troops. Now if there were proof (*a*) that the letter did belong to this year and (*b*) that Bruce obeyed it, it would be evidence. But there is no evidence that Bruce did obey it, and none either that the letter belongs to this year : the date is a pure guess of Bain's in 1881. The other of these documents is a letter bearing the date ' 3rd July,' *but no year.* It is from Bruce to Edward to ask for a renewal of protection for three named knights ' in the King's service.' Now, two of these knights are known to have been, from 1297 to 1301, on the Scottish side : the only reason for assuming it to belong to 1297-1298 is simply another casual guess of Bain's, while the letter itself contains strong evidence that it cannot possibly be of either year !

Yet on this airy foundation certain historians have built a really spectacular structure of tergiversation upon Bruce's part. Sir Herbert Maxwell, who goes so far as gravely to tabulate these conjectural changes, talks in pained tones of his conduct in these years. The process of his narrative is worth study. On pp. 98-9 of what long has been the standard life of Bruce, he does quote both Hemingburgh and these letters, as contradicting each other, and does admit that the authority of the letters is doubtful : but he does it in such a way, and with such a shocked countenance over his inference from them, that the reader who has not all his wits about him, and one of the greater libraries within reach in which to look up the cryptic references, would assume them, none the less, the superior evidence : and on p. 121 he actually makes this assumption himself, citing their content as ascertained fact, without any suggestion of dubiety, and then holding forth on ' the ugly details ' of it. Lang also accepts Bain's conjectures quite un-examined (Bain did have the decency to query them, too) and talks of ' the conscience of that ever-shifting politician ' Bruce condemning him after Falkirk. And a large number of gentlemen, impressed by footnote references to Bain and Stevenson, and unwilling to go to the trouble of verifying these for themselves, have gladly adopted the calumny as gospel. One cannot but recall a remark of Hill Burton's, who as a lawyer knew something both of evidence and of juries. ' His-torians seem to have found . . . in the charge of treachery a sort of revenge for the perplexities they have had to endure from the indistinct and unaccountable movements of many of these barons.'

APPENDIX III

' THESE Scottishmen are right hardy and sore travailing in
harness and in wars, for when they will enter into England,
within a day and a night they will drive their whole host
twenty-four mile. For they are all a-horseback, without it
be the truants and the laggards of the host, who follow after
afoot. The knights and squires are well horsed, and the
common people and other on little hackneys and geldings, and
they carry with them no carts or charrets for the diversities of
the mountains that they must pass through in the country of
Northumberland. They take with them no purveyance of
bread nor wine : for their usage and soberness is such in time
of war that they will pass in the journey a great long time with
flesh half sodden (i.e. stewed) without bread, and drink of the
river water without wine, and they neither care for pots nor
pans. For they seethe beasts in their own skins. They are
ever sure to find plenty of beasts in the country they will pass
through. Therefore they carry with them no other purveyance,
but on their horse between the saddle and the panel they truss
a broad plate of metal, and behind the saddle they will have a
little sack full of oatmeal, to the intent that when they have
eaten of the sodden flesh, then they lay their plate on the fire,
and temper a little of the oatmeal, and when the plate is hot
they cast of the thin paste thereon, and so make a little cake in
manner of a cracknel or biscuit, and that they eat to comfort
withal their stomachs. Wherefore it is no great marvel though
they make greater journeys than other people do.'

BIBLIOGRAPHY

THE primary sources are what has survived of the state papers and correspondence of the time. These are collected in Thomas Rymer's great *Foedera*, vols. ii and iii, in vol. i of *The Acts of the Parliament of Scotland*, in vols. i and ii of *The Exchequer Rolls of Scotland*, in vols. i and ii of *Parliamentary Writs and Writs of Military Summons*, in vol. i of *Rotuli Scotiae*, in vol. i of *Registrum Magni Sigilli*, in Sir Francis Palgrave's *Documents and Records Illustrating the History of Scotland*, Joseph Stevenson's *Illustrations of Scottish History* and *Historical Documents of Scotland*, and in Joseph Bain's *Calendar of Documents relating to Scotland*, which last is a collection not of actual texts but of abridgments in English—a useful guide, but to be handled with care, as some of the conjectural dates are very uncertain.

The contemporary chronicles are a valuable supplement to these, being equivalent, from the historian's point of view, to the newspapers of a later period. They have the same limitations as newspaper record : one can rely on them for what was generally believed at the time (and these beliefs have an influence on action) but with regard to fact their authority varies, both with the chronicler and with the type of fact. Few historians now, for instance, would consider that ' Herod, Nero, and the accursed Ham ' is an accurate comparison for William Wallace : and unluckily we have only the ' press ' of one side : no *contemporary* Scottish chronicle has survived. The chief name here is Walter of Hemingburgh, an Austin Canon of Gisburne in Yorkshire, whose *Chronica* go up to 1346, the year before his death : he gives a sober and well-informed account, and ranks, so to speak, as *The Times* among his brethren. Nicholas Trivet, a Dominican, in his *Annales*, is of the same class, and in fact makes use of Hemingburgh's work. With these may be placed the body of work referred to, sometimes rather loosely, as that of William Rishanger, a monk of St Alban's, whose name is

368

attached to a good deal of history written at that abbey during the period. John Trokelowe, whose work covers the reign of Edward II, may have been a monk of the same abbey. An anonymous monk of Malmesbury produced a rhetorical but lively *Vita Edwardi Secundi*, which is one of the major authorities for Bannockburn. The sobriety of these gentlemen is not found in the *Chronicon de Lanercost* or the *Flores Historiarum*, which represent the *Daily Mail* of the war, but the fact that the former was written by the Friars Minor of Lanercost near Carlisle, who moved freely about the Border at the time it covers, makes it none the less of great value, and the immensely popular *Flores*, if violently biassed, is very lively : it is usually referred to as ' Matthew of Westminster,' though according to Luard the writer for this period was probably one Robert of Reading, a monk of Westminster Abbey.

With them may be ranked the historians of a generation later, who are known to have had (and taken) opportunities of obtaining material from eyewitnesses. These are, in chief, two Scots, an Englishman writing in Scotland, and a Fleming. The Scots are John Barbour, Archdeacon of Aberdeen (d. before 1395) and John of Fordun (? d. 1387) probably a chantry priest of the same cathedral. Barbour's *Brus*, in English, is a lively and scholarly biography of the King from his coronation to his death : the order of events is sometimes confused, but the account of the events themselves, when it can be tested, is singularly accurate in detail. Fordun's *Scotichronicon* does not actually reach this period, but he seems to have left very copious notes covering this time, which were later worked up by Walter Bower, Abbot of Inchcolm, in a supplement called *Gesta Annalia* : it is customary, and justifiable, to refer to their joint work as either ' Fordun ' or ' the *Scotichronicon*.' Both Fordun and Barbour had been a good deal in England, and both had access to Scots sources no longer extant. Sir Thomas Gray of Heton in Northumberland, as a prisoner of war in Scotland in the 1350's, wrote a Norman-French *Scalacronica* which covers this time : his father had actually fought through most of the war. The *Chroniques* of the admirable Jean Froissart begin too late for more than the last campaign of the war, but give an extremely vivid account of that : he was in Scotland in 1365.

Of modern writing, even beginning ' modern ' with Lord Hailes,

2 A

whose *Annals* of 1797 are still a valuable commentary on certain legal and diplomatic points, there is surprisingly little of any value. Burton's delightfully racy and human work is still the best exposition of these aspects. For the military side, Sir Charles Oman's *History of the Art of War in the Middle Ages* is the standard work, though its detailed account of Bannockburn is unfortunately vitiated by the assumption of an impossible terrain : its general picture of mediaeval strategy, tactics, and armament is invaluable. Dr Mackay Mackenzie's *Scottish Mediaeval Castles* supplements it usefully. Difficult as it sometimes is to read, by far the best general study of the period, considered as a piece of scholarship, is Mr E. H. Barron's *Scottish War of Independence* : it is very fully documented, but unfortunately stops short at Bannockburn. For the movements of that battle, Dr Mackay Mackenzie's study may be recommended : the credit of clarifying them is his more than any man's. For the terrain, see the Rev. Thomas Miller's detailed study in his Historical Society Pamphlet. The family relationships which play so great a part in the politics may be studied in the *Scots Peerage* of Sir James Balfour Paul and the excellent series of small genealogies prefixed to Professor C. S. Terry's *History of Scotland.*

For contemporary foreign affairs there is ample material. Classical short studies are, for England, Professor Tout's volume in *A Political History of England*; for France, M. Funck-Brentano's *Le Moyen Âge*; for Norway, H. H. Boyesen's *History of Norway*; and for Europe generally, Professor Tout's *The Empire and the Papacy* (918-1273) and Sir Richard Lodge's *The Close of the Middle Ages* (1273-1494).

INDEX

PRINTED IN GREAT BRITAIN
BY BRADFORD AND DICKENS, LONDON W.C.1

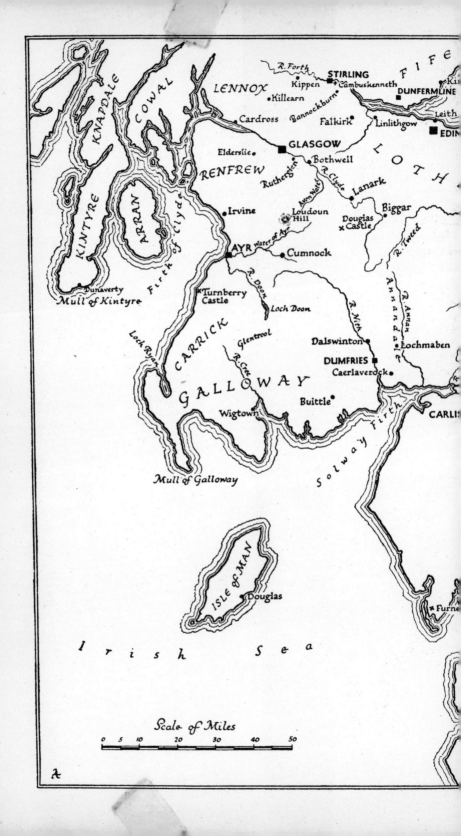